The Spirit of T[illegible]

The Institute of Ismaili Studies

OCCASIONAL PAPERS, 4

1. *The Poetics of Religious Experience: The Islamic Context* by Aziz Esmail
2. *Mysticism and the Plurality of Meaning: The Case of the Ismailis of Rural Iran* by Rafique Keshavjee
3. *Spiritual Quest: Reflections on Qur'ānic Prayer According to the Teachings of Imam ʿAlī* by Reza Shah-Kazemi

The Spirit of Tolerance in Islam

REZA SHAH-KAZEMI

I.B.Tauris *Publishers*
LONDON • NEW YORK
in association with
The Institute of Ismaili Studies
London, 2012

Published in 2012 by I.B.Tauris & Co. Ltd
6 Salem Road, London W2 4BU
175 Fifth Avenue, New York, NY 10010
www.ibtauris.com

in association with The Institute of Ismaili Studies
210 Euston Road, London NW1 2DA
www.iis.ac.uk

Distributed in the United States and Canada Exclusively by Palgrave Macmillan,
175 Fifth Avenue, New York, NY 10010

ISBN: 978 1 78076 131 2

A full CIP record for this book is available from the British Library
A full CIP record for this book is available from the Library of Congress

Library of Congress catalog card: available

Typeset in Minion Tra for The Institute of Ismaili Studies
Printed and bound in Great Britain by TJ International Ltd, Padstow, Cornwall

MIX
Paper from responsible sources
FSC® C013056

The Institute of Ismaili Studies

The Institute of Ismaili Studies was established in 1977 with the object of promoting scholarship and learning on Islam, in the historical as well as contemporary contexts, and a better understanding of its relationship with other societies and faiths.

The Institute's programmes encourage a perspective which is not confined to the theological and religious heritage of Islam, but seeks to explore the relationship of religious ideas to broader dimensions of society and culture. The programmes thus encourage an interdisciplinary approach to the materials of Islamic history and thought. Particular attention is also given to issues of modernity that arise as Muslims seek to relate their heritage to the contemporary situation.

Within the Islamic tradition, the Institute's programmes promote research on those areas which have, to date, received relatively little attention from scholars. These include the intellectual and literary expressions of Shiʿism in general, and Ismailism in particular.

In the context of Islamic societies, the Institute's programmes are informed by the full range and diversity of cultures in which Islam is practised today, from the Middle East, South and Central Asia, and Africa to the industrialized societies of the West, thus taking into consideration the variety of contexts which shape the ideals, beliefs and practices of the faith.

These objectives are realised through concrete programmes and activities organized and implemented by various departments of the Institute. The Institute also collaborates periodically, on a programme-specific basis, with other institutions of learning in the United Kingdom and abroad.

The Institute's academic publications fall into a number of interrelated categories:

1. Occasional papers or essays addressing broad themes of the relationship between religion and society, with special reference to Islam.
2. Monographs exploring specific aspects of Islamic faith and culture, or the contributions of individual Muslim thinkers or writers.
3. Editions or translations of significant primary or secondary texts.
4. Translations of poetic or literary texts which illustrate the rich heritage of spiritual, devotional and symbolic expressions in Muslim history.
5. Works on Ismaili history and thought, and the relationship of the Ismailis to other traditions, communities and schools of thought in Islam.
6. Proceedings of conferences and seminars sponsored by the Institute.
7. Bibliographical works and catalogues which document manuscripts, printed texts and other source materials.

This book falls into category one listed above.

In facilitating these and other publications, the Institute's sole aim is to encourage original research and analysis of relevant issues. While every effort is made to ensure that the publications are of a high academic standard, there is naturally bound to be a diversity of views, ideas and interpretations. As such, the opinions expressed in these publications must be understood as belonging to their authors alone.

Contents

Acknowledgements

I would like to express deep gratitude to Dr Farhad Daftary, Head of Department at the Department of Academic Research and Publications and Co-Director of The Institute of Ismaili Studies, for ensuring that I had the time and space, alongside my other duties at the IIS, to conduct the research needed to write this monograph. I would also like to thank Kutub Kassam for his careful editing of this text; Nadia Holmes for her kind and efficient help on the editorial front; Asad Zaydi for providing me with some key sources pertaining to Ottoman history; and my wife, Nureen, for many valuable suggestions regarding this essay as a whole, and particularly the section on the Cordoban Umayyads.

Reza Shah-Kazemi

Introduction

The Trajectory of Tolerance

> The most beloved religion to God is primordial, generously tolerant faith (*al-ḥanīfiyya al-samḥa*).
>
> The Prophet Muḥammad[1]

Since September 11, 2001, the word 'Islam' hardly conjures up the principle of tolerance in the minds of most people living in the West. Quite the contrary: if one were to ask the average Westerner which of the world's religions is the most *intolerant*, the answer, most likely, would be Islam. It would therefore come as something of a shock for those holding such a negative view of Islam to read the following sentences from, arguably, the leading British scholar of Islam of his generation, Sir Hamilton Gibb:

> It possesses a magnificent tradition of interracial understanding and co-operation. No other society has such a record of success in uniting, in an equality of status, of opportunity, and of endeavour, so many and so various races of humanity.[2]

In the same generation, we find the following objective appraisal of Islam by Sir Thomas Arnold in the conclusion to his far-reaching—and still unsurpassed—study of the spread of the faith, *The Preaching of Islam*:

> On the whole, unbelievers have enjoyed under Muhammadan rule a measure of toleration, the like of which is not to be found in Europe until quite modern times. Forcible conversion was forbidden, in accordance with the precepts of the Quran . . . The very existence of so many Christian sects and communities in countries that have

> been for centuries under Muhammadan rule is an abiding testimony to the toleration they have enjoyed, and shows that the persecutions they have from time to time been called upon to endure at the hands of bigots and fanatics, have been excited by some special and local circumstances rather than inspired by a settled principle of intolerance . . . But such oppression is wholly without the sanction of Muhammadan law, either religious or civil.[3]

Such scholarly objectivity towards the tolerance which has historically characterised the Islamic tradition as a whole, is, alas, in short supply these days. Through an insidious symbiosis between fanatical Muslims and hysterical Islamophobes, the very opposite image of Islam has emerged as one of the most malevolent stereotypes of our times: the image of the rabidly intolerant Muslim is paraded, not as the grotesque caricature of authentic Islam that it is, but rather as the 'true' Muslim. It is this kind of Muslim who ostensibly expresses the grim reality of the Islamic faith, the tolerant Muslim being regarded as a kind of anomaly if not an oxymoron. The most cursory glance at history will reveal the falsity of this view of Islam, for to speak of the Islamic tradition is to speak of an explicit recognition of the divinely-inspired phenomenon of religious plurality; it is therefore to speak of profound respect for, and not simply legal tolerance of, the religious Other.

In his classic work on comparative religion, *The Meaning and End of Religion*, Wilfred Cantwell Smith argues convincingly that, among the religions of the world, Islam has a unique approach to the question of religious plurality. He demonstrates that Islam is a 'special case' within the religious phenomenon in that it explicitly acknowledges the category of religion *per se*, within which there are various instances of 'religion', the word *dīn* possessing an intelligible and immediately recognisable plural, *adyān*. Such religions as Christianity, by contrast, recognise only themselves as constituting 'religion', a phenomenon which is strictly *sui generis*, not one among others in a category embracing kindred phenomena.[4] Bernard Lewis makes the same point, adding that, in a context of religious plurality, the crucial verse, 'There is no compulsion in religion' (2:256), enjoins tolerance and forbids the use of force in matters concerning religious faith; he then provides this useful starting-point for any discussion of the practice of tolerance in the Islamic tradition:

> Islam, from the beginning, recognized that it had predecessors, and that some, having survived the advent of Islam, were also contemporaries. This meant that in Muslim scripture and in the oldest traditional theological and legal texts, certain principles were laid down, certain rules were established, on the treatment of those who follow other religions. This pluralism is part of the holy law of Islam, and these rules are on many points detailed and specific. Unlike Judaism and Christianity, Islam squarely confronts the problem of religious tolerance, and lays down both the extent and the limits of the tolerance to be accorded to the other faiths. For Muslims, the treatment of the religious other is not a matter of opinion or choice, of changing interpretations and judgments according to circumstances. It rests on scriptural and legal texts, that is to say, for Muslims, on holy writ and sacred law.[5]

Lewis is one of the most stringent critics of the intolerance manifested by various contemporary Muslim groups; his testimony to the tolerance that characterises Muslim history is thus all the more striking. What is also striking is the contrast he highlights between Muslim traditions of tolerance and Christian traditions of intolerance, the seventeenth century marking a certain turning-point in this regard:

> Until the seventeenth century, there can be no doubt that, all in all, the treatment by Muslim governments and populations of those who believed otherwise was more tolerant and respectful than was normal in Europe . . . there is nothing in Islamic history to compare with the massacres and expulsions, the inquisitions and persecutions, that Christians habitually inflicted on non-Christians, and still more on each other. In the lands of Islam, persecution was the exception; in Christendom, sadly, it was often the norm.[6]

This statement, coming from one who can hardly be described as biased towards Islam, helps to demonstrate the extent to which it is incorrect to identify the intolerance of some contemporary Muslims with Islam *per se*; rather, such intolerance must be seen as a deviation from the norms established by Muslim praxis, and enshrined in Islamic principle. In objective, historical terms, the Islamic world should be seen as having provided living models of tolerant conduct for an evidently intolerant Christian world. It is thus one of the supreme ironies of our times that prominent and apparently well-educated figures are calling out for Muslims to learn about tolerance from the West, and even that Islam needs to undergo, in its fifteenth century, a Reformation such as Christianity underwent in its own fifteenth century: that very Reformation which was the prelude to the worst bouts of religious intolerance, fanatical inquisitions and bitter internecine wars that Europe—indeed the world—has ever seen. A modicum of historical research will reveal that, in fact, it was the Christian world which learnt about the meaning of tolerance from the Muslims: the trajectory of tolerance was from East to West.

In 1689 John Locke, one of the founding fathers of modern liberal thought, wrote a historic treatise, 'A Letter Concerning Toleration'. This letter is widely viewed as instrumental in the process by which the ethical value of religious tolerance was transformed into a human right, as far as individual conscience is concerned; and into a legal obligation, incumbent upon the upholders of political authority, as far as the state is concerned. It is evident from this letter that Locke was deeply struck by the contrast between paradoxically tolerant 'barbarians'—the Muslim Ottomans—and violently intolerant yet ostensibly 'civilised' Christians. The contrast was compounded by the fact that Muslims exercised more tolerance towards non-Muslims than Christians did to their co-religionists, let alone non-Christians. In his letter, Locke ruefully reflected on the absurdity that Calvinists and Armenians were free to practise their faith if they lived in the Muslim Ottoman Empire, but not in certain parts of Christian Europe: would the Turks not 'silently stand by and laugh to see with what inhuman cruelty Christians thus rage against Christians?'[7]

Locke passionately proclaimed the need for universal tolerance, whatever one's religious beliefs were. Following on logically from this principle of tolerance was the right for non-Christians to live unmolested in the state of England, and be accorded full civil and political rights: '… neither pagan nor Mahometan [sic] nor Jew ought to be excluded from the civil rights of the Commonwealth because of his religion.'[8] In other words, political or outward obedience was to take precedence over the question of inward belief as far as public life was concerned.

Locke had laid the foundations for a new paradigm. This paradigm of tolerance, enshrining the right of freedom of religious belief and worship in the Western world, is thus not simply a corollary of the liberal political philosophy expounded by Enlightenment thinkers like Locke: it must also be seen as at least partly a product of the historical contrast between mutually intolerant Christian states and denominations on the one hand, and a spectacularly tolerant Muslim polity on the other. In other words, the Western notion and practice of religious tolerance is derived—to a not inconsiderable degree—from the example of Islam. The highly respected scholar, Norman Daniel, author of the seminal study *Islam and the West: The Making of an Image* (Edinburgh, 1958), states the case quite plainly in another work: 'The notion of toleration in Christendom was borrowed from Muslim practice.'[9]

There is abundant evidence to substantiate this claim, which can be made, however, without descending into polemics or one-upmanship. To demonstrate that, historically, the West had much to learn about tolerance from Islam is not to engage in 'competitive' as opposed to 'comparative' religion, to score points or to point fingers; rather, such a demonstration simply helps debunk the following kind of reasoning, all too commonly encountered in our times: 'In principle, Islam is an intolerant religion, and in practice, Muslims have always been intolerant; Muslims, therefore, need to learn about tolerance from the West, as they have no tradition of tolerance of their own.' One of the main purposes of this essay is to show the falsity of this view both as regards Islamic principle and Muslim practice. The latter will be treated in the first part of the monograph, through a brief overview of the manifestation of tolerance in specific historical contexts; the principle or spirit of this tolerance will then be explored in the second part of the monograph, through an evaluation of its Qur'ānic and prophetic wellsprings.

Locke was, of course, not alone in noticing the embarrassing discrepancy between the undeniably tolerant practices of the Muslims and the increasingly intolerant nature of Christianity. As noted by Mohammed Sharafuddin, there was a constructed literary form, 'the orient', in terms of which the Muslim world was a foil against which the oppressive and indeed murderous intolerance of Europe could be contrasted.[10] For example, Voltaire, one of the most influential of the French *philosophes* of the Enlightenment, pointed to the 'sociable and tolerant religion' of Islam in contrast to the rabid intolerance characterising the relationship between rival Christian sects. Like Locke, Voltaire also 'pointed out that no Christian state allowed the presence of a mosque; but that the Ottoman state was filled with churches.'[11]

The impact of Islamic modes of tolerance upon the Western conscience needs to be situated in the context of the wider and deeper currents of culture and thought emanating from the Muslim world to the West. Although this is not the place to go into the details of this extraordinary inter-civilisational transmission of knowledge,[12] one should at least note that it is possible to argue as follows: the transmission to the West of the idea of religious tolerance is but the tip of an iceberg of Islamic influence on Western civilisation, impartial cognisance of which has been all but submerged beneath the tidal waves of passion and prejudice against Islam in recent times. The spirit of tolerance can hardly flourish in an environment dominated by parochial notions of religious exclusivism.[13] Medieval Western Christendom was plunged in ignorance about Islam, and for this reason could only see it, in religious terms, as a dangerous heresy, and, in political–military terms, as an even more dangerous rival. Just as, in the Christian world, ignorance of Islam bred intolerance of Islam, so, conversely, as we shall see, in the Muslim world, knowledge of Christianity as a revealed faith produced tolerance of Christianity. At the risk of simplification, we might say that ignorance breeds fear, and fear in turn produces intolerance; knowledge, by contrast, engenders respect which in turn leads to tolerance.

How did Western Christendom emerge from its parochialism, and begin to develop modes of objective investigation in such domains as philosophy and science, which in turn led to a more objective and tolerant appreciation of Islam and other religions? Any answer to this question would have to draw attention to the instrumental role played by the transmission of knowledge—chiefly through translations from Arabic into Latin—from Islam to the West. It is often blithely stated that modern European culture began with the Renaissance, and the Renaissance in turn means the 'rebirth' in the West of Greek philosophy, logic and science. What is overlooked here is, firstly, that Greek thought was overwhelmingly transmitted to the West through Islamic sources, and secondly, that these same Islamic sources were, for centuries before the Renaissance, introducing much more than just a rehashed form of Hellenism. Wave after wave of translations from Arabic into Latin, from the eleventh to the fifteenth century, transformed Western thought in virtually every field of intellectual endeavour. By the end of the fourteenth century, according to Eugene Myers, who has conducted comprehensive research into this issue, 'there was little of real importance in the Arabic scientific literature which scholars had not made accessible to the Europeans . . . The cultural importance of the work of Islamic scholars and translators for the development of science and literature can hardly be overestimated.'[14]

Myers, building upon the research of scholars such as Robert Hammond in theology and philosophy,[15] claims that 'By the middle of the thirteenth century, there had finally developed in Western Europe the core of a new civilisation, a core essentially Greco–Arabic–Latin . . . When the West became sufficiently mature to feel the need for deeper knowledge, when it wanted to renew its contact with ancient thought, it turned to Arabic sources . . . knowledge was won not by fresh and independent investigation but by translation, chiefly from Arabic.'[16]

As regards the most obvious and well-researched aspect of Islamic influence on the West, that of science and medicine, suffice to quote this remarkable affirmation by Briffault in his *The Making of Humanity*. He argues that what was transmitted from the Arabic sources to the West was much more than simply Hellenic data:

> The debt of our science to that of the Arabs does not consist in startling discoveries of revolutionary theories; science owes a great deal more to Arab culture, it owes its existence . . . The Greeks systematized, generalized and theorized, but the patient ways of investigation, the accumulation of positive knowledge, the minute methods of science, detailed and prolonged observation, experimental inquiry, were altogether alien to the Greek temperament . . . What we call science arose in Europe as a result of a new spirit of inquiry, of new methods of investigations, of the methods of experiment, observation and measurement, of the development of mathematics in a form unknown to the Greeks. That spirit and those methods were introduced into the European world by the Arabs.[17]

As regards culture and learning more generally, George Makdisi employs an immense amount of erudition to substantiate his convincing argument that the philosophy of 'humanism' underpinning the Renaissance owes much to Muslim perspectives on the meaning and nature of the human being. These perspectives, he claims, were expressed in the tradition of Islamic *adab*, that is, the field of what today would be called generally the liberal arts. The reason why this claim is important for our purposes is that the ethic of tolerance is deemed by scholars to have been rooted in the humanistic philosophy which in large part defined the Renaissance movement. According to Giorgio de Santillana, the notion of *humanitas*, revalorised from late antiquity, comes to imply not only man's higher nature but also his fallibility; acknowledgement of his fallibility renders man open in a new way to 'venture, risk, responsibility, freedom, *tolerance*.'[18]

Although, as noted by Charles Glenn Wallis, the Renaissance is a multi-faceted phenomenon, 'so complex and ambiguous that it eludes attempts at definition', nonetheless many of its foremost thinkers, such as Nicholas of Cusa, Marsilio Ficino and Giovanni Pico della Mirandola 'often exhibited a tolerant eclecticism, an open-minded, receptive attitude toward foreign and ancient philosophies'. Moreover, they believed that a 'continuous religious revelation ran through the apparent diversity of human cultures'.[19] Such views clearly echo the Islamic conception of *tawḥīd* (divine unity), the universality of revelation, and the intrinsic dignity of man, expressed by the concept of *al-fiṭra*—themes which we will explore in more detail in the second part of this monograph. At this point we simply wish to draw attention to Makdisi's assertion of Islamic influence on the currents of thought that defined the Renaissance, in order to underscore the relationship between Muslim learning and culture, on the one hand, and the evolution of the concept of tolerance in the West, on the other.

Makdisi notes that in the literature dealing with the origins of humanism, what is left unexplained is why the movement began in Italy instead of France, which at the time (fifteenth century) boasted a much greater classical tradition. He argues that the explanation lies in the close connection between Italy and the Islamic world, and refers to the essay by Jacob Burckhardt, written in 1877, 'The Civilisation of the Renaissance in Italy: An Essay'; this work emphasises in particular the great admiration felt for many dimensions of Islamic culture by the Emperor, Frederick II, earlier in the thirteenth century, seeing this as an expression of a strong and continuing tendency in pre-Renaissance Italy:

> The knowledge and admiration of the remarkable civilisation which Islam had attained was peculiar to Italy from the time of the Crusades. This sympathy was fostered by the half-Mohammedan government of some Italian princes, by dislike and even contempt for the existing Church, and by constant commercial intercourse with the harbours of the eastern and southern Mediterranean. It can be seen that in the thirteenth century the Italians recognized a Mohammedan ideal of nobleness, dignity and pride which they loved to connect with the person of the Sultan.[20]

Makdisi reinforces this argument by quoting from *The Dignity of Man* by the above-mentioned Pico della Mirandola (d. 1494), whose thought is described as disclosing 'the spirit of the Italian Renaissance';[21] similarly, this work is described as the very epitome of the Renaissance outlook: 'I have read, revered fathers, in the works of the Arabs, that when Abdala the Saracen was asked what he regarded as most to be wondered at on the world's stage . . . he answered that there is nothing to be seen more wonderful than man.' Makdisi asserts that the reference must be to 'Abd Allāh b. Qutayba (d. 276/889) from whose book, *Khalq al-insān* ('The Creation of Man'), the quotation in question comes; this book was widely published in both East and West.[22] Indeed, in his work Pico refers to such Muslim luminaries as al-Fārābī, Ibn Sīnā and Ibn Rushd, remarking in particular that there is something 'divine and Platonic' in Ibn Sīnā.[23]

Makdisi points also to the evidence of Islamic influence upon the Western scholastic method of inquiry: that of the developed dialectic as found in Islamic jurisprudence. He shows that certain key features are identical, indicating unacknowledged borrowing from the Islamic sources: the *summa* genre itself parallels such works as Ibn 'Aqīl's (d. 513/119) *Clear Book on the Sources and Methodology of the Law*; the use of 'articulus' for article is an equivalent of the Islamic *faṣl*, both words having the root meaning of 'joint' – i.e., of a finger; a specific problem is referred to as a *quaestio* (question), which is the counterpart to the Arabic *su'āl*; and the question is usually introduced under the aspect of alternatives: the Latin *utrum* (whether) here corresponding to the Arabic *hal.*[24] One should also mention in this context Makdisi's remarkable analysis of the rise of colleges and universities in the West. This is not the place to enter into the wealth of scholarly evidence he brings to bear on this subject; suffice to mention a single but vital aspect of learning in the Western university system, the principal means of teaching: the lecture. The word is derived from the Latin *lectio*, 'reading', and its precise meaning was debated by Western schoolmen. Hugh of St Victor is quoted by Makdisi as follows:

> Reading consists of informing our minds by rules and precepts taken from books. There are three kinds of reading: the teacher's, the learner's and the independent reader's. For we say, 'I am reading the book to him', 'I am reading the book under him', and 'I am reading the book'.

Makdisi shows that this tripartite definition of 'reading' mirrors the Muslim definition of *qara'a*:

> Thus the equivocal meaning of the verb to read (*qara'a*) and its infinitive noun, reading (*qirā'a*) is native to Islam, and goes back to the recitation and reading of the Koran. The Arabic *qara'a 'alā*, verb and preposition, had a double meaning: 1) to read aloud, or recite, to; and 2) to read aloud, or recite, under. The sentence *qara'a'l-kitāba 'alā Zayd*, meant 'he read the book to Zayd (the student)', as well as 'he read the book under Zayd, under the direction of Zayd (the professor)'. In other words, the preposition *'alā*, in this context, had the meaning of the Latin *illi*, to him, as well as the meaning of *ab illo*, under him, in the statement of Hugh of St Victor quoted above.[25]

Given the fact that the ethic of tolerance finds its natural place in a constellation of kindred virtues, together with an open-minded attitude towards knowledge and learning, it would not be out of place to mention here another aspect of Islam's transmission of culture to the West. This is the whole notion of chivalry, within which tolerance functions as a key value, as we shall see in more detail in Part 1 of this monograph. According to Sir John Glubb, the eight centuries of Muslim rule on the Iberian peninsula resulted in the establishment of a refined conception of the nature and purpose of warfare. War was seen by Muslims 'as a means of gaining honour rather than of destroying their enemies . . . With the return of classical ideas at the Renaissance, war in the West gradually became "rationalised" once more, the only object being the destruction of the enemy, by fair means or foul.'[26]

It should be remembered that war in the pre-modern period was an intrinsic and inevitable concomitant of imperial rivalry. The distinction between fighting for honour and fighting to destroy assumes particular significance in a context where international law was non-existent, and where justice or fair-play depended crucially upon the sense of honour which, alone, ensured that treaties and agreements would be upheld. Glubb makes a telling point about the so-called 'rationalisation' of war in the West, it being more 'rational' to destroy the enemy than be distracted by notions of honour. This helps explain the genocidal extermination of peoples undertaken by ostensibly 'humanist' Christians in the Renaissance period. Nasr notes the paradox of 'how fewer than two hundred men from Western Spain could defeat the entire Incan empire in Peru, and bring about the death of four million of the eight million inhabitants of that land in a decade, while debating whether the people the invaders were slaughtering had souls, and whether or not they were human'.[27]

One such debate was that held between the Dominican missionary Bartholomé de Las Casas and the historian Ginés de Sepúlveda at Valladolid in 1550. The latter held that both political necessity and religious principle required the dominion 'of perfection over imperfection, of force over weakness, of eminent virtue over vice'; Indians were related to Spaniards 'as children are to adults . . . women to men . . . wild beasts to civilized people'. Las Casas, on the contrary, appalled by the slaughter, mutilations and burnings taking place in the name of Christian conquest, pleaded for an abandonment of conquest and enforced slavery—but still sought the total conversion of Indians by peaceful means.[28]

As will be seen in the course of this monograph, such a debate would have been inconceivable in a traditional Muslim context. Not just the more learned among the community, but even the most unlettered among those engaged in Muslim wars of conquest would have found utterly reprehensible such wanton disregard for the intrinsic dignity of the human being, *per se*. The Muslim attitude towards human beings is essentially defined by the Qur'ānic doctrine of *al-fiṭra*, the primordial, inalienable substance of humanity: 'So set your purpose for religion as one by nature upright (*ḥanīfan*): the *fiṭra* of God, that according to which He created man' (30:30).[29] Similarly, at Q 17:70: 'We have bestowed dignity on the progeny of Adam'. Hashim Kamali refers to various commentaries on this verse in his fine work, *The Dignity of Man: An Islamic Perspective*, pointing out that they all concur as regards its basic implication: regardless of race, colour, ethnicity or even religion, every human being is endowed with inalienable dignity.[30] Innumerable sayings and deeds of the Prophet Muḥammad reinforce the principle in question here, the sense that humanity is essentially one and the same in all human beings, whatever their religious affiliation or lack thereof.

Kamali cites the following instructive examples. On one occasion, the Prophet stood up respectfully when a funeral procession passed by. Upon being told that the deceased was not a Muslim, he replied: 'Was he not a human being?' He said: 'People are the children of God (*ʿīyāl Allāh*); and those most loved by God are those who are most compassionate to His children (*arḥamuhum li-ʿīyālihi*).' The Prophet was angered when he heard someone abusing a person by calling him 'Ibn al-Sawdā'' (son of a negress), and said: 'The son of a white woman has no superiority over the son of a black woman except on grounds of God-consciousness (*taqwā*).'[31] One of his companions, Abū Mūsā al-Ashʿarī said to the Prophet: 'You remind us so frequently about *raḥma* (compassion), even though we actually think that we are compassionate toward one another.' The Prophet replied: 'But I mean *raḥma* to all! (*innamā urīd al-raḥma bi'l-kāffa*)'.[32] It is also worth mentioning here the famous guidance of Imam 'Alī b. Abī Ṭālib in his letter appointing Mālik al-Ashtar as governor of the province of Egypt: 'Infuse your heart with mercy for the people in your charge, have love for them and be kind to them. Be not like a ravenous beast of prey above them, seeking to devour them. For they are of two types: either your brother in religion or your equal in creation.'[33]

Such an understanding of the nature of humanity is part of the spirit of tolerance proper to the Islamic revelation, which will be addressed in its own right in Part 2 of this monograph. For now, let us note that such a view of the human being strictly precluded any possibility of regarding some human beings as savages and treating them abominably, even in the midst of battle. Precepts deriving from the prophetic period form the basis for an elaborate structure of rules of warfare in Islamic law, among which mutilation of any kind—and even striking the face of one's enemy—is prohibited.

The contrast between Muslim and Christian notions of humanity during the pre-modern era is deepened when one considers that the worst episodes of Spanish genocide were being perpetrated in the 'New World' at precisely the time when humanistic philosophy was being expounded in Europe, as Nasr remarked. This was also a period coinciding with the expulsion of the last Muslims from Spain. The year 1492 is highly significant in this regard. As noted by Todorov:

> The year 1492 already symbolizes, in the history of Spain, this double movement: in the same year the country repudiates its interior Other by triumphing over the Moors in the final battle of Granada and by forcing the Jews to leave its territory; and it discovers the exterior Other, that whole America which will become Latin.[34]

John Phelan's description of the Spanish sense of 'mission' subsequent to 1492—both in relation to the Americas and the Philippines—helps throw into stark relief precisely what Spain was rejecting by repudiating 'its interior Other'; that is, both the chivalric codes which governed the Muslim conduct during times of warfare, and the tolerance that was granted by Muslims during times of peace:

> The Spanish race appeared to them as God's new chosen people, destined to execute the plans of providence. Spain's mission was to forge the spiritual unity of all mankind by crushing the Protestants in the Old World, defending Christendom against the onslaughts of the Turks, and spreading the gospel among the infidels of America and Asia . . . with the conversion of the peoples of Asia, all the races of mankind would be brought into the fold of Christianity.[35]

* * *

Tolerance is a multi-faceted concept comprising moral, psychological, social, legal, political and religious dimensions. The dimension of tolerance addressed here is specifically religious tolerance, such as this principle finds expression within the Islamic tradition. We could define religious tolerance in two ways: in minimalist or 'secular' terms on the one hand, and in maximalist or 'sacred' terms on the other. Minimally, tolerance is equated with an open-minded attitude towards all religions and their adherents, an attitude which engenders actions, policies and laws aimed at protecting the rights of all religious communities to uphold and implement their religious beliefs without prejudice or hindrance. This secular approach to tolerance has achieved considerable success in establishing the inviolability of the principle of freedom of religion and conscience in the Western world, to such an extent that tolerance is widely regarded as one of the hallmarks of a progressive, modern and enlightened society. Its opposite, intolerance, has come to be seen as backward and oppressive, harking back to the 'dark ages' of medieval obscurantism and religious dogmatism. The current religious revival—in all religious traditions—raises for many the fear that an over-zealous advocacy of one's faith will inevitably resurrect the dogmatic intolerance of the Other which characterised Western Christendom in the pre-modern period.

Maximally, religious tolerance can be defined in terms of a positive spiritual predisposition towards the religious Other, a predisposition fashioned by knowledge of the divinely-willed diversity of religious communities. If the diversity of religions is perceived to be an expression of the will of God, then the inevitable differences between the religions will be not only tolerated but also celebrated: tolerated on the outward, legal and formal plane, celebrated on the inward, cultural and spiritual plane. As is the case with secular tolerance, here also one will in principle encounter a positive and open-minded attitude, one capable of engendering actions, policies and laws of a tolerant nature towards the religious Other, but the root of this attitude derives from a principle going beyond the secular domain: a tolerant attitude emerges as the consequence of a kaleidoscopic vision of unfolding divine revelations, a vision which elicits profound respect for the religions of the Other. This contrasts sharply with an external, purely formal mode of tolerance which can in fact be accorded reluctantly, begrudgingly or condescendingly. From profound respect, tolerance cannot but emerge; but the converse does not hold: one can be tolerant outwardly and legally, without this being accompanied by sincere respect for the religion of the Other. Moreover, the purely secular approach to tolerance carries with it the risk of falling into a corrosive relativism of the 'anything goes' variety. It can lead to the normativity and particularity of one's own faith being diluted, if not sacrificed, for the sake of an abstract social construct. Does tolerance of the Other necessarily compromise the absoluteness of one's dedication to one's own faith, or does faithful practice of one's own faith, on the contrary, call out for tolerance of the Other?

The Islamic tradition, in principle as well as in practice, provides important answers to this and many questions pertaining to the relationship between religious tolerance and the practice of one's own faith. One of the chief lessons here is that tolerance of the Other is in fact integral to the practice of Islam; it is not some optional extra, some philosophical or cultural indulgence, or, still less, something that one needs to import from some other tradition. This being said, one needs to take note of an irony: the essential sources of the Islamic faith reveal a sacred vision of diversity and difference, plurality and indeed universality, which is unparalleled among world scriptures; the actual conduct of contemporary Muslim states, however, not to mention many vociferous extra-state groups and actors, falls lamentably short of the standards of tolerance set by the secular West.[36] In consequence, it is hardly surprising that many argue that what the Muslim world needs in order to become more tolerant is to learn to become more modern and secular, and less traditional and religiously idealistic. This kind of argument, however, ignores and marginalises the vast treasury of ethical and spiritual resources within the Islamic tradition, and in so doing only strengthens the case of the most intolerant voices within the Muslim community, whilst weakening the position of those calling for greater tolerance—those calling, precisely, for a return to the normative tradition of tolerance which has overwhelmingly characterised Muslim praxis throughout the centuries, and which is entirely in harmony with the spiritual ethos of the Qur'ān and the prophetic paradigm of impeccable virtue.

The argument we wish to make in this essay is close to that articulated by Ashis Nandy, who calls out for the 'recovery of religious tolerance'; this recovery must be made in a manner which is organically related to the religions themselves. Nandy is speaking in the context of the Indian subcontinent, but the argument in question can be applied to the Muslim world generally, *mutatis mutandis*:

> The time has come for us to recognise that, instead of trying to build religious tolerance on the good faith or conscience of a small group of de-ethnicized, middle-class politicians, bureaucrats and intellectuals, a far more serious venture would be to explore the philosophy, the symbolism and the theology of tolerance in the faiths of the citizens, and hope that the state systems in South Asia may learn something about religious tolerance from everyday Hinduism, Islam, Buddhism, and Sikhism, rather than wish that the ordinary Hindus, Muslims, Buddhists and Sikhs will learn tolerance from the various fashionable secular theories of statecraft.[37]

As regards the contemporary practice of religious tolerance, Muslims lose nothing in acknowledging that the secular West has indeed set high institutional standards in this domain, albeit as a consequence of the decline of religious values in public life, rather than as an expression of its own specifically religious traditions. As was implicit in what we noted above, secularism in the West was seen as the only way of preventing intra-Christian intolerance from continuing to infect and disrupt public life; emerging from a period dominated by wars of religion, it seemed entirely reasonable to promote a secular ideal for the sake of civil society, and leave religion to the domain of personal conscience. With the decline of specifically Christian principles in society, then, there arose codes of conduct within which the principle of religious tolerance assumed central importance.

Instead of demonstrating the intrinsic incapacity of religion as such to promote and implement tolerance, however, one should evaluate the Western experience in its own historical, political and religious context, and not pretend to arrive at universal laws such as would equate religion with intolerance on the one hand, and secularism with tolerance on the other. For, as is evident, tolerance goes hand in hand with Islam at its height, while the spirit of tolerance declines with the decline of Islamic civilisation itself; in other words, the decline of the influence of traditional Islamic values has brought in its wake that peculiar inferiority complex of which religious intolerance is a major symptom. In Europe, by contrast, intolerance reigned supreme when Christianity was at its height, and it was only with the decline of Christian values in public life that religious tolerance emerges as a laudable principle and becomes enshrined in legal codes. This is not to belittle the value of such codes, for whether inspired by secular values or religious ones, tolerance remains what it is. It is when tolerance goes hand in hand with a diminution of commitment to one's own faith that it can be seen to exert a negative influence, but this is not to cast aspersions on tolerance *per se*; it is simply to note that its role varies according to the ideological or religious context in which it is located. In other words, tolerant codes of conduct can be seen, objectively, as formal expressions of the universal principle of tolerance, a principle which is inherent to the vision of Islam itself, but is not the 'property' of Islam any more than is knowledge, piety, or any fundamental—hence universal—virtue. Tolerance as such is neither 'secular' nor is it 'Islamic' in any exclusive sense. It can fall prey to a corrosive relativism in the measure that it becomes indiscriminate, unthinking and mechanical; but it can be seen to express a sacred truth—the plurality of paths which lead to God is itself a reflection of the infinitude of God—if it be guided by revealed principles: then it can contribute to what Tim Winter most aptly referred to as a 'transcendently-ordained tolerance'.

This phrase comes in the course of an appeal to Muslims not to regard Christianity or 'the West' as a monolithic force, inherently hostile to Islam, but rather to see that even if the Islamophobes in the West are part of the 'problem' in Muslim-Christian relations, there is another part which, he argues, is 'emphatically part of the solution, advocating hospitality in a world which has never been more in need of a transcendently-ordained tolerance.'[38] Elsewhere, Winter makes a telling point about the lesson which Islam can impart as regards this 'transcendently-ordained tolerance', a point which echoes that made by Hamilton Gibb about Islam's unique success 'in uniting, in an equality of status, of opportunity, and of endeavour, so many and so various races of humanity'. Winter writes: 'No pre-modern civilisation embraced more cultures than that of Islam . . . [this fact] demonstrates the divine purpose that this Ishmaelite covenant is to bring a monotheism that uplifts, rather than devastates, cultures.'[39]

In the contemporary world Muslims and Christians alike need to be reminded of this basic truth about Islam's role in relation to diverse human cultures. It is a lesson which teaches that all that deep commitment to the faith of Islam, far from implying any kind of 'nationalist' or chauvinistic sentiment, on the contrary causes human diversity to flourish. According to Islam's all-inclusive vision, such principles as truth, virtue and holiness transcend all national, racial, ethnic—and, at the highest levels of thought, religious—boundaries. This is a valuable lesson for the West, both in its Christian and secular aspects. For, although the Western world is so often referred to as 'post-Christian', it is clear that Christianity is undergoing a revival in the twenty-first century. This might resurrect, for some, the terrifying ghosts of the age of the inquisitions; but there are also some—especially Christians who are keen to reconcile religious commitment with religious diversity—who might benefit from making an objective evaluation of the Islamic experience, and to see the way in which fervent faith in one's religion, far from logically entailing exclusivist intolerance of the Other, can on the contrary generate a spirit of sincere tolerance and profound respect for the religious Other. One might go so far as to say that a Muslim cannot be true to the deepest intentions of Islam unless his soul radiates that 'primordial, generously tolerant faith' (*al-ḥanīfiyya al-samḥa*) which the Prophet referred to, and to which we will return in Part 2 of this monograph.

Even if, as we hope to show, tolerance is a particularly striking characteristic of Islamic faith and Muslim praxis, tolerance as such should be seen as a universal principle, and not as the exclusive preserve of any religion or culture. Different religions and cultures, at different times, may manifest more or less tolerance, but this does not allow tolerance *per se* to be exclusively identified with one religion rather than another, or one civilisation rather than another. It is self-evidently absurd for any religion, civilisation or culture to claim a monopoly on tolerance. For such a claim violates the very nature of the principle itself, or at least, contradicts the philosophical basis of the ethic of tolerance: one tolerates the religious Other not least because truth, beauty, wisdom and virtue are present in the religions of the Other; these universal principles are not the exclusive property of any group or religion, but rather form part of the patrimony of the whole of humanity. To tolerate the Other means to celebrate the values of the

Other; respecting their right to manifest these values, however different such manifestations might be from one's own customs or traditions, follows as a logical consequence. Tolerance expresses therefore both an obligation and a right: the obligation to permit people of different faiths to manifest their own specific ways of embodying and radiating the spiritual, intellectual, legal and cultural values which are universally recognisable as such, and the right of all to benefit from the unique and therefore irreducible manifestations of these universal values. This is one important aspect of the purpose of human diversity, according to a key verse in the Qur'ān which we shall discuss further in Part 2 of this monograph: 'O mankind, We have created you male and female, and We have made you into tribes and nations in order that you might come to know one another' (49:13).

Part 1

A Glance at the Historical Record

It was stated above that a modicum of historical research suffices to refute the claim that the only true Muslim is an intolerant one. It was also made clear that John Locke and other European thinkers of the Enlightenment period were painfully aware of the contrast between a broad-minded and tolerant Ottoman Muslim polity on the one hand, and a dogmatically and mutually intolerant set of Christian nations and churches on the other. It would be appropriate at this point to sketch out some of the ways in which Muslim tolerance was manifested in different historical contexts, before proceeding in the second part of this essay to explore the roots of the spirit of tolerance so evidently characterising the history of Muslim relations with followers of other faiths. We do not mean to imply that the Muslim record is impeccable on this score;[1] only that, in stark contrast to Christendom throughout much of its history, those instances of dogmatic intolerance in Islamic history are exceptions that prove the rule. What follows, then, is a series of snapshots of four dynasties, starting with the most recent, the Ottomans and Mughals, then proceeding to the Fatimids, and finishing with the earliest, the Cordoban Umayyads. Our principal aim here is to show how the Muslim spirit of tolerance is brought to light in these different dynasties; a secondary aim being to highlight some of the distinguishing features or particular accentuations of this spirit as they came to be expressed within each of these Muslim contexts.

The Ottomans

In their introduction to a comprehensive two-volume history of the Ottoman empire, Benjamin Braude and Bernard Lewis sum up the essential features of this remarkable dynasty which was, for nearly seven hundred years (1280–1924), the principal Muslim 'Other' in relation to Christendom.

> For nearly half a millennium the Ottomans ruled an empire as diverse as any in history. Remarkably, the polyethnic and multireligious society worked. Muslims, Christians and Jews worshipped and studied side by side, enriching their distinct cultures. The legal traditions and practices of each community, particularly in matters of personal status—that is, death, marriage and inheritance—were respected and enforced throughout the empire. Scores of languages and literatures employing a bewildering variety of scripts flourished. Opportunities for advancement and prosperity were open in varying degrees to all the empire's subjects. During their heyday the Ottomans created a society which allowed a great degree of communal autonomy while maintaining a fiscally sound and militarily strong central government. The Ottoman Empire was a classic example of the plural society.[2]

The *millet* system (Arabic: *milla*, 'religious community') was the chief instrument by means of which the multi-religious empire functioned. The spirit of religious tolerance was the guiding principle of this system within which religious communities were permitted to govern themselves, in return for the payment of the *jizya* (poll-tax) and recognition of the political authority of the Ottoman rulers. The system was established under Mehmet II (r. 1451–1481) who conquered Constantinople in 1453. One of his first acts was to appoint Gennadius Scolarius as patriarch of the Greek Orthodox community now referred to as a *millet*. The Patriarch was given the rank of a *paşa* 'with three horsetails'; he had the right to apply the laws of the Orthodox faith to his followers, in both religious matters and such secular domains as education, hospitals, social security and justice. As noted by Ottoman historian Stanford Shaw:

> The *millet* leaders found their self-interest cemented to that of the sultan, since it was by his order that that they were given more extensive power over their followers than had been the case in the Christian states that had previously dominated the area. The

> complete Ottoman conquest of southeastern Europe once again united most of the Christians in the area, Greek and Slav alike, under the authority of the Greek patriarchate, making the Church a particular beneficiary of the Ottoman expansion.[3]

Such was the respect granted by the Ottomans to the Orthodox Patriarch Gennadios and his church that the Greeks preferred Muslim rule to that of the Latin Franks or the Venetians. The clergy taught that the sultan had a divine sanction to rule, and had a mandate to do so not only as leader of the Muslims but also as the protector of the Orthodox Church. The degree of religious tolerance granted to all Christian denominations was such that the Calvinists and Unitarians of Hungary and Transylvania 'long preferred to submit to the Turks rather than fall into the hands of the fanatical house of Habsburg'.[4] It is not hard to see why. After complaining bitterly at the massacre of thousands of Russian Orthodox by Polish Catholics in the seventeenth century, Macarius, Patriarch of Antioch, exclaimed: 'God perpetuate the empire of the Turks for ever and ever! For they take their impost [the *jizya*] and enter into no account of religion, be their subjects Christians or Nazarenes, Jews or Samarians.'[5] Similarly, when the Ottomans conquered Constantinople it is said that 'the Easterners [Greek Orthodox Christians] declared that they preferred the Sultan's turban to the Pope's tiara'. The bitter memory of what had happened to their city in 1204, two centuries earlier, during the so-called 'Fourth Crusade', was still fresh in their minds: the Catholic Venetians sacked the capital of the Byzantine Empire in the most despicable manner, committing 'one of the most abominable outrages in history'.[6]

One should stress here that not only did the *millet* system provide Christian leaders with a degree of autonomy greater than that which was possible for these religious leaders under the earlier Christian regimes in the region,[7] it also brought about—or rather, enforced—a degree of intra-Christian tolerance that was noticeably lacking under Christian rule: such denominations as the monophysite Armenians, to mention one of the key examples, were considered heretical by the Greek Orthodox church, whereas under the Ottomans the Armenian Church was recognised as an independent *millet* in 1461. This *millet* came to include a host of other smaller Christian groups, and this diverse group of denominations co-existed peacefully for centuries within the framework of the Ottoman empire.

Shaw's point above regarding the coincidence between the 'self-interest' of the sultan and that of the *millet* leaders needs to be re-formulated somewhat, for it was not simply a question of a pragmatic convergence between political interests. Rather, one needs to take cognisance of the fundamental nature of the system within which these interests were brought into a mutually beneficial mode of convergence, a system governed more than any other single variable by the spirit of Islamic law and the tolerance it enjoined. Indeed, it was at times when the political self-interest of the sultan clashed with the imperatives of tolerance inherent in Islamic law that one observed deviations from the norm, and lapses into what Braude and Lewis rightly refer to as 'atypical' intolerance: 'persecution was rare and atypical, usually due to specific circumstances'. The tolerance that typified Ottoman rule stemmed not from any exceptional circumstances, still less from the whim of the rulers, but from the very nature of the system *per se*, the system which was 'maintained by both Holy Law and common practice'.[8]

Braude and Lewis, in common with many other historians who have studied this period, also refer to the fact that religious discrimination was operative within this system, Muslims being clearly the ruling class. Such discrimination shows that Ottoman tolerance cannot be equated with the modern ethos of religious egalitarianism, but it also goes to show that even when Muslims were in the ascendant, the hierarchical organisation of religious communities did not entail persecution or intolerance, only the relegation of the minorities to what would be called today 'second-class' status. The inequalities inherent in such a religious hierarchy are to be evaluated according to the medieval standards of the time, not those of the modern world; and according to imperial political structures, not democratic ones.[9] At a time when anti-Semitism was rife in Christendom, and when the existence of any kind of Muslim community within Christendom was largely unthinkable, Ottoman standards of religious tolerance should be seen not only as highly exceptional, but also as expressive of the spirit of tolerance central to the Islamic ethos. This spirit logically implies equality in matters of religious conscience, even if the political manifestation of this spirit in the imperial and medieval context of the Ottoman world led to the observed socio-political inequalities between Muslims and non-Muslims. These inequalities are of the contingent order, being particular outcomes of a specific historical context; whereas the principle of tolerance, logically implying religious equality, is of the essence, which transcends such contingencies. If one wishes to distinguish between the essential and the contingent as regards Ottoman conduct towards the non-Muslim Other, therefore, one's focus should be on the fundamental principle at work, which generated tolerance and respect, and not on political contingencies which may have entailed intolerance and disrespect.

Another factor to note as regards the Ottoman system—which was *inherently* tolerant—as opposed to the role of the sultan—which was *possibly* capricious—is that in actual practice the sultan had, in the words of Stanford Shaw, 'very limited power'. This was because so much power was *de facto* delegated not only to the autonomous *millet*s, but also to the professional guilds, various corporations and religious societies, including the *futuwwa* (chivalric) orders, Sufi *tarīqa*s and *waqf* organisations. If the sultan's role was largely symbolic, what was it that made these social and religious forces work together in harmony? Shaw answers as follows:

> The most concrete binding force of the system was the corporative substructure of society that brought together Muslims and non-Muslims alike as a result of common pursuits for union with God, and common economic activities and interests. Products of the society that had evolved in the Middle East over the centuries to meet the needs of all its people, these institutions harmonized conflicting interests in a way that the Ottoman political structures never did, nor aspired to do. One result of this was that decay within the political structures of empires such as that of the Ottomans had much less effect on the operation of the system than one might imagine.[10]

Whilst on one level the point being made here appears to be presenting tolerant co-existence as a systemic norm which operated quasi-independently of the Ottomans, or any empire in the Middle East, one should note that at a deeper level what is being implied is that the spirit of tolerant Islam was the operative principle at work here, that principle which, precisely, made room for 'Muslims and non-Muslims alike' to engage in their 'common pursuits for union with God, and common economic activities and interests'. Again, one need only contrast this state of affairs with the conditions which prevailed under Christian states of Europe to appreciate that tolerant co-existence and religious harmony in pursuit of a common life of service to God and to society was much more a 'product' of the Islamic ethos, than simply of 'the Middle East', conceived as some supra-religious force transcending Islam and all other religious traditions.

As Yusuf Ibish explains, the Ottomans saw themselves not as 'colonisers' but as 'incorporators'; their role was to look after a garden: 'they might extend the boundaries of the garden, but aimed to disturb the gardeners as little as possible; as long as taxes were paid and allegiance proffered, the gardeners would be left in peace to cultivate the garden. The Ottomans should rather be remembered for this policy of what might be called in modern parlance "laissez-faire", rather than cast as the embodiment of the political type "oriental despotism".'[11] The key point here is that it was their fidelity to Islam that allowed the Ottomans to adopt this attitude to rule—as opposed to, let us say, the Spanish model of conquest from the fifteenth century onwards, based upon plunder and tyranny; and it was likewise the tolerance at the heart of the Islamic conception of the non-Muslim Other that propelled the Ottomans into adopting a policy of religious tolerance and communal autonomy.

Although all of the sultan's subjects were considered as part of his 'protected flock', the benefits of the *millet* system extended to foreigners also, who 'gained many of the advantages of *millet* status, and an exemption from Ottoman laws that provided them with such a privileged position that they were, for all practical purposes, "nations within nations" . . . able to do what they pleased without interference by the Ottoman authorities.'[12]

But of course it was first and foremost the members of the *millet*s who benefited from the system, and the extent to which this was appreciated can be observed in the following fulsome tribute to the Ottomans given by the Greek Patriarch of Jerusalem in the late eighteenth century, looking back at what had transpired for his Church after living for four hundred years under Ottoman rule:

> See how clearly our Lord, boundless in mercy and all-wise, had undertaken to guard once more the unsullied Holy and Orthodox faith . . . He raised out of nothing this powerful empire of the Ottomans, in place of our Roman [Byzantine] empire, which had begun, in a certain way, to cause to deviate from the beliefs of the Orthodox faith, and He raised up the empire of the Ottomans higher than any other kingdom so as to show without doubt that it came about by divine will, and not by the power of man . . . The all-mighty Lord, then, has placed over us this high kingdom, 'for there is no power but of God', so as to be to the people of the West a bridle, to us, the people of the East, a means of salvation. For this reason He puts into the hearts of the sultans of these Ottomans an inclination to keep free the religious beliefs of our Orthodox faith, and, as a work of supererogation, to protect them, even to the point of occasionally chastising Christians who deviate from their faith, that they have always before their eyes the fear of God.[13]

Some might regard these words as expressing the craven capitulation of a loyal Ottoman Christian to his sultan, but the language used here subtly indicates that the Christians really did feel that the integrity of their faith—which was far more important to them than their socio-political subordination to their overlords—owed much to the conditions maintained by the Ottomans for centuries. Eastern Orthodox Christians were proud to preserve what they perceived to be the pristine identity of the faith in the face of the 'deviations' of Western Christianity.[14] As noted earlier, the Eastern Orthodox 'preferred the Sultan's turban to the Pope's tiara': the statement by the Patriarch of Jerusalem above shows why.

The same pattern of Catholic persecution and Muslim toleration is visible in the case of the conversion of half of the Christian population of Crete. Under Muslim control from 825–961, it reverted to Byzantine administration until the thirteenth century, when the Latin Venetians purchased the island, and instituted a tyrannical regime of persecution against the Orthodox population. When the Ottomans conquered the island the old Greek Bishops were reinstated, and the Patriarch in Constantinople was bidden by the Ottomans to appoint an archbishop for the province; as a result of the freedom and the respect granted them by the Muslims, half of the island's population had freely converted to Islam within one hundred years of Ottoman rule.[15] In regard to the vast numbers of captured slaves who converted to Islam, Arnold writes: 'Many who would have been ready to die as martyrs for the Christian religion if the mythical choice between the Qur'ān and the sword had been offered them, felt more and more strongly, after long years of captivity, the influence of Muhammadan thought and practice, and humanity won converts where violence would have failed.'[16]

The spectacle of Muslim tolerance as exercised by the Ottomans, then, was nothing new for the Christian world inhabited by John Locke in the seventeenth century. Ottoman conquest was followed almost without exception by Islamic tolerance. 'Tolerance', according to (Reverend) Susan Ritchie, 'was a matter of Ottoman policy and bureaucratic structure, and an expression of the Ottoman interpretation of Islam, which was in most instances stunningly liberal and cosmopolitan.'[17] Indeed, Susan Ritchie argues convincingly that this Ottoman tolerance decisively influenced the process leading to the famous Edict of Torda in 1568, issued by King John Sigismund of Transylvania (which was under Ottoman suzerainty), an edict hailed by Western historians as expressing 'the first European policy of expansive religious toleration.'[18] It is thus hardly surprising that, as noted above, Norman Daniel should allow himself to make the simple—but to many, startling—claim: 'The notion of toleration in Christendom was borrowed from Muslim practice.'[19]

Ottoman tolerance of the Jews provides an illuminating contrast to the anti-Semitism of Christendom, which resulted in the regular pogroms and—what would be labelled today—'ethnic cleansing' which took place in the medieval Christian world. Many Jews fleeing from persecution in Central Europe would have received letters like the following, written by Rabbi Isaac Tzarfati, who reached the Ottomans just before their capture of Constantinople in 1453. This is what he replied to those Jews of Central Europe who were calling out for help:

> Listen, my brethren, to the counsel I will give you. I too was born in Germany and studied Torah with the German rabbis. I was driven out of my native country and came to the Turkish land, which is blessed by God and filled with all good things. Here I found rest and happiness . . . Here in the land of the Turks we have nothing

> to complain of. We are not oppressed with heavy taxes, and our commerce is free and unhindered . . . every one of us lives in peace and freedom. Here the Jew is not compelled to wear a yellow hat as a badge of shame, as is the case in Germany, where even wealth and great fortune are a curse for the Jew because he therewith arouses jealousy among the Christians . . . Arise, my brethren, gird up your loins, collect your forces, and come to us. Here you will be free of your enemies, here you will find rest . . .'[20]

We might profitably conclude this brief survey of tolerance under the Ottomans by referring to the salutary influence of the numerous Sufi orders which permeated the length and breadth of the Ottoman world. These orders (Turkish: *tarikat*s, Arabic: *ṭuruq*, sing. *ṭarīqa*) aerated the religious ambience of the entire empire with a spiritual fragrance, affording greater access to the core values of love, respect, tolerance at the heart of the Qur'ānic message and the conduct of the Prophet. Tim Winter gives a useful overview of the variety of the Sufi orders in the different parts of the Ottoman empire, showing how the orders performed particular functions in respect of different social, economic, political, military and religious groups.[21] All these functions worked together to provide what Marshall Hodgson appropriately called a 'subtle leaven', without which, he argues, the Shariʿa could not have operated so effectively. What he writes about Sufism in the 'Middle Periods' of Islamic history accurately describes the effect of Sufi *tarikat*s in the Ottoman empire:

> Sufism . . . became the framework within which all popular piety flowed together; its saints, dead and living, became the guarantors of the gentle and co-operative sides of social life. Guilds commonly came to have Sufi affiliations. Men's clubs claimed the patronage of Sufi saints. And the tombs of local saints became shrines which almost all factions united in revering. It is probable that without the subtle leaven of the Sufi orders, giving to Islam an inward personal thrust and to the Muslim community a sense of participation in a common spiritual venture quite apart from anyone's outward power, the mechanical arrangements of the Shariʿah would not have maintained the loyalty essential to their effectiveness.[22]

Sufi orders in the Ottoman empire varied greatly, from the Bektaşī *tarikat* which incorporated so much popular folklore and culture[23] to the highly elitist Mevleviye (Arabic: Mawlawiyya), based on the teachings and practices of Jalāl al-Dīn Rūmī (d. 1273), described by A. J. Arberry as 'surely the greatest mystical poet in the history of mankind'.[24] In the words of Halil Inalcık: 'As Maulānā [Rūmī] himself had been, his successors also were usually close to the ruling class, and from the fifteenth century, the Mevlevīs established themselves in many Ottoman cities as a *tarīkat* appealing to the elite. In time, fourteen large and well-organized *tekke*s [lodges] were founded in the cities, and seventy-six minor *tekke*s in small towns. All the Ottoman sultans, in particular Murād II, Bāyezīd II, Selīm I, and Murād III, took a close interest in the Mevlevīs. Murād II founded a large Mevlevī lodge in Edirne'.[25]

Winter notes that 'the early Ottoman rulers and princes wore the woollen Mevlevi ("Hurasani") cap, while the reforming Selim III (1789–1808) was an enthusiastic member and patron of the order.'[26] The refined ecumenism and love-mysticism of Rūmī, therefore, is by no means irrelevant to a consideration of the religious attitude of Ottoman elites in general, and their embrace of the principle of tolerance in particular. Much has been written on Rūmī's ecumenical spirit, as expressed in his poetry, and especially his masterpiece, the *Mathnawī*, suffice to cite here the following couplet: 'The religion of Love is separate from all religions/for lovers, the religion and creed is—God.'[27] Also from the latter work, one reads these remarkable lines on the ultimate metaphysical meaning of *tawḥīd*, which indicate the transcendence of the essence of religion over all its forms, including even Islam:

> What is to be done, O Muslims? for I do not recognise myself.
> I am neither Christian, nor Jew, nor Gabr [i.e. Zoroastrian], nor Muslim.
> I am not of the East, nor of the West, nor of the land, nor of the sea.
> …
> My place is the Placeless, my trace is the Traceless;
> 'Tis neither body nor soul, for I belong to the soul of the Beloved.
> I have put duality away, I have seen that the two worlds are one;
> One I seek, One I know, One I see, One I call.
> *He is the First, He is the Last, He is the Outward, He is the Inward.*[28]

It is also important to take note of key passages in the prose work, *Kitāb fīhi mā fīhi* ('A book which contains what it contains'), consisting of oral discourses given by Rūmī to his disciples on different occasions; these passages give us a vivid sense of the spirit underlying Rūmī's respect and tolerance vis-à-vis the Christians and Jews among whom he lived and died, and should be viewed as an indication of one of the major sources of the attitudes and dispositions adopted by his innumerable disciples and followers. First, as regards the importance of ecumenism and tolerance within Islam itself:

> Though the ways are various, the goal is one. Do you not see that there are various roads to the Kaaba? For some the road is from Rūm, for some from Syria, for some from Persia, for some from China, for some by sea from India and Yemen. So if you consider the roads, the variety is great and the divergence infinite; but when you consider the goal, they are all of one accord, and one. The hearts of all are upon the Kaaba. The hearts have an attachment, an ardour, and a great love for the Kaaba, and in that there is no room for contrariety. That attachment is neither infidelity nor faith; that is to say, that attachment is not confounded with the various roads which we have mentioned. Once they have arrived there, that disputation and war and diversity touching the roads—this man saying to that man, 'You are false, you are an infidel', and the other replying in kind—once they have arrived at the Kaaba, it is realized that that warfare was concerning the roads only, and that their goal was one.[29]

Second, as regards the essence of spiritual truth transcending and encompassing all true faiths:

> I was speaking one day amongst a group of people, and a party of non-Muslims was present. In the middle of my address they began to weep and to register emotion and ecstasy. Someone asked: What do they understand and what do they know? Only one Muslim in a thousand understands this kind of talk. What did they understand, that they should weep? The Master [i.e. Rūmī himself] answered: It is not necessary that they should understand the form of the discourse; that which constitutes the root and principle of

> the discourse, that they understand. After all, every one acknowledges the Oneness of God, that He is the Creator and Provider, that He controls everything, that to Him all things shall return, and that it is He who punishes and forgives. When anyone hears these words, which are a description and commemoration (*dhikr*) of God, a universal commotion and ecstatic passion supervenes, since out of these words come the scent of their Beloved and their Quest . . . all men in their inmost hearts love God and seek Him, pray to Him and in all things put their hope in Him, recognizing none but Him as omnipotent and ordering their affairs. Such an apperception is neither infidelity nor faith. Inwardly it has no name.[30]

Finally, it is important to stress that the tolerance cultivated by Rūmī and his followers is not some independent poetic creation of Rūmī himself, but is rather a faithful expression of the spirit pulsating from the Qurʾānic revelation. The *Mathnawī* is often referred to as 'the Persian Qurʾān',[31] but more importantly, it is also regarded as a poetic commentary on the Qurʾān; it has been calculated that approximately six thousand verses of Rūmī's *Dīwān* and *Mathnawī* are 'practically direct translations of Qurʾānic verses into Persian poetry.'[32] Rūmī and his fellow Sufis should therefore be seen not as isolated mystics marginalised from mainstream society, but as infusing a certain ethos into all levels of Ottoman society, from the simple craftsmen to the sultans themselves. They therefore complemented—in esoteric, poetic and mystical mode—the efforts of the jurists, theologians and even administrators and governors of the Ottoman empire to be faithful to the Islamic revelation in respect of the dignity, the status and the rights of the non-Muslim Other.

The Mughals

Thanks to the centuries of predominantly peaceful contact between Islam and Hinduism dating from the Muslim conquest of Sind in the early eighth century, elements of Indic culture had entered into and enriched the forms taken by the Islamic faith in India, and Islam in its turn, influenced the development of certain expressions of Hindu religious and social life. The work of figures such as Kabir, Guru Nanak and Dadu Dayal manifested this trend towards mutual rapprochement, compromise and synthesis that were at work in medieval Indian society at this time, trends that were reinforced on the Muslim side by Sufism, and on the Hindu side by the Bhakti movements. It is against this background that one should view the peak of tolerance attained during the Mughal period, and, in particular, with the rule of Akbar, though the rule of Babur, the founder of the dynasty, and that of Humayun, his son and successor, were also characterised by a spirit of ecumenism and tolerance. However, it was Akbar who, during his long reign of almost fifty years in the second half of the sixteenth century, was to weave these religious and social tendencies into a culture which was altogether dominated by the principle of tolerance; a culture that was, moreover, eminently successful in purely political terms, and at the same time immensely fruitful in the field of spirituality, literature and the arts. Indeed, it was under Akbar that Mughal culture really took root, that culture that was such a marvellous blend of Islamic and Indic tradition, and which must go on record as one of the most tolerant of all cultures in the pre-modern period.

Akbar established at his court an ambience in which Hindus and Muslim notables were linked, often by marriage, in a culture dominated by mutual respect. The royal court was thus intended to be a microcosm of the mutual religious tolerance that Akbar wished to see replicated throughout society. In 1575, at the height of the conflict between Catholics and Huguenots in France, he established a 'house of worship', (*'ibādat khānah*) at Fatehpur-Sikri, 'where Muslims of different sects, Jesuit fathers from Goa, Zoroastrians, Hindu pundits and others gathered together to discuss religion with Akbar and among themselves'.[33] He allowed a whole array of Hindu festivals to be celebrated at court, such as *Diwali* and *Shivaratri*. Such an attitude of religious tolerance was all the more appreciated by the Hindus insofar as it went hand in hand with a policy of opening up the administration of the empire to Hindu notables and officers. Akbar's genius for administration enabled him to forge, out of the various elements of the ruling classes, a homogeneous elite that found itself very much at home in the *mansabdār* system.[34] The mutual tolerance characterising the members of this Muslim-Hindu elite exerted a positive radiance throughout society.

It is not out of place to take note here of some political manifestations of Akbar's tolerance. A Hindu, Todar Mal, was made Finance

Minister in 1564; by the 1570s eight out of the twelve revenue officers of the provinces of the empire were Hindu,[35] and several of Akbar's closest friends and advisers were Hindus.[36] These changes at the top of the administrative hierarchy were reflected at the grass-roots level by two key policy changes: the abolition of the *jizya*, or poll-tax paid by non-Muslims to the state, and the abolition of the tax on Hindus performing pilgrimages. The impact of the *jizya* abolition was particularly far-reaching, according to Sri Ram Sharma.[37] However controversial it may have appeared, there was a religious logic which justified the abolition of the *jizya*; for if Hindus were fully participating in all aspects of state administration, from military service to financial management, it was inappropriate for them to pay a discriminatory tax. As we shall see below, in the section on the *dhimma*, this is evident in the earliest history of Muslim statecraft. Akbar was no doubt made aware of the precedents in Islamic history and jurisprudence where the *jizya* was waived for non-Muslims who were actively involved in the state system.[38] Here again we observe the operation of the following principle: the universal spirit of religious tolerance at once inspires and takes precedence over the specific forms by which it is expressed. These forms are secondary, contingent and variable, being dependent upon a host of conditions, while the spirit is primary, principal and invariable, being rooted in the Qur'ānic revelation itself.

Akbar promulgated laws allowing Hindus to build new temples, and Christians to build churches and schools.[39] He also permitted those Hindus who had been forcibly converted to Islam to revert to their Hindu faith.[40] To quote Professor Ikram, 'For this policy of religious tolerance, and of giving an adequate share in the administration to all classes, there can be nothing but praise; and it became a part of the Mughal political code.'[41]

In addition to these socio-political bridges, Akbar was instrumental in building spiritual, intellectual, cultural and aesthetic bridges between the two faiths. This he did through a sustained programme of court patronage of architecture as well as art, music and poetry;[42] and perhaps most significantly of all, through the commissioning of translations of religious scriptures. Akbar's efforts at bridge-building in this domain made a profound and enduring impact on the culture of India and significantly contributed to the articulation of one of the major expressions of Islamic civilisation. As Annemarie Schimmel writes, in respect of the translation of the *Mahabharata* into Persian, the manuscript, 'produced in a cooperative effort of Muslim and Hindu artists, belongs to the most fascinating works of Islamic art.'[43] In addition to the *Mahabharata* and the *Ramayana*, other scriptures such as the *Atharva Veda*, the *Harivamsa Purana*, and Valmiki's *Yogavasistha* were also translated into Persian.[44] These translations gave a new impetus to Persian literature in India, Persian being the language of court culture. This wave of translations of Hindu classics into Persian had a deep impact on the religious sensibilities of the elites of the Indian subcontinent at the time, and for generations to come. But the concepts, idioms and terms of this cosmopolitan culture did not remain restricted to the higher reaches of philosophy; according to Rizvi, 'they percolated down to several regional languages and enriched them. The typical Mughal culture would have been much poorer without this intellectual and artistic contribution.'[45]

In the light of such impressive achievements it is easy to see why contemporary Hindu writers, in particular, refer to Akbar as one of the greatest rulers India has ever had, and why liberal Muslims see his rule as a forerunner to modern cosmopolitan culture and liberalism. One of the mainsprings of his religious policies was his undoubted sensitivity to the sacred dimension of life, and, hand in hand with this, an appreciation of the idea that no one religion has a monopoly on the sacred, an idea which, as we shall see in Part 2 of this monograph, is clearly expressed in the Qur'ān. One should also note here the influence of the Sufi accentuation of this idea, and in particular, the doctrines of the Andalusian mystical authority, Muḥyi'd-Dīn Ibn al-ʿArabī (d. 1240). Akbar's religious predilections were clearly influenced by the perspectives of this great master of Sufi metaphysics, as mediated through his chief religious adviser and court historian, Abu'l-Faḍl ʿAllāmī.

Abu'l Faḍl was not just a courtier *par excellence*, encouraging and flattering his master; he also articulated in a philosophical manner his master's innermost thoughts and desires.[46] The writings of Abu'l Faḍl are, according to the other great historian of this period, Rizvi, 'articulated within the general framework of the spiritual and mystical philosophy of Ibn Arabi.'[47] For example, the following statement can be seen as an echo of Ibn al-ʿArabī: 'There are wise men to be found ready at hand in all religions, and men of asceticism and recipients of revelation . . . Truth is the inhabitant of every place; and how could it be right to consider it as necessarily confined to one religion or creed . . . ?'[48] The following passage is found in Ibn al-ʿArabī's *Fuṣūṣ al-ḥikam*, the best known and most commented upon of all his works:

> Beware of being bound up by a particular creed and rejecting others as unbelief! Try to make yourself a prime matter for all forms of religious belief. God is greater and wider than to be confined to one particular creed to the exclusion of others. For He says 'To whichever direction you turn, there is the face of God'.'[49]

The influence of Ibn al-ʿArabī's universalism upon Akbar's religious attitudes and policies cannot be denied. But one should not conclude from this that Akbar's position was based more on the Sufi doctrine of Ibn al-ʿArabī than on the Qurʾānic ethos of tolerance. For, as is clear in the above citation from the *Fuṣūṣ*, Ibn al-ʿArabī's doctrine is itself based completely on the Qurʾān, so much so that it can be argued that his entire corpus is nothing more than an extended commentary on the Qurʾān. He affirms as much himself: 'Everything we have spoken about in our sessions or written about in our books proceeds from the Qurʾān and its treasures.'[50]

One must also note, however, the argument that Akbar's tolerant religious policies alienated significant sections among the Muslim *'ulamā'*, leading to the political backlash of Awrangzeb, two generations later, and the religious backlash of Shaykh Aḥmad Sirhindī, who criticised Ibn al-ʿArabī's doctrine of *waḥdat al-wujūd* ('oneness of being') in the name of what he considered a more appropriate mystical doctrine, *waḥdat al-shuhūd* ('oneness of witnessing'). Sirhindī, known as the *mujaddid* ('spiritual renewer') of his age, traced back to the doctrine of *waḥdat al-wujūd* much of what he saw as the religious laxity of the time, and was a vociferous advocate for reform. It has been argued by some modern Muslim scholars that Awrangzeb's more severe treatment of the Hindus in the eighteenth century was the culmination of the religious programme inaugurated by Sirhindī.[51] This programme in turn was a reaction to Akbar's policies, deemed not only to be too tolerant to non-Muslims, but also too aggressive to the Muslim clergy.

K. A. Nizami, in his seminal study of Akbar's religious outlook, notes that Akbar's relationship with the Muslim exoteric authorities passed through three distinct phases: beginning with sympathy, then lapsing into apathy, and finally hardening into antipathy.[52] What seemed more than anything else to have turned Akbar against the clerics was the series of acrimonious and petty debates conducted in his presence by various scholars in his debating chamber, the *ʿibādat khānah*, mentioned above, in the 1570s. The two main results of Akbar's disenchantment with ultra-orthodox exoteric Islam were the promulgation of his own rather mysterious and convoluted *dīn-i ilāhī* ('divine religion') on the one hand, and certain policies aimed at reducing the influence of the exoteric authorities as a class on the other. While the labels 'heretic' and 'apostate' were hurled at Akbar largely because of his *dīn-i ilāhī*, it might be argued that his policy of reducing imperial patronage of the religious classes was the underlying cause of these accusations. For his *dīn-i ilāhī* really only affected a tiny minority of people at court: it is said that there were only eighteen fully-fledged members of this 'religion', which in all likelihood was nothing but a set of esoteric opinions. But it was largely because of the diminution of the power of the Muslim clerics as a class that the tolerance Akbar accorded to other religious communities came to be seen as having been purchased at the price of Islam's pre-eminence.

I. M. Qureshi charts Akbar's policies towards the Muslim clerical class, which principally took the form of banishment of individuals deemed dangerous, and cuts in state funding for certain activities connected with this class. He shows how this resulted in damage to various Muslim institutions, with mosques becoming derelict, and religious schools forced to close for lack of funding.[53] Nonetheless, it cannot be denied that the positive influence of Akbar's tolerant policies, in particular towards the Hindu majority, was a significant factor contributing to the harmony that, in large part, characterised Muslim–Hindu relations throughout the rest of the Mughal period. Even during the time of the more stringent emperor, Awrangzeb, for example, when the *jizya* tax was re-imposed upon the Hindus, the treatment of non-Muslim minorities was still largely characterised by tolerance. The compendium of legal judgements known as *Fatāwā-yi ʿĀlamgīri* describes the treatment of the *dhimmī*s under Awrangzeb as follows:

> The *dhimmīs* do not have to bow down before the law of Islam, whether in religious matters, such as fasting and prayer, or in secular matters, such as selling wine or pork, which are proscribed by Islam but are legal for them. We [i.e., the jurists] are commanded to allow them freedom in matters covered by their own laws.[54]

Even if, for some Muslim commentators, Akbar's ecumenism was deemed excessive, none can deny that his policies, attitudes and bridge-building efforts in relation to the religious Other deepened and consolidated the ethos of tolerance which was already characteristic of the evolving Mughal culture into which he was born and brought up; and that he imparted to that ethos an impetus which guaranteed that this dimension of tolerance would persist right up to and beyond the demise of the Mughal empire. Even in later, more turbulent times, this ethos served to attenuate any tendencies towards harshness or intolerance that may have emerged under the influence of different political and ideological currents. Underlying this ethos, needless to say, was the power of the spirit of tolerance proper to the Islamic revelation; and it was from this spirit that the Mughal ethos of tolerance derived both its ultimate sanction and its ability to radiate throughout society, rather than remain confined within the culture of the court. This is clearly discernible in the simple statement of the jurists quoted above from the time of Awrangzeb: 'We are commanded to allow them freedom in matters covered by their own laws.' The jurists are 'commanded' by the sacred law of Islam to allow religious minorities the freedom to be governed by their own laws; and that law is itself but the surface expression of the tolerant spirit of the Islamic revelation, a spirit which, in Mughal India, manifested itself in the form of some of the most stunning cultural and artistic achievements in history.

The Fatimids

One of the key distinguishing features of the Fatimid dynasty was the tolerance it extended not only to non-Muslim minorities, but also to different schools of thought within Islam itself. Although themselves adhering to the Shiʿi Ismaili school of thought and law, the Fatimids scrupulously upheld the right of the majority of the peoples over whom they ruled to abide by their own confessional allegiances. This feature of Fatimid rule was particularly noteworthy in Egypt, which was peacefully conquered in 969. The famous *amān*, or pledge of security, granted by Jawhar, commanding the Fatimid army on behalf of the Imam-caliph al-Muʿizz, contained various promises to the peoples of Egypt in return for their acceptance of Fatimid rule,[55] amongst which was an important extension of the notion of *dhimma* or protection:[56] the whole population of Egypt, including all the Muslims, together with the Christians and Jews, were now to be protected under the unified *dhimma* of the Fatimids. The key passage of this historic pledge to the people of Egypt is the following:

> You shall continue in your *madhhab* [legal school]. You shall be permitted to perform your obligations according to religious scholarship, and to gather for it in your congregational and other mosques, and to remain steadfast in the beliefs of the worthy ancestors and from the Companions of the Prophet, may God be pleased with them, and those who succeeded them, the jurists of the cities who have pronounced legal judgements according to their *madhhab*s and *fatwas*.[57]

The Fatimids saw not just the 'People of the Book' (*ahl al-kitāb*, i.e., Christians and Jews), but also all Muslims as being protected by their *dhimma*. The idea of the *dhimma* pertaining in the first instance to Muslims, and being thereafter extended to non-Muslims, was seen to be rooted in a clause expressed in the Prophet's 'Constitution' of Medina, in which it was stated that 'the *dhimma* of God is one and the same'; and which was echoed in a prophetic tradition transmitted on the authority of Imam ʿAlī b. Abī Ṭālib: 'the *dhimma* of the Muslims is one and the same'.[58]

The Fatimids were to remain faithful to this pledge to protect the religious freedom of all faith communities, including the majoritarian Sunni Muslims who did not adhere to the Shiʿi Ismaili confession. As Farhad Daftary notes, although the Fatimids gradually introduced their school of law (*madhhab*), and changed certain aspects of public ritual—such as the call to prayer, which was made in accordance with Shiʿi law—'they never attempted forced conversion of their subjects, and the bulk of Egyptians remained Sunni, belonging to the Shāfiʿī *madhhab*, in addition to a large community of Christian Copts. Prior to the Fatimid arrival, the Shīʿa represented a minority in Egypt, and their minoritarian status remained unchanged throughout the two centuries of Fatimid rule.'[59]

Even though the Ismailis were known for their missionary activity, there was no attempt by the holders of power in Egypt and other lands ruled by the Fatimids to impose Ismaili Shiʿism upon the Sunni populace. On the contrary, the authorities within all four schools of Sunni jurisprudence were respected and received state support for their legal and educational institutions. The Ismaili *daʿwa* or 'missionary call', by which people were invited to consider and to adhere to the Ismaili creed, did not translate into any kind of ideological or polemical attack upon the beliefs or practices of the majority. Rather, the *daʿwa* operated as an invitation to study the wisdom pertaining to the inner or esoteric aspect (*al-bāṭin*) of the faith, and to explore the complementary relationship between the *sharīʿa* and the *ḥaqīqa*. The *daʿwa* was conducted in what were called the 'sessions of wisdom' (*majālis al-ḥikma*), which, as Heinz Halm notes, 'no one was compelled to attend'.[60] Thus, one of the distinctive features of the tolerance practised under the Ismaili Fatimids was this intra-faith Muslim ecumenism, which complemented interfaith tolerance and co-existence. Such ecumenism went hand in hand with a profoundly philosophical spirit of inquiry, a respect for knowledge and science, and an open-minded attitude on the part of the elites governing Fatimid state and society. As stated by Halm:

> The reign of the Fatimid imam-caliphs was one of the most brilliant periods of Islamic history, both politically and in terms of its literary, economic, artistic and scientific achievement . . . Fatimid traditions of learning have spread their influence geographically far beyond the limits of the Fatimid empire itself—as far as India and Western Europe—and chronologically beyond the political end of the dynasty.[61]

One of the most famous surviving monuments to this spirit of inquiry is the university of al-Azhar, the foundations of which were laid in 970 by Jawhar. The original structure of the mosque was completed two years later, and in 989 it was established as a university, which has been called 'the first in the world' by Farhad Daftary. 'It has remained the principal institution of religious learning in the Muslim world.'[62]

The peaceful co-existence between the different faith communities throughout the Fatimid period in Egypt is vividly portrayed in the historical vignettes emerging out of what are known as 'the Geniza documents' of Cairo, documents of the Jewish community, written mostly in Hebrew script, but in the Arabic language, dating from the tenth to the thirteenth century, describing in great detail all sorts of legal cases, economic transactions, private correspondence, accounts, marriage and divorce proceedings, etc. They constitute 'a primary source for social and economic history during the Fatimid and Ayyubid periods'.[63] The documents afford the historian a view from the grass-roots, allowing one to see how Muslim tolerance operated in the concrete social and economic relationships by which the different faith-communities were bound together in a unified, and largely harmonious, social system. The picture which emerges from these precious documents is indeed one of remarkable cohesion between the different communities, the Fatimid rulers doing little more than establishing the general parameters within which the communities were free to operate in conformity with their own religious norms and customs, and according to the laws of the market-place, within an over-arching framework defined by the principles of Islamic law. Goitein notes that mutual respect between the religious scholars of the different faith communities is expressed in many of the documents:

> Particularly noteworthy are the friendly relations between the religious scholars and dignitaries of the various denominations. Throughout the Geniza letters and in the queries addressed to Maimonides and his son Abraham, as well as their *responsa*, the Muslim judges and jurists are referred to reverentially, and rarely without a comment wishing them temporal or spiritual success, or both.[64]

Historians across the board are in no doubt about the tolerance and liberality of the ruling Fatimids, but appear divided over the question of the extent to which 'the tenets and theology' of the Ismaili Fatimids 'were responsible for the character of the new state'. Goitein himself opines that the Fatimids 'did not create the comparatively liberal spirit of the period'; rather, the fact that they were 'only a small minority' within a predominantly Sunni land 'contributed to a trend of tolerance in their conduct of government, and to a general leniency toward other minority groups.'[65]

By contrast, Bernard Lewis argues that the Ismaili appeal to all religions and races was an inherent part of their theology, coming close to being a form of 'interconfessionalism . . . verging at times on complete rationalism'. By 'rationalism' he appears to mean an absence of fanaticism. He asserts that the Ismailis developed 'a coherent system in which the relative truth of all religion was freely recognised, and fanaticism definitely renounced.'[66] He cites passages from the 'epistles' (*rasā'il*) of a group of Ismaili philosophers known as al-Ikhwān al-Ṣafā' ('Brethren of Purity'), probably writing in the late ninth/early tenth century. These passages indicate that the ideal philosophical approach to the phenomenon of religious diversity is to have empathy for all, to pray for all, and to avoid all polemics in matters of religion. Lewis further cites the work of the tenth century Ismaili missionary, Ja'far b. Manṣūr al-Yaman, who asserted that not only the Christians, Jews and Sabeans, but also 'people of any other religion who believe in God and in an afterlife, who do good and obey God, have a place in heaven.'[67] Samuel Stern concurs with Lewis, and also cites passages from the Ikhwān al-Ṣafā' expressing their tolerance and open-mindedness. For example: 'It befits our brothers that they should not show hostility to any kind of knowledge or reject any book. Nor should they be fanatical in any doctrine, for our opinion and our doctrine embrace all doctrines and resume all knowledge.'[68]

The two contrasting explanations of Fatimid tolerance are by no means mutually exclusive. One can argue that purely political and demographic factors predisposed the rulers to a tolerant mode of governance; for a fundamental *intolerance* would no doubt have weakened the already limited power base of the state, eliciting a hostile reaction from the religious minorities, and possibly pushing them into forging an alliance with the Sunni majority against the Fatimids. However, such political considerations do not render irrelevant the universal spirit inherent in the Ismaili philosophy guiding the Fatimids. Rather, the dictates of political pragmatism and the tenets of theology happened to dovetail quite neatly: tolerance was not just good politics, it was also sound theology. Trying to determine which came first is not as important as acknowledging that the spirit of tolerance penetrated the entire political and social domain within which policies were to be decided upon and implemented. This spirit palpably informed the Ismaili outlook, which, in turn, cannot be divorced from the ecumenical spirit of the Qur'ān itself. Hence, one can dismiss the opinion of Stern, who claims that the universal spirit of the Ikhwān al-Ṣafā' was far from 'orthodox Islam'.[69] It may well have been far from 'fundamentalist' or fanatical Islam, but it was completely in accord with the basic thrust of the Islamic approach to knowledge generally[70] and to religious minorities in particular, as will be made clear in the second part of this monograph. For the moment, though, let us note that the opinion of Ja'far b. Manṣūr al-Yaman, cited above, is clearly an echo of this Qur'ānic verse, which definitively affirms the universal criteria for salvation:

> Truly those who believe, and the Jews, and the Christians, and the Sabeans—whoever believes in God and the Last Day and performs virtuous deeds—surely their reward is with their Lord, and no fear shall come upon them, neither shall they grieve (2:62; repeated almost verbatim at 5:69).

Stern goes on to claim that official Ismailism only manifested 'latitude' regarding the religious Other by using the scriptures of the People of the Book as prophecies regarding the advent of the Ismailis themselves. He concludes: 'There appears absolutely no sign of an attitude towards other religions which could be characterised as deviating from the common opinion of Islam'—a point with which one cannot but agree, insofar as the 'common opinion of Islam' regarding other religions be understood as stemming from verses such as 2:62 and 5:69. In other words, the 'common opinion of Islam' is precisely what leads to 'latitude' and tolerance vis-à-vis other religions. The most commonly found Muslim 'opinion' regarding other religions is that which is based on the Qur'ānic ethos of religious plurality, an ethos which logically entails the ethics of tolerance and respect, and it is this which was upheld as normative by the Fatimids.

As regards the Ismaili use of scriptures of the People of the Book, it may well be true that in certain polemical debates these scriptures were interpreted, through *ta'wīl*, as prophesying certain events connected with the Ismailis, but such exegetical exercises in no way compromised or diluted the basic Qur'ānic position as regards the scriptures of the People of the Book. This position was one of reverence and not merely tolerance. Such reverence is clearly manifested in a variety of early Ismaili sources. For example, in Ibn Haytham's *Kitāb al-munāẓarāt* written some time after 946, it is said that the Ismaili missionary, Abū ʿAbdallāh al-Shīʿī asked Ibn Haytham if he had read the epistles (*mayāmīr*) of St Paul. 'He then launched forth into the substance of them, and it was as if he had a copy in front of him, and he went over it chapter by chapter.'[71]

One should also note the work of the great Fatimid philosopher, Abū Ḥātim al-Rāzī (d. 934), entitled *Aʿlām al-nubuwwa* ('Signs of Prophecy'). In this work one finds an ecumenical approach to the question of religious truth, which is upheld through arguments drawing in an unbiased manner from Christian and Jewish scriptures as well as from the Qur'ān. The book takes the form of a series of debates between Abū Ḥātim and Muḥammad b. Zakariyyā al-Rāzī on questions of revelation and the multiplicity of religions. As Seyyed Hossein Nasr notes, in his introduction to a recent edition of this work:

> Abū Ḥātim answers Muḥammad b. Zakariyyā' Rāzī's criticisms and displays a remarkable knowledge not only of the Holy Qur'ān but also the Old and New Testaments. In answer to the criticism of the multiplicity of religions, Abū Ḥātim strongly defends the transcendent unity of religions and the celestial origin of all authentic religions ... *Aʿlām al-nubuwwa* is without doubt one of the most important Islamic works in what is known today as comparative religion.[72]

The position of Christians and Jews under the Fatimids is described by Goitein as 'both safeguarded and precarious'. By this he meant that Islamic law did indeed protect life, property and freedom while allowing the Jews and Christians the right to practise their faith unimpeded. But the 'precarious' nature of their condition was on account of the fact that, according to Goitein, Islamic law also 'demanded from them segregation and subservience, conditions that under a weak or cruel government could and did lead to situations bordering on lawlessness and even to outright persecution.' He does, however, concede that during most of the Fatimid period 'the protective principles of Islamic law were more conspicuous than its dark side.'[73] This last sentence is questionable, just as his claim that Islamic law demanded 'segregation and subservience' is mistaken. What might be described as 'dark' is, rather, the precise opposite or absence of Islamic law; that is to say, violations of, or deviations from, the norms established by what Goitein rightly refers to as 'the protective principles of Islamic law'. As Goitein observed himself, it was under 'weak or cruel' governments that one found such lapses into an uncharacteristic persecution. The spirit of tolerance governing Islamic law is what strikes the objective observer of Islamic history as the rule, intolerance being evidently the exception.

While some might point to the segregation of the People of the Book and the imposition upon them of distinctive apparel as a sign of their subjection to the Muslim state, one should note that there is nothing in the Qur'ān or Hadith justifying such practices, as will be further argued in the second part of this monograph. One can rightly regard such practices as contingent and somewhat artificial creations of the jurists, which are in fact antithetical to the spirit defining the fundamental attitude to religious minorities in the Islamic revelation. In any case, Goitein notes the discrepancy between theory and practice on this point. Even though there are 'countless references' to the imposition of distinctive dress upon the Jews and Christians in Arabic literary sources, 'the Geniza documents prove, however, that practice during the Fatimid and early Ayyubid periods must have differed widely from theory . . . nowhere do we find any allusion to a specific "Jewish" attire. On the contrary, there is much evidence that there was none.'[74]

In regard to the issue of places of worship, one notes that the Fatimid imam-caliphs, particularly al-Muʿizz and al-ʿAzīz, granted full rights to Christians and Jews both to build and to restore their churches and synagogues. This tolerant policy was continued into al-Ḥākim's rule, so much so that it led to criticism from some quarters that he was unduly favourable to the Christians at the expense of the Muslims. It was al-Ḥākim's attempts to contain mounting tensions between the two communities that appears to have provoked some of the contradictory edicts which were issued during his rule—most importantly, the order to destroy the Church of the Holy Sepulchre in Jerusalem, which was under the suzerainty of the Fatimids at this time.[75] This tragic event did not, however, signal a 'general persecution of Christians, as has been falsely maintained again and again', as Halm notes. Rather, that towards the end of his reign, al-Ḥākim 'returned to the Christians the expropriated churches and convents, as well as their lands, and allowed them to reconstruct the demolished buildings'.[76]

For most of al-Ḥākim's rule (996–1021), what is evident is his effort to establish harmonious relations between all faith communities, and also between different Muslim schools of thought. This effort culminated in the edict (*sijill*) of tolerance in 399/1009, which legally put Sunni rites on a par with Shiʿi rites. In support of this edict he referred to the well-known Qurʾānic verse, 2: 256, 'There is no compulsion in religion'. As Halm notes: 'The differences between the Islamic confessions remained, but were tolerated. Al-Ḥākim's *sijill* ended with the liberal principle: "Each Muslim may try to find his own solution within his religion (*li-kulli muslim fī dīnihi ijtihād*)".'[77]

A fundamentally benevolent attitude towards the Christians and Jews, as well as towards non-Ismailis, continued to characterise Fatimid rule after al-Ḥākim. Yaacov Lev refers to the royal support granted to churches, monasteries and synagogues throughout the Fatimid period, and draws attention to such Jewish institutions as the Jerusalem Yeshiva, which received important assistance from the Fatimids. Both Christians and Jews were 'employed massively in the Fatimid administration', he notes, and this extended right up to the post of wazir. The wazir of al-ʿAzīz was the Jew Ibn Killis who converted to Islam; the wazir of al-Ḥāfiẓ was the Christian Bahrām; and the head of al-Mustanṣir's mother's office—an extremely powerful position—was the Jew Abū Saʿd al-Tustarī.[78] However, rather like Goitein and Stern, Lev fails to see the organic connection between the ethos of the Qurʾān and the tolerant attitudes of the Fatimids, arguing instead that such tolerance had more to do with the fact that the imam-caliph had no need to consult religious scholars and did whatever he thought was appropriate.[79] Lev appears to be arguing that the tolerant policies of the Fatimids were the result of arbitrary decisions; that these policies emerged *despite* the Qurʾān rather than *because* of the Qurʾān. As will be made clearer in the second part of this monograph, one can make the contrary argument: the attitudes and policies of the Fatimids as regards non-Muslims were not only in harmony with the Qur'ānic principle of tolerance, they were substantially determined by this principle and faithful expressions of it.

The Umayyads of Cordoba

At the very same time as the Christian West was indulging in periodic anti-Jewish pogroms, the Jews were experiencing what some Jewish historians themselves have termed a kind of 'golden age' under Islamic rule generally, but in Muslim Spain in particular. As Erwin Rosenthal writes, 'The Talmudic age apart, there is perhaps no more formative and positive time in our long and chequered history than that under the empire of Islam.'[80] This point of view is strongly reinforced by Samuel Goitein:

> Judaism could draw freely and copiously from Muslim civilisation and, at the same time, preserve its independence and integrity far more completely than it was able to do in the modern world or in the Hellenistic society of Alexandria . . . Judaism inside Islam was an autonomous culture sure of itself despite, and possibly because of, its intimate connection with its environment. Never has Judaism encountered such a close and fructuous symbiosis as that with the medieval civilisation of Arab Islam.[81]

Let us again quote from that fierce critic of contemporary Muslim movements, Bernard Lewis, who cannot but confirm the facts of history as regards the true character of Muslim–Jewish relations until recent times. In his important book, *The Jews of Islam*, he writes that even though there was a certain level of discrimination against Jews and Christians under Muslim rule:

> Persecution, that is to say, violent and active repression, was rare and atypical. Jews and Christians under Muslim rule were not normally called upon to suffer martyrdom for their faith. They were not often obliged to make the choice, which confronted Muslims and Jews in reconquered Spain, between exile, apostasy and death. They were not subject to any major territorial or occupational restrictions, such as were the common lot of Jews in premodern Europe.[82]

This pattern of tolerance characterised the nature of Muslim rule vis-à-vis Jews and Christians until modern times, with very minor exceptions. As the Jewish scholar Mark Cohen notes:

> The Talmud was burned in Paris, not in Cairo or Baghdad. More secure than their brethren in the Christian West, the Jews of Islam took a correspondingly more conciliatory view of their masters. In Europe, the Jews nurtured a pronounced hatred for Christians, whom they considered to be idolators subject to the anti-pagan discriminatory provisions of the ancient Mishnah. Moreover, when faced with the choice between death and conversion, the Jews of northern Europe usually chose martyrdom rather than 'the polluting waters of the baptismal font' as they called it in Hebrew. The Jews of Islam had a markedly different attitude towards the religion of their masters. Staunch Muslim opposition to polytheism convinced Jewish thinkers like Maimonides of Islam's unimpeachable monotheism. This essentially 'tolerant' view of Islam echoed Islam's own respect for the Jewish 'People of the Book' . . .[83]

One particularly rich episode in the 'golden age' of the Jews took place in Andalusia. As has been abundantly attested in contemporaneous sources, the Jews enjoyed not just freedom from oppression, but also an extraordinary revival of cultural, religious, theological and mystical creativity. As Titus Burckhardt writes, 'The greatest beneficiaries of Islamic rule were the Jews, for in Spain (*sephārād* in Hebrew) they enjoyed their finest intellectual flowering since their dispersal from Palestine to foreign lands.'[84] Jewish poetry acquired an entirely new idiom: the renowned poet Dunash Ben Labrat adopted Arabic poetic metres in Hebrew verse, thus establishing a precedent for future generations of Jewish poets in Spain. Similarly, Samuel Ha-Nagid, Solomon ibn Gabirol and Judah Ha-Levi are described as having produced a veritable 'renaissance' in Jewish poetry in the eleventh century, matching the composition of such philosophical classics as Maimonides' *Guide for the Perplexed*, and Ha-Levi's *Kuzari*.[85]

In her eloquent testimony to the tolerance characterising Muslim Spain,[86] Maria Rosa Menocal vividly depicts the extraordinarily rich culture of the Cordoba caliphate within which the spirit of tolerance was so vibrant. She reveals that the Muslims did not so much introduce tolerance into the existing culture in Christian Visigothic Spain; rather, it introduced culture *per se* into what was a wasteland, in terms of most of the indices of authentic culture. Although, as she notes, one of the virtues of 'Arabic-Islamic civilisation' was its ability 'to assimilate and even revive the rich gifts of earlier and indigenous cultures',[87] what one observes in the case of Muslim Spain was in fact the grafting by the Umayyads of this civilisation—already enriched in its original Syrian milieu—upon a land devoid of literary culture, let alone tolerance. The description 'ornament of the world' comes from the pen of the tenth-century Saxon writer Hroswitha, as she tried to convey to her sisters at the convent at Gandersheim the scarcely imaginable beauty and splendour of Cordoba at that time: 'The brilliant ornament of the world shone in the West . . . Cordoba was its name and it was wealthy and famous and known for its pleasures and resplendent in all things, and especially for its seven streams of wisdom [the trivium and quadrivium].'[88] Hroswitha's informant was no less a figure than Racemundo, the bishop of Elvira, metropolitan see of al-Andalus, and 'an esteemed member of the caliph's diplomatic corps'.[89]

Menocal notes that it was its 'intellectual wealth' rather than its material wealth or simply outward beauty that made Cordoba famous as the 'ornament of the world.' As will be argued in the second part of this essay, authentic knowledge of the Other is what carries in its train the ethic of tolerance; it is this that, among other things, characterised the spirit of the Islamic revelation, and is manifested with particular clarity in the case of the Cordoban caliphate. The centrality of knowledge to the material and cultural success of the 'ornament of the world' is well expressed by Menocal:

> The rich web of attitudes about culture, and the intellectual opulence that it symbolized is perhaps only suggested by the caliphal library of (by one count) some four hundred thousand volumes, and this at a time when the largest library in Christian Europe probably held no more than four hundred manuscripts. Cordoba's caliphal library was itself one of seventy libraries in a city that apparently so adored books that a report of the time indicated that there were seventy copyists in the book market who worked exclusively on copying Qurans . . . the catalogues alone of the Cordoba library ran to forty-four volumes.

Prior to the advent of the Umayyads, the Iberian peninsula was nominally Christian under Visigothic rule, but basically still pagan, and the Jews who had arrived with the Romans centuries earlier 'lived in nearly enslaved squalor'.[90] Under 'Abd al-Raḥmān—the sole survivor of the massacre of the Umayyads by the 'Abbāsids in 750—and his successors, the situation was to change dramatically. Along with a dynamic culture, political stability and economic prosperity, the Muslims brought to the peoples of Andalusia a degree of religious tolerance, inclusiveness and broad-mindedness that was difficult to match in any part of the world of that time: 'Here the Jewish community rose from the ashes of an abysmal existence under the Visigoths to the point that the emir who proclaimed himself caliph in the tenth century had a Jew as his foreign minister.'[91] Menocal connects the Jewish 'Golden Period' in Andalus with a particular feature of Andalusian tolerance, its generous embrace of the apparently contradictory internal Other:

> God's universe, in al-Andalus, had three principal and interlocking features which are at the heart of its importance for us, and which were in its own time at the heart of that culture's extraordinarily vigorous well-being: ethnic pluralism, religious tolerance, and a variety of important forms of what we could call cultural secularism—secular poetry and philosophy—that were not understood, by those who pursued them, to be un- or anti-Islamic. Of course, all three are inherently possible in Islam. One might even say they are inherently mandated by Islam. But few Islamic polities have done it as well as al-Andalus did, nor for as long, nor with greater long-term impact and dazzling results.[92]

As mentioned above, the Umayyads brought to Spain an entirely new culture, which was perpetually enriched by streams of influence from the Islamic heartlands of the East. It was also enriched by the dynamism of the *muwallad*s, that is, the indigenous converts to Islam who were Celto-Iberians, Visigoths and Romans. Within the course of one or two generations, the relationship between religious identity and ethnicity in Cordoban society was totally transformed: the ruling Arab minority was swamped by waves of converts in the tenth century, such that approximately eighty per cent of the original indigenous population had converted to Islam. The result was 'a different kind of society, an Islamic one in which indigenous peoples predominated, replacing the imperial state ruled by an Arab minority.'[93]

Those who remained Christian were soon named *Mozarab* (from the Arabic *mustaʿrab*, 'one has become Arabised' or *mustaʿrib*, 'one who seeks to be Arabised'),[94] and while benefiting from the protection afforded by their *dhimmī* status, simultaneously threw themselves into the rich Arabic culture that Menocal refers to as 'secular', although a better word to describe the openness of the developing culture would be 'universal'. Menocal waxes lyrical about the ability of the Cordoban culture to cultivate a 'first-rate mind', which she defines, using F. Scott Fitzgerald's terms, as a mind which could hold two contrary ideas at the same time. This, she argues is what one sees in the 'true religious tolerance and the sort of cultural vitality' that characterised Andalusian society under the Muslims. For Menocal, the key to this 'secular' culture was the Arabic language, and particularly its poetry, which was so important for a correct understanding of Qurʾānic Arabic. The enthusiasm with which Jews adopted the Arabic medium, alongside a cultivation of Hebrew in fields outside of theology and law, can only be explained with reference to a fundamental attitude which celebrated otherness and not merely tolerated it:

> Tolerance of 'others' is one thing, and a very good thing indeed, but the effects of taking pleasure in contradiction within one's own identity can be even richer. It became possible to be a pious Jew who could recite a pre-Islamic ode . . . or take the peripatetic tradition seriously, in great measure because pious Muslims did it. The community of Jewish intellectuals and leaders absorbed and came to believe in the fundamental moral of the story: internal tolerance of contradictory identity is the basis of a superior and first-rate language and identity.[95]

One of the results of this inclusive culture concerned Hebrew: for the first time in a thousand years it was 'brought out of the confines of the synagogue' and became as versatile an instrument as Arabic for the expression of such universal themes as philosophy and love. Sephardim poetry is an eloquent testament to the dynamism of this 'golden age' of Judaism. Menocal rightly mentions the fact that the ultimate source of the tolerance of the Muslims in Cordoba was their conception of God, who, it turns out, 'had a first-rate mind Himself, and perhaps not only tolerated but enjoyed contradictions'. She does not adequately elaborate on this, but it seems clear that she has in mind such verses of the Qur'ān as follows:

> We have revealed unto you the Scripture with the Truth, as a confirmer of whatever [revealed] Scripture came before it, and a protector thereof... For each We have appointed a Law and a Way. Had God willed, He could have made you one community. But in order that He might try you by that which He has given you [He has made you as you are]. So vie with one another in good works. Unto God you will all return, and He will inform you of that wherein you differed (5:48).

> O mankind, We have created you male and female, and We have made you into tribes and nations in order that you might come to know one another. Truly, in the sight of God, the most honoured amongst you is the most pious amongst you (49:13).[96]

The 'contradiction' here might more accurately be described as a divinely-willed diversity which is intended not only to enhance the richness of human culture and the depth of human knowledge, but also contribute to 'piety' or God-consciousness (*taqwā*). Menocal's stress on the 'secular' nature of Cordoban culture, whether Muslim, Jewish or Christian, does not sufficiently take into account the scope of the piety or God-consciousness which remained the fundamental goal of the religious communities in Cordoba. The culture nurtured by the Muslim elites was one in which this goal could be pursued by all, within a common medium, the Arabic language; so what one observes is not so much a 'secular' culture being pursued outside the framework of religion, but rather the opposite: Muslim tolerance allowed Jews and Christians, as well as Muslims, to express in their own unique ways their deepest spiritual aspirations. These aspirations came to encompass the whole of one's cultural and psychological identity, and not simply one's theology, and in this manner, no domain was left outside of, or apart from, one's faith. The search for love, interest in philosophy, appreciation of virgin nature, cultivation of fine taste, humour, wit, etc.—Muslims, Jews and Christians came to express these universal themes in a common cultural medium which enriched their respective religious identities, and did not necessarily dilute or impoverish this identity by any implication of compromise with 'the world', that is, with a putatively 'secular' or non-religious dimension.

The example set by ʿAbd al-Raḥmān II during his thirty-year rule (822–852) is instructive in this regard. Described by E. Lévi-Provençal in his monumental and now classic three-volume study, *Histoire de l'Espagne musulmane*, as undoubtedly 'the most cultivated of all the Hispano-Umayyad emirs', with the exception of his descendant, al-Ḥakam II.[97] He was a great patron of the arts—the famous musician Ziryāb introduced new genres of music, such as what became the origin of Flamenco—and sciences, both religious and natural, drawing to court a large entourage of experts in fields as diverse as *ḥadīth* interpretation and love poetry, astronomy and dream-interpretation, philosophy and music. It is clear that for such a ruler, the distinction between the religious and the secular would not have made much sense; the category of 'religion' or 'faith' was simply expanded beyond the fields of theology and law and thus came to encompass all that was noble, beautiful and true. It was this cosmopolitan culture that both Jews and Christians found irresistible: they were invited to extend their own religious identity to embrace these diverse domains of life and culture. The result was the creation of a universal cultural milieu or 'space' in which all three religions found a home, interacting fruitfully with each other in the language proper to this new space, even while retaining, on the specifically theological and juridical planes, their own unique and thus irreducible confessional identity.

This was certainly the case, by and large, for the Muslims and Jews; for Christians, however, the relationship between religious identity and the new cosmopolitan culture was more complex. For although there is no serious dispute about the fact of Muslim tolerance of Christians, there is evidence that the Christian community felt its integrity to be increasingly undermined by the huge mass of conversions to Islam. This was bitterly lamented, by the Christian clergy in particular. First, though, as regards tolerance, we have the following interesting contemporaneous testimony to the practice of Muslim tolerance, which comes from within the Christian community itself. In the middle of the tenth century embassies were exchanged between the court of Otto I of Germany and the court of Cordoba. One such delegation was led by John of Gorze in 953. At Cordoba, he met the resident bishop, John of Cordoba, who explained to John of Gorze how the Christians survived:

> We have been driven to this by our sins, to be subjected to the rule of the pagans. We are forbidden by the Apostle's words to resist the civil power. Only one cause of solace is left to us, that in the depths of such a great calamity, they do not forbid us to practise our own faith . . . For the time being, then, we keep the following counsel: that provided no harm is done to our religion, we obey them in all else, and do their commands in all that does not affect our faith.[98]

This statement was made one hundred years after the anomalous set of executions of the so-called 'Cordoban martyrs'. On the surface, it would appear that the execution for heresy of forty-eight Christians by the caliphal authorities between 850 and 859 supplies evidence of Muslim intolerance. But upon closer inspection, it bears witness, in a certain sense—relative to the context—to the very opposite. During the summer of 851 thirteen Christian monks and clerics deliberately sought martyrdom by publicly abusing the Prophet of Islam and calling him an imposter. Around the same number is recorded as having been executed the following year.[99] These executions do not, however, signify any lapse by the Muslim authorities into active persecution of Christians. On the contrary, those who sought martyrdom were hoping to elicit from their Muslim overlords the kind of persecution which, precisely, Muslims were *not* guilty of. What most concerned those seeking martyrdom was the very congeniality and tolerance of the Arab–Islamic culture, which made conversion to Islam so attractive a proposition for Christians. Many of these martyrs were aiming at transforming the Christian community in Cordoba into 'a martyr Church, following the pattern set in the great Diocletianic persecution of 303–312. Their aim was to halt the slide into Arabicising and into Islam by setting their Church into violent opposition to the Muslim establishment.'[100]

Just as Muslim tolerance of Christians in Cordoba was at the very antipodes of Roman persecution of Christians under Diocletian, so the Muslim judges in the trials of the Cordoban martyrs cannot be compared to the pagan governors of Rome. There is abundant evidence that the Muslim *qāḍī*s strove as far as they could to avoid the death penalty. When conversion to Islam was the only legal alternative to execution, they went so far as to invite the accused to make a purely nominal conversion, after which they could go and practise their Christian faith without fear of further investigation: 'Say only a word in this hour of need', said a *qāḍī* to Eulogius, one of those seeking martyrdom, 'and afterwards practise your faith where you will. We promise not to search for you'.[101] Eulogius was in fact one of the chief propagandists on behalf of the martyrs before he himself became one of their number. He complained at how the Cordoban Christians 'consider it a delight to be subject to these people [the Muslims], and do not resist being led by the yoke of the infidels. They even make use of many of their sacrileges on a day to day basis and seek their company rather than trying to save themselves like the Patriarch Lot, who departed Sodom for the mountains'. The close friend and biographer of Eulogius, Paul Albar, wrote the following, which can be taken as evidence of the success of the Cordoban cultural venture, if success be defined in terms of creative synthesis between Christian faith and Arabic culture:

> The Christians forgot their language to the point that you would not find among a thousand of them one person who could write a letter to a friend in Latin which is free from error. As for writing Arabic, you will certainly find a large number who master that language, possessing an elegant style, writing poetry that at times surpasses in quality that which is composed by the Arabs themselves.[102]

The martyrs' movement created a split in the Christian community. Many supported the cause and upheld the underlying theological position motivating the movement. Eulogius and his friend (and biographer) Paul Albar wrote vicious polemics against Islam in their justification of the martyrs' actions. 'They condemned Islam as both a social and theological entity. Islam, they argued, encouraged moral depravity as well as corruption and exploitation in government. At the same time, they dismissed its theology as trivial and superstitious.'[103]

By contrast, those Christians who were either employed by the government or closely involved with Muslims in business and commerce, together with significant sections among the clergy, were appalled by the martyrs' actions, which did, indeed, result in the harsh retaliatory measures that the martyrs were hoping for. However, these measures were short-lived: 'the radical Christian movement had little long-term effect.'[104]

It is of course simplistic and erroneous to claim that, prior to the fifteenth century massacres and expulsions, tolerance was exclusively practised by Muslims, and intolerance exclusively by Christians—there are clearly examples of Muslim intolerance and Christian tolerance throughout the long history of Islam's encounter with Christianity on the Iberian peninsula. But what should be clear is that Muslim tolerance was the norm, from which intolerance was a deviation; a norm, moreover that was not simply observable, *ex post facto*, as an empirical pattern, but rather was *a priori* rooted in Islamic law and governed by an ethical spirit fashioned by the Islamic revelation. Instances of Christian tolerance, by contrast, are haphazard and occasional exceptions to a general attitude of antipathy if not hostility towards non-Christians. One of the main reasons for the immense contrast between the Muslim treatment of Jewish and Christian minorities, on the one hand, and the Christian treatment of Jewish and Muslim minorities, on the other, consists of their different conceptions of sacred law and the spiritual root and concomitant of that law. Thomas Glick expresses this point as follows in his *Islamic and Christian Spain in the Early Middle Ages*:

> The reason for the discrepancy, and the erosion of the social status of subject Jews and Muslims from the start, lies in the differing conceptions of law prevailing in the two cultures. Islamic law, although subject to a relatively limited range of differing interpretations, was universal and unchangeable. The safeguards afforded to the People of the Book were the norm, and suffered erosion only at the hands of weak rulers, who permitted unlawful contraventions of minority rights, or of despots whose fanaticism led to direct contraventions of law. In the Christian kingdoms, there was no general norm, except for vague guarantees of freedom of worship and group autonomy, but rather the rules were pacted with local

> groups by specific rulers and were subject either to ratification or change by each successive ruler.[105]

Moses ben Ezra, poet and courtier of Granada arrived in Castille in 1095, as one of the wave of Jewish migrants who left Muslim Spain for Christian Spain as a result of the Berber invasions of the eleventh and twelfth centuries. His bitter complaint is evidence of the contrast between the two cultures in Spain at that time: 'I have come to the iniquitous domain of a people scorned by God and accursed by man, amongst savages who love corruption'; his homeland, the Muslim state of Granada was like 'the gardens of truth', whilst he is now reduced to hewing 'the wood of forests and folly' in Castille.[106]

One can gauge the extent of the contrast between the two contexts by noting that the caliph al-Ḥakam II (961–976) went so far in his respect for Jewish learning that he employed Joseph ibn Shatnash (a disciple of Rabbi Moses) to explain to him, in Arabic, the whole of the Talmud.[107] One might contrast this Muslim interest in and respect for the Jewish scriptures with the difficulty encountered by Peter the Venerable, Abbot of Cluny, in his effort to find someone willing and able to translate the Qurʾān into Latin.

With the expulsion, murder or forced conversion of all Muslims and Jews following the Reconquista of Spain—brought to completion with the fall of Granada in 1492—it was to the Ottomans that the exiled Jews turned for refuge and protection. They were welcomed in Muslim lands throughout North Africa, joining their co-religionists already settled there, and also establishing new Jewish communities. The Ottoman sultan Bāyazīd II, in 1509, made the famous remark about King Ferdinand of Spain, who was busy expelling all the Jews (and Muslims) from Spain: 'Can you call such a king wise and intelligent? He is impoverishing his country and enriching my country.' Commenting on this remark, Eliahu Klein writes that 'the influx of these Sephardic Jews into the Turkish empire was one of the factors that helped the Turks become a world economic power at that time.'[108] Thus, the radiance of the Jewish 'golden age' experienced in Spain under Muslim rule was not altogether eclipsed by the Christian Reconquista; thanks to the warm welcome received from the Ottomans, Sephardic Judaism became the bearer of a rich cultural tradition, comprising a newly valorised dimension of the Kabbalah, the mystical tradition of Judaism. Spanish Jewry was enabled by the Ottomans to lay the roots of Safed Kabbalah in Palestine, from where it spread the teachings of the *Zohar*, the Spanish-Jewish magnum opus of the Kabbalah, to nearly all parts of the globe, and continues to do so to this day.[109]

If the Jews of Muslim Spain were granted legal toleration and also the cultural freedom to engage with their tradition in a manner which produced such a 'golden age', this was not only thanks to a particularly enlightened attitude on the part of the Muslim rulers of Spain. Rather, these rulers had an enlightened and tolerant attitude because they were particularly well-attuned to the spirit of the Islamic revelation. One can well appreciate how the following lines of poetry by Spain's most celebrated Sufi, Muḥyī'd-Dīn Ibn al-ʿArabī, could have been penned by one reared in the multi-religious and tolerant milieu of Andalusian Islam:

> My heart has become capable of every form: it is a pasture for gazelles,
> and a convent for Christian monks,
> And a temple for idols, and the pilgrim's Kaʿba, and the tables of the Tora,
> and the book of the Koran.
> I follow the religion of Love: whatever way Love's camels take, that is my religion and my faith.[110]

As noted in the section on the Mughals, the perspective of Ibn al-ʿArabī is rooted in the Qur'ān; his all-embracing universality is therefore not to be reduced to the status of a mystical or rhetorical expression of a spectacularly cosmopolitan Andalusian spiritual culture. Rather, Ibn al-ʿArabī is simply transcribing, in poetic and mystical mode, the essential message of the Qur'ān as regards the religious Other. We might note here that he claims, in *al-Futūḥāt al-Makkiyya*, that the culminating point in his spiritual ascent was the realisation of the meaning of the Qur'ānic verse, 3:84; he describes this verse as 'the key to all knowledge': 'Say: we believe in God and that which is revealed unto us and that which was revealed unto Abraham and Ishmael and Isaac and Jacob and the tribes [of Israel] and that which was given unto Moses and Jesus and the prophets from their Lord. We make no distinction between any of them, and unto Him we have surrendered'.[111]

This all-encompassing view of revelation fundamentally fashioned both Ibn al-ʿArabī's metaphysical universality and the culture of Andalusian religious tolerance. Ibn al-ʿArabī merely disclosed the mystical dimensions of the spirit of the Qurʾānic message concerning the religious Other; he did not create that spirit any more than did Andalusian culture.

It might also be noted that the same principle applies in regard to the famed Andalusian dedication to beauty—to the beauties of art and architecture, as well as the beauties of virgin nature, so eloquently described in innumerable poems in all the languages being spoken and written at the time. Ibn al-ʿArabī tellingly begins his famous poem above with a reference to the 'pasture for gazelles'. This may be taken as an allusion to the revelation inherent in the cosmos as such, which is a constellation of infinite 'signs' (*āyāt*, sing. *āya*) pointing to the all-encompassing reality of God—a perspective central both to Sufi metaphysics and Andalusian culture. Again, this is a perspective that is entirely Qurʾānic. On the one hand: 'We shall show them Our signs on the horizons and in their own souls, so that it be clear to them that He is the Real' (41:53); and on the other, 'Unto God belong the East and the West; and wherever ye turn, there is the Face of God' (2:115).

Dhimmīs: 'Protected Minorities'

In the previous sections mention has been made repeatedly of the term *dhimmī*, and it may be helpful to discuss some of the issues, both theological and historical, pertaining to this concept before addressing, in Part 2 of this monograph, the spirit of tolerance in the Qurʾān and the Sunna of the Prophet. The word *dhimmī* comes from a root meaning 'blame': the idea here is that any violation of the religious, social or legal rights of the protected minority was subject to the 'censure' (*dhamāma, madhamma*) of the Muslim authorities, who were charged with the protection of these rights; the implication is further extendable to mean that these authorities are themselves subject to divine censure if they violate the rights of those under their protection. The lexical meaning here is worth noting, as it is closely related to the idea of *ḥurma*, something inviolable, sacrosanct: '. . . a thing which one is under an obligation to reverence, respect or honour and defend . . .

every *ḥurma* for the neglect or non-observance of which one is to be blamed'.[112] Several points need to be made in regard to this issue, given the extent to which it has been bound up with the practice of tolerance in Muslim history.

First, let us note that the protected minorities are not only the Jews, Christians and Sabeans—the religious communities named in the Qur'ān as belonging to the 'People of the Book' (*ahl al-kitāb*); the *dhimmī* category was de facto expanded to include such religions as Zoroastrianism,[113] Hinduism and Buddhism. The inclusion of Hinduism and Buddhism into this juridical category, at the very outset of Islam's expansion into India in the eighth century, is important and highly instructive. During the short Indian campaign of Muḥammad b. Qāsim, launched in 711, the young Umayyad general received petitions from the indigenous Buddhists and Hindus in the city of Brahmanabad in Sind regarding the restoration of their temples and the upholding of their religious rights. He consulted his superior, the governor of Kūfa, Ḥajjāj b. Yūsuf, who in turn consulted his religious scholars. The result of these deliberations was the formulation of an official position which was to set a decisive precedent of religious tolerance for the ensuing centuries of Muslim rule in India. Ḥajjāj wrote to Muḥammad b. Qāsim a letter which was translated into what became known as the 'Brahmanabad settlement':

> The request of the chiefs of Brahmanabad about the building of Budh and other temples, and toleration in religious matters, is just and reasonable. I do not see what further rights we can have over them beyond the usual tax. They have paid homage to us and have undertaken to pay the fixed tribute [*jizya*] to the caliph. Because they have become *dhimmī*s we have no right whatsoever to interfere in their lives and property. Do permit them to follow their own religion. No one should prevent them.[114]

The Arab historian, al-Balādhurī, quotes Muḥammad b. Qāsim's famous statement made at Alor (Arabised as 'al-Rūr'), a city besieged for a week, and then taken without force, according to strict terms: there was to be no bloodshed, and the Buddhist faith would not be opposed. Muḥammad was reported to have said: 'The temples [lit. al-Budd, but referring to the temples of the Buddhists and the Hindus, as well as the Jains] shall be treated by us as if they were the churches of the Christians, the synagogues of the Jews, and the fire temples of the Magians'.[115] It is thus not surprising to read, in the same historian's work, that when Muḥammad b. Qāsim died, 'The people of India wept at the death of Muhammad, and made an image of him at Kiraj'.[116]

Although subsequent Muslim rulers varied in their degree of fidelity to this precedent—the notorious destruction of the monastery at Valabhi by the Abbasid army in 782 being an exception which proves the rule[117]—it is important to note, first, that the precedent decisively established a standard of tolerance for subsequent Muslim rulers in India to live up to; that this norm was in accordance with the Qur'ānic paradigm regarding the religious Other; and finally that the precedent extended the category of 'protected peoples' to include even non-theistic Buddhists,[118] and apparently polytheistic Hindus.[119] Although not necessarily included in the theological category of *ahl al-kitāb*, both Buddhists and Hindus were included in the juridical category of the *dhimma*, and thus were entitled to the same religious and legal recognition as the *ahl al-kitāb*. The implication of this act of recognition is clear: the religions of India could not be regarded as analogous to the pagan polytheistic religions of Mecca, whose adherents were not granted such privileges. The category of 'protected peoples' is thus open-ended and extendable; this might be seen as a juristic counterpart to the Qur'ānic doctrine that God has sent messengers to every community on earth: 'For every community (*umma*) there is a Messenger' (10:47). The Qur'ān mentions some but not all of the messengers (traditionally given as 124,000 in number): 'Truly, We sent Messengers before you; among them are those about whom We have told you, and those about whom We have not told you' (40:78).

The origin of the institution of the *dhimma* lies in a series of agreements made by the Prophet Muḥammad with various tribes and groups in the Arabian peninsula. The following pact, concluded with the Christians of Najran, to whom we shall return below, is a primary example of what the *dhimma* of the Prophet meant. According to this pact, legal recognition, religious tolerance, political protection and socio-economic rights were granted by the Muslim state in return for the payment of the *jizya*:

> Najrān and their followers are entitled to the protection of Allah and to the security of Muḥammad the Prophet, the Messenger of Allah, which security shall involve their persons, religion, lands, possessions, including those of them who are absent as well as those who are present, their camels, messengers, and images [*amthila*, referring to crosses, icons, etc.]. The state they previously held shall not be changed, nor shall any of their religious services or images be changed. No attempt shall be made to turn a bishop, a monk from his office as a monk, nor the sexton of a church from his office . . . They shall neither be called to military service nor compelled to pay the tithe [i.e., *zakāt*].[120]

This precedent was faithfully followed by the Prophet's immediate successors, and established a standard of tolerance by which all subsequent Muslim regimes could be judged. It is this standard and the spirit determining it which is essential, and not the various ways in which medieval jurists and rulers lived up to this standard or failed to live up to it. As noted in the previous sections, the historical record of the Muslims is in fact an impressive one in this regard, especially when judged according to the standards of the medieval world dominated as it was by imperial rivalry; the instances of intolerance, persecution or coercion that have taken place are overshadowed if not eclipsed by evidence of tolerance as the prevailing norm. Even if it be true that, according to contemporary Western standards of tolerance, the *dhimmī* was still something of a second-class citizen compared to the Muslim, the anachronism at the root of such a comparison vitiates its relevance to the discussion. If, instead, the standards of tolerance established by the Muslim institution of the *dhimma* be compared to the Christian record of the same period, one will be better able to discern the extent to which the spirit was operative, and to appreciate the degree to which it was—and remains, in principle—an inseparable corollary of the Islamic faith. Furthermore, even if the institutional forms taken by this spirit may not satisfy current Western expectations of tolerance, what such an evaluation helps us to see is that there is nothing incompatible between contemporary standards and expectations regarding the principle of religious tolerance, on the one hand, and the spirit of Islam, on the other. Quite the contrary: the trajectory established by the spirit of tolerance in Islamic history can be seen to harmonise with the finest aspects of religious tolerance enshrined in Western legal codes. And, as we have seen, the process by which these codes were themselves established cannot be divorced from the models of tolerance fashioned by Muslims according to the spirit of tolerance inherent to Islam itself.

In recent times, however, it has become somewhat fashionable for critics of Islam to stress the 'second-class' status of *dhimmī*s, while ignoring or belittling the ethical values and spiritual principles of which the *dhimma* was a more or less faithful institutional embodiment; the implication here is that those who wish to retain any commitment to 'Islamic tradition' are by that very token supporting the restoration of a system which perforce degrades non-Muslims, even if it legally tolerates their existence. This argument ignores the self-evident principle that Muslims are bound by the principle of tolerance, and all the concomitants of that principle which the contemporary context engenders; they are not bound to the institution of the *dhimma* as the sole administrative apparatus by which tolerance can be administered. In other words, the argument against the *dhimma* ignores the fact that, for intelligent contemporary Muslims, the *dhimma* is a medieval socio-religious construct, appropriate and even 'progressive' for its times, but not necessarily so for ours. It is the spirit animating the institution that is timeless, not the institution itself; and, being timeless, it must be manifested in a manner that is 'timely', that is, in accordance with the conditions of the time.

Bat Ye'or has promoted the pejorative term 'dhimmitude'[121] to express the inferior status or servitude putatively imposed as a matter of religious principle, and not just state policy, on religious minorities in Muslim ruled societies. Similarly Yohanan Friedmann explores issues of 'tolerance and coercion'[122] with an almost exclusive emphasis upon medieval juridical thought and the coercive impact of that thought as regards questions of religious freedom. However, as pointed out by such scholars as 'Abdul Ḥamīd Abū Sulaymān,[123] the positions adopted by medieval jurists—positions in large part engendered by defensive attitudes and reflexes of thinkers living in a context of imperial rivalry—are not to be taken as the criteria by which to judge the Islamic principles of tolerance, justice and respect in regard to the religious Other. Rather, it is the Qur'ān and the Sunna that must be taken as the criteria by which to judge medieval jurisprudential thought on such issues of religious tolerance in particular, and the justice and rectitude of Muslim rule in general.[124]

A key issue in the historical debate about the *dhimma* pertains to the humiliation that is supposed to be entailed by the payment of the *jizya*. Abū Sulaymān argues against those jurists who stress that belittlement or humiliation (*ṣaghār*) is a necessary part of the enactment of the *jizya* laws, based on the final words of Q. 9:29, which speak about making the People of the Book 'pay the *jizya* readily, while they are in a subdued conditioned (*wa hum ṣāghirūn*)'. He argues that the word *ṣāghir* simply means 'vanquished' or 'overpowered', and implies that a previous state of war has been brought to a peaceful conclusion. Instead of reading these words in the context of a specific war, 'the jurists simply extended a treatment intended for an assumed aggressive, corrupt enemy to include all non-Muslims, regardless of their actual attitudes, and of the total meaning and basic objective of Islam to guide and serve man.' He makes the point that the pact with the Najrānī Christians must be taken into account in any discussion of the issue of the *jizya*, for this pact makes it clear that *ṣaghār* was not intended to apply automatically to all non-Muslims. Rather, '*ṣaghār* is an attitude and punishment not for choosing a different belief but for [manifesting] a hostile and treacherous attitude against Muslim peoples in opposition to justice and to the Islamic obligation to protect man's right to safety and freedom of belief'.[125]

This kind of thoughtful re-evaluation of the medieval heritage in the light of the Islamic revelation would appear to be what Tim Winter is referring to when he writes: 'Thinkers such as Abdul-Hamid Abu Sulayman and several others have already urged the abolition or radical recasting of the bulk of the *dhimma* laws as medieval constructs whose relationship to the divine predicate of justice appears extremely problematic.'[126] Earlier in this monograph, reference was made to the importance of Sufism in the articulation of tolerant attitudes towards the non-Muslim Other. In this seminal article Winter formulates the underlying theological rationale for tolerance, which is arguably even more important than Sufism as regards the treatment of religious minorities in the Islamic tradition, in that it was *kalām* (theology), rather than *taṣawwuf* (Sufism), that provided the Shari'a 'with the immediate moral and theological context of its provisions in the area of the treatment of non-Muslims'.[127] The theological position here is based on what he calls the 'non-categoric' supersession of Islam. That is, Islam's supersession or abrogation (*naskh*) of other faiths 'is not construed as absolute or categoric in its displacement of what preceded ... For Islam, then, pre-Koranic history is not mere pre-history. Humanity did not have to wait for Muḥammad in order to gain the opportunity of complete "success" [*falāḥ*]'.[128] Other faiths are thus viewed by the theologians as retaining a certain salvific efficacy, on account of the inaugural revelation inaugurating their tradition, even if the tradition itself may be deemed to have become corrupted to some degree over time and on account of innovations.

Returning to Q. 9:29, Abū Sulaymān makes it clear that the context of the verse implies that those who are to give the *jizya* in a state of humility or lowness (*wa hum ṣāghirūn*) are those who had already initiated hostilities and were now defeated; the verse is not to be interpreted as entailing a universal injunction to humiliate those who pay the *jizya*, to impose dress restrictions upon them, refuse them the right to build places of worship—in short, to engage in those very acts which contemporary Muslims are right to regard as inappropriate for our times, and which moreover militate against the spirit of tolerance proper to the Islamic revelation, and against the absolute imperative of justice on all planes and in all respects, which is the core of the Qur'ānic message. Observing the practice of the Prophet and his immediate successors—and many of the rulers thereafter—it is clear that the *jizya* was supposed to be received in a spirit of magnanimity and justice, without any hint of condescension or contempt for those paying the tax. On the contrary, it is the 'kind' and 'just' conduct referred to in Q. 60:8 which was supposed to determine the spirit in which *jizya* was taken: 'As for those who do not fight you on account of your religion, nor expel you from your homes, God does not forbid you from dealing kindly and justly with them. Indeed, God loves the just.' The eminent contemporary Syrian scholar, Ramaḍān al-Būṭī, lays great stress on this principle, and calls attention to the fact that the Prophet and the first four caliphs are all reported to have encouraged their agents to collect the *jizya* with kindness and justice.[129] Ignaz Goldziher reinforces this point as follows:

> Just as the principle of toleration ruled in matters of religion, forbearance and moderation were to have the force of law in the treatment

> of non-Muslims in the areas of civil law and economic relations. Oppression of non-Muslims under the protection of Islam (*ahl al-dhimma*) was condemned by the believers as sinful excess. When the governor of Lebanon used great severity against the population that had rebelled because of an oppressive tax-collector, that governor could be warned with a reminder of the Prophet's teaching: 'On the Day of Judgement I myself will act as accuser of any man who oppresses a person under the protection of Islam.'[130]

It would not be out of place to substantiate this argument by the evidence provided by some further historical narratives. One of the most momentous and far-reaching acts of tolerance established by the Prophet's successors was that enshrined by the second caliph, 'Umar b. al-Khaṭṭāb, at the conquest of Jerusalem in 638. The Patriarch of Jerusalem, Sophronius, refused to hand over the keys of the city to anyone but the caliph in person, who agreed to this condition and came to the city not as a proudly triumphant conqueror but as a humble pilgrim. After entering the city, the muezzin made the call to prayer. The Patriarch invited 'Umar to perform his prayers in the Church of the Holy Sepulchre, but 'Umar declined, and prayed outside the church, for fear his action would later be taken as a pretext to convert the church into a mosque. Not only did he guarantee security and freedom of worship to the Christian inhabitants but he showed equal reverence to the holy sites of the Jews, personally taking part in the cleaning of the Temple Mount, which had been converted into a rubbish dump under the Christians. It is recorded that as 'Umar gazed in awe at the rock (*al-sakhrā'*), called 'the navel of the earth'—the place where David was held by tradition to have sung his psalms to his Lord, and from where Muḥammad was taken on his *mi'rāj* (ascent) through the heavens—Sophronius whispered in Greek to one of his aides: 'Behold, the Abomination of Desolation spoken of by the Prophet Daniel that standeth in the Holy Place.' The irony of this remark has been well captured by Barnaby Rogerson:

> This oft-quoted stage whisper, such a perennial favourite of Western historians and tour guides, has always seemed to me an extraordinary instance of doublethink. Leaving aside the ingratitude with which Sophronius repaid Omar's extraordinary respect for Jerusalem,

> for the Patriarch, for the city's Christian holy places and his own modest role as a pilgrim, Daniel's vision has itself always been taken to apply to the Roman invasion and its desecration of Jerusalem with graven images—which would ultimately be fulfilled with the destruction of both city and temple. As Omar had just vanquished the direct heirs of the Romans and brought an imageless worship of the One God back to the Holy Place raised up by Solomon, there seems little doubt whom Daniel would have considered to have been the Abomination of Desolation.[131]

Indeed, one of the most important results of the Muslim conquest of Palestine was that a Jewish population was reinstated in Jerusalem after an absence of five hundred years.[132] Moreover, as the Jews began to return to the Old City, 'Umar interceded on their behalf against the Christians who were opposed to the Jewish resettlement.[133] The agreement contracted between the caliph and the inhabitants of Jerusalem was recorded as follows:

> This is the assurance of safety which the servant of God 'Umar, the Commander of the Faithful, has granted to the people of Jerusalem. He has given them an assurance of safety for themselves, for their property, their churches, their crosses, the sick and healthy of the city, and for all the rituals that belong to their religion. Their churches will not be inhabited [by Muslims] nor will they be destroyed. Neither they, nor the land on which they stand, nor their crosses, nor their property will be damaged. They will not be forcibly converted.[134]

The Jacobites, Melkites and Nestorians were the main Christian sects in the territories conquered by the Muslims in the eastern part of the Byzantine empire, principally Syria, Mesopotamia and Persia, in the first wave of the expansion of Islam. As Sidney Griffith shows clearly, these Christian sects, in addition to being granted tolerance by the Muslims, were able to forge a specific cultural identity compounded out of the Arabic language and elements of their Islamic milieu, on the one hand, and their own specific religious doctrines and rites, on the other:

> It is seldom recognized that the establishment of Islamic, Arabic-speaking culture in the caliphate by the end of the ninth century

> . . . provided the circumstances for two important developments in Christian life in early Islamic times. It fostered the articulation of a new cultural expression of Christian doctrine, this time in Arabic, and it provided the cultural framework within which the several Christian denominations of the Orient ultimately came to define their mature ecclesial identities.[135]

Returning to the precedent established by the Prophet and his immediate successors, let us note the following important statement by ʿAlī b. Abī Ṭālib, fourth caliph and first of the Shiʿi Imams; it helps to disclose the essence of the *dhimma* institution, that is, the underlying trajectory intended by the spirit of Muslim tolerance of the religious Other: 'Those who have contracted the agreement of *dhimma* have done so such that their lives and their properties should be as inviolable as our own'. He further underscored the legal equality between Muslims and the protected minorities by saying that the compensation for the killing of a Christian or Jew was the same as that for a Muslim.[136] This resonates with the famous injunction, cited in the Prologue, to Mālik al-Ashtar, his appointee as governor of Egypt: 'Infuse your heart with mercy for the people in your charge, have love for them and be kind to them. Be not like a ravenous beast of prey above them, seeking to devour them. For they are of two types: either your brother in religion or your equal in creation.'[137]

Moving forward to a period closer to our times, it would not be out of place to refer here to the actions taken by the Emir ʿAbd al-Qādir in Damascus, in 1860; actions which were motivated by the very principles of egalitarianism and humanitarianism expressed by Imam ʿAlī in the above statements, and which are so integral to the spirit of tolerance in Islam.[138] Having been defeated by the French after a gallant defence of his Algerian homeland from 1830 to 1847, the Emir, now in exile in Damascus, found himself confronted by a potentially catastrophic conflagration. When civil war broke out between the Druzes and the Christians in Lebanon, the Emir wrote letters to all the Druze shaykhs, requesting them not to 'make offensive movements against a place with the inhabitants of which you have never before been at enmity', that is, not to attempt to provoke an attack by the Muslims of Damascus upon the Christian inhabitants of the city.

The Emir's letters proved to no avail. When the Druzes—whose numbers were now swelled by members of the Damascus mob—were approaching the Christian quarters of the city, the Emir confronted them, urging them to observe the rules of religion and of human justice: 'What', they shouted, 'you, the great slayer of Christians, are you come out to prevent us from slaying them in our turn? Away!' 'If I slew the Christians,' he shouted in reply, 'it was ever in accordance with our law—the Christians who had declared war against me, and were arrayed in arms against our faith.'[139]

This had no effect upon the mob. As the Turkish authorities stood by, either unable or unwilling to intervene, the Christian quarters were attacked and many Christians killed. The Emir and his small band of Algerian followers sought out as many of the terrified Christians as they could, giving them refuge in his own home. News of this spread, and on the morning of July 10, an angry crowd gathered outside the Emir's house, demanding that he hand over the Christians. Alone, he went out to confront them, and fearlessly addressed them thus: 'O my brothers, your conduct is impious . . . How low have you fallen, for I see Muslims covering themselves with the blood of women and children? Has God not said: "He who kills a single soul . . . it is as if he hath killed the whole of humanity [5:32]"? Has he not also said: "There is no compulsion in religion, the right way is clearly distinguished from error [2:256]"?' This only enraged the mob further. The leaders of the crowd replied to him: 'O holy warrior! We do not need your advice . . . Why are you interfering in our affairs? You, who used to fight the Christians, how can you oppose our avenging their insults? Disbeliever, deliver up those you have hidden in your house; otherwise we will strike you with the same punishment we have meted out to the disbelievers: we will reunite you with your brothers.' Further words were exchanged, the Emir retorting that 'I did not fight "Christians", I fought the aggressors who called themselves Christians.' The anger of the mob increased and at this point the tone of the Emir changed, his eyes flashed with anger, he sensed the possibility of battle, for the first time since he had left Algeria. He hurled one last warning to the crowd, saying that the Christians were his hosts, and that for as long as one of his soldiers lived, the Christians would not be handed over. Then, addressing his own men: 'And you, my Maghrebis, may your hearts rejoice, for I call God to witness: we are going to fight for a cause as holy as that for which we fought before!' The mob dispersed and fled in fear.[140]

One should note carefully the words of the Emir to his own men, preparing them to lay down their lives for the Christians: this act of defence is as holy as the war which was fought to defend their own land and people against the French colonialists in Algeria. His action can be seen as an expression of the spirit of reverence—and not just tolerance—in regard to the rights of religious minorities in Islam; and also as a graphic response to, and thus commentary upon, the call made in the following verse: 'O you who believe! Stand up for justice, as witnesses to God, even against your own souls, or your parents or your kin, whether rich or poor, for God protects both. Follow not passion lest you deviate . . .' (4:135).

The Emir then sent 200 of his men to various parts of the Christian quarters to find as many Christians as they could. He also offered fifty piastres to anyone who brought to him a Christian alive. His mission continued thus for five days and nights. As the numbers swelled to several thousand, the Emir escorted them all to the citadel of the city. It is estimated that in the end, no less than fifteen thousand Christians were saved by the Emir in this action, including all the ambassadors and consuls of the European powers together with their families. As Charles Henry Churchill, his biographer, prosaically puts it, just a few years after the event:

> All the representatives of the Christian powers then residing in Damascus, without one single exception, had owed their lives to him. Strange and unparalleled destiny! An Arab had thrown his guardian aegis over the outraged majesty of Europe. A descendant of the Prophet had sheltered and protected the Spouse of Christ.[141]

The Emir received the highest possible medals and honours from all the leading Western powers. The French Consul himself, representative of the state that was still very much in the process of colonising the Emir's homeland, owed his life to the Emir. When the Bishop of Algiers, Louis Pavy, praised the Emir's actions, the latter replied: 'The good that we did to the Christians was what we were obliged to do, out of fidelity to Islamic law and out of respect for the rights of humanity. For all creatures are the family of God, and those most beloved of God are those who are most beneficial to his family.' Then follows this passage which expounds clearly the theology underpinning of the spirit of tolerance in Islam.

> All the religions brought by the prophets, from Adam to Muhammad, rest upon two principles: the exaltation of God Most High, and compassion for His creatures. Apart from these two principles, there are but ramifications, the divergences of which are without importance. And the law of Muhammad is, among all doctrines, that which shows itself most attached to, and most respectful of, compassion and mercy. But those who belong to the religion of Muhammad have caused it to deviate. That is why God has caused them to lose their way. The recompense has been of the same nature as the fault.[142]

What we are given here is a concise and irrefutable diagnosis of the contemporary malaise within the Muslim world: since the tolerant compassion that is so central to this great religion has been subordinated to anger and bitterness, the mercy of God has been withdrawn from those 'who have caused it to deviate'. In so heroically upholding the inviolable rights of the religious Other, the Emir's action speaks louder than words, delivering to both contemporary Muslims and Islamophobes alike an eloquent lesson on the depth and power of the spirit of tolerance in Islam. Indeed, his heroism is all the more relevant to the contemporary crises wrought by Muslim extremism, in that his actions so unequivocally opposed fanatically intolerant Muslims who were intent on violating the Islamic ideal of tolerance.[143]

It is interesting to note that another great warrior of Islam, Imam Shamīl of Dagestan, hero of the wars against Russian imperialism,[144] wrote a letter to the Emir when he heard of his defence of the Christians. He praised the Emir for his noble act, thanking God that there were still Muslims who behaved according to the spiritual ideals of Islam:

> Know that when my ear was struck with that which is detestable to hear, and odious to human nature—I allude to the recent events in Damascus concerning the Muslims and the Christians, in which the former pursued a path unworthy of the followers of Islam . . . a veil was cast over my soul . . . I cried to myself: 'Corruption has

> appeared on the earth and at sea, because of what men's hands have wrought' [30: 41]. I was astonished at the blindness of the functionaries [the Muslims] who have plunged into such excesses, forgetful of the words of the Prophet, peace be upon him, 'whoever shall be unjust towards a tributary [that is, a *dhimmi*], whoever shall do him wrong, whoever shall deprive him of anything without his own consent, it is I who will be the accuser on the day of judgement.' Ah, what sublime words! But when I was informed that you have sheltered the tributaries beneath the wings of goodness and compassion; that you had opposed the men who militated against the will of God Most High . . . I praised you as God Most High will praise you on the day when neither their wealth nor their children avail [3:10]. In reality, you have put into practice the words of the great apostle of God Most High, bearing witness to compassion for His humble creatures, and you have set up a barrier against those who would reject his great example. May God preserve us from those who transgress His laws![145]

In response to this letter the Emir wrote the following, which expresses so well the malaise prevailing to an even more shameful degree in our own times: 'When we think how few men of real religion there are, how small the number of defenders and champions of the truth—when one sees ignorant persons imagining that the principle of Islam is hardness, severity, extravagance and barbarity—it is time to repeat "Patience is beautiful, and God is the source of all succour" [12: 18].'[146]

One must also take care to note well the following point: the Emir, when fighting the French in Algeria, went to great lengths to ensure that his French prisoners of war were enabled to perform their regular worship, requesting the Bishop of Algiers to send a priest to his camp to administer the sacraments for the prisoners. As Colonel Gery confided in the Bishop of Algeria: 'We are obliged to try as hard as we can to hide these things [the treatment accorded French prisoners by the Emir] from our soldiers. For if they so much as suspected such things, they would not hasten with such fury against Abd el-Kader.'[147] Over one hundred years before the signing of the Geneva conventions, the Emir demonstrated the meaning not only of the rights of prisoners of war, but also of the innate and inalienable spiritual dignity of the human being, whatever be his or her religion.

Such attitudes go far beyond a merely formal or even reluctant tolerance of the Other; rather, they stem from a particular vision, being infused by a particular spirit proper to the heart of Islam. This spirit guarantees that tolerance will be manifested as an outward expression of inner respect for the Other, being based upon acknowledgement of the divine source of the religion of the Other, however much one may disagree with certain theological tenets of that religion.

The institution of the *dhimma* is thus predicated on the universal principle of tolerance; it is not to be thought that the principle of tolerance should be restricted in its application to the particular institutional form it assumes as the *dhimma*. Indeed, as Khaled Abou El Fadl notes, the Prophet did not collect the *jizya* from every non-Muslim tribe that submitted to the Muslim state. Some tribes in fact were themselves paid from the Muslim treasury, being deemed to fall within the category of 'those whose hearts are to be reconciled'. The caliph 'Umar entered into a peace settlement with Arab Christian tribes who objected to paying the *jizya*; they were permitted to pay a tax which was referred to as *zakāt*, the same kind of tax paid by Muslims.[148]

It is clear, then, that the institution of *dhimma/jizya* is more a historically conditioned contingency than an unconditional theological necessity. It met the requirements of a particular historical context, which was governed by the exigencies of imperial politics; the *dhimma* effectively introduced a mode of tolerance into that context, without this implying that the principle of tolerance is exhausted by, or restricted to, this particular institutional form. As noted above, while the 'protected' status of religious minorities under Muslim rule falls short of contemporary standards of religious equality and tolerance, the status enjoyed by these minorities was far in advance of anything that could be expected by minorities in Christendom. The institution of the *dhimma* manifested an underlying principle of tolerance which was itself rooted in the Islamic revelation. The institutional form, however, is contingent, whereas the principle of tolerance is necessary. It is therefore not so much a possibility as a necessity for this principle to be adapted to the conditions of the contemporary world; for it is this universal applicability that demonstrates or proves that it does indeed arise out of the Qur'ānic revelation itself, rather than being defined in its essence by any medieval institutional forms. For that which arises out of the Qur'ānic revelation is principial and perpetually valid, while the institutional forms are contingent, dependent upon their specific context.

Part 2

The Spirit of Tolerance

Our aim in this part of the essay is to explore the roots of the tradition of tolerance in Islam, historical evidence of which was presented above. This impressive tradition did not emerge out of a void; nor can it be explained simply by reference to benevolent Muslim rulers or the precepts of Islamic law. Rather, the spirit of tolerance that normally characterised the legal and political attitudes of Muslims towards the religious Other should be appreciated as a direct consequence of the spiritual ethos of the Islamic revelation. As we hope to demonstrate in this part of the essay, the contemplative vista of religious plurality opened up by the Qurʾānic revelation goes well beyond the Muslim traditions of legal, political and theological tolerance observed in the medieval and pre-modern period. It is important to be aware that the Qurʾānic vision both provides the foundation for these traditions and infinitely transcends them. For these traditions of tolerance were articulated in contexts of imperial power: the Muslim authorities tolerated the largely powerless religious minorities. The spiritual ethos of tolerance emerging from reflection upon the sources of the Islamic revelation, however, should not be viewed through the prism of this historical context; on the contrary, the historical record is to be evaluated in terms of the principles revealed in the Qurʾān.

Therefore, any contemporary effort to review or revive the integral tradition of tolerance in Islam should be focused first and foremost on the verses of the Qurʾān, and the acts and deeds of the Prophet; the medieval standards of Muslim medieval tolerance, while impressive and enlightened for their times, ought not constitute the yardstick—or the sole yardstick—by which contemporary Muslim tolerance or intolerance is judged. The Qurʾānic perspective on religious plurality clearly opens up contemplative angles of vision which go far beyond mere tolerance of the powerless by the powerful. The religious Other is not just tolerated but respected; indeed, at a higher level, the religion of the Other can become a source of inspiration for the Muslim who is sensitive to the deeper currents of the Qur'ānic discourse on religion and religions. The Muslim record of tolerance is therefore to be regarded as an empirical, historically contingent expression of a spiritual ethos which comprises trans-historical, universally valid principles. These call out to be reflected upon by each generation of Muslims, and creatively applied by them in accordance with the conditions of their time, not those of the past. Such a moral, intellectual and spiritual endeavour can be characterised as 'traditional' in the sense described so well by Henri Corbin:

> A Tradition transmits itself as something alive, since it is a ceaselessly renewed inspiration, and not a funeral cortège or a register of conformist opinions. The life and death of spiritual things are our responsibility; they are not placed 'in the past' except through our own omissions, our refusal of the metamorphoses that they demand, if these spiritual things are to be maintained 'in the present' for us.[1]

Tolerance and Revealed Knowledge

There is a close relationship between revealed knowledge and the spirit of tolerance in the Islamic context. The central argument we wish to make here is this: the spirit motivating the ethic of tolerance in Islam is a corollary of, not simply knowledge, but *sacred* knowledge, derived from divine revelation and assimilated by intellectual reflection. Sincere and respectful tolerance—as opposed to formal, begrudging tolerance—of the Other flows forth in the measure that the Muslim *knows* that the religions of the Other are also divinely revealed, and this knowledge stems from what is revealed by the Qur'ān itself about other religions.

One may of course arrive at such knowledge by dint of one's own intellectual reflection. But, for the Muslim, what is decisive is not so much one's personal intuition of the divine origin of other faiths, but the point of view and fundamental orientation furnished by the Qur'ānic revelation. The Qur'ān provides the believer with spiritually irrefutable evidence that religious diversity is brought about by the will of God and is not a regrettable accident of history; and that this divine will manifests profound wisdom, and not caprice or whim. One of the key texts in this connection, which will form the basis of our reflections in this part of the essay, is the following, the second part of the Qurʾānic verse 48 from the chapter entitled 'The Table Spread' (*al-Māʾida*):

> For each We have appointed a Law and a Way. And had God willed, He could have made you one community. But in order that He might try you by that which He has given you [He has made you as you are]. So compete with one another in good works. Unto God you will all return, He will disclose to you [the truth] of that about which you had different opinions (5:48).

God Himself has willed that humanity be made up of different religious communities—different *umma*s, even if, at a higher level, the whole of mankind constitutes one *umma*. In the chapter entitled 'The Prophets', verses 48 to 92 present brief references to a whole series of Biblical figures—Moses, Aaron, Abraham, Lot, Isaac, Jacob, Noah, David, Solomon, Job, Ishmael, Enoch, Ezekiel, Jonah, Zechariah, Mary and Jesus. Then comes the following verse: 'Indeed, this *umma* of yours is one *umma*, and I am your Lord, so worship Me' (21:92). The implication here is that the whole of humanity consists of one community, even if it be internally divided into different religious communities configured around one prophet or a group of prophets.[2]

Even if the Muslim may feel incapable of understanding all the complex—apparently contradictory—implications of the phenomenon of religious diversity, no doubts can be entertained about the simple, uncomplicated and immediately intelligible principle: God has willed that there exist different religious traditions and communities. Logically flowing from this spiritual principle is the ethical obligation of religious tolerance. The ethic of tolerance in Islam is therefore rooted in the knowledge revealed in the Qurʾān; whence the remarkable, if not unique, quality of specifically Islamic faith—tolerance of the religious Other is a corollary of the Muslim's belief in the very nature of divine revelation. God's reveals Himself not once to a single community selected from among mankind, but repeatedly through different modes of prophetic revelation which encompass the whole of humanity.

Religious tolerance is therefore a moral imperative derived from one's belief in the way in which God reveals Himself, and cannot be regarded simply as a possible option dependent upon one's personal opinion.

The spiritual basis of tolerance—belief in the diverse forms assumed by divine revelation—enters into the very articulation of the Muslim credo. The verses which inaugurate the first chapter after 'The Opening' (*al-Fātiḥa*) define the true believers and their success or salvation (*falāḥ*) in terms which render central and necessary—not marginal or merely possible—the principle of belief in *all* of God's revelations, not just the Qur'ān:

> *Alif-Lām-Mīm.*[3] This is the Scripture, whereof there is no doubt, a guidance unto those who are pious; those who believe in the Unseen, and establish worship, and spend of that which We have bestowed upon them; and who believe in that which is revealed unto you (Muḥammad) and that which was revealed before you, and who are certain of the Hereafter. These depend on guidance from their Lord; these are the successful (2:1–5).

Near the end of the same chapter, the nature of specifically Islamic faith is again described in terms of the universality of revelation; this time, stress is placed on the strict equivalence of all the revelations in which the Muslim must believe:

> The Messenger believes in that which has been revealed unto him from his Lord, and [so do] the believers. Every one believes in God and His angels and His scriptures and His Messengers [saying]: We make no distinction between any of His Messengers . . . (2:285).

The Muslim's faith in all divine revelations—all the scriptures and the Messengers through whom they were revealed—entails a particular form of knowledge, a specific content of consciousness, which fashions the spirit of tolerance in Islam. One knows, with a confidence born of faith, that the various religious traditions of mankind are ultimately rooted in the divine will, and are thus expressions of divine wisdom. The inevitable differences between the traditions—on the level of doctrines, rites, and spiritual 'styles'—may be difficult to understand or resolve, but 'Unto God you will all return, He will disclose to you [the truth] of that about which you had different opinions.' Differences are therefore inevitable, and are the consequences of the divinely-willed phenomenon of religious diversity. It is therefore a part of wisdom to refrain from polemically attacking those aspects of other religions which one does not understand; in the Hereafter, such apparent contradictions will be resolved according to a mode of wisdom which may presently elude the scope of one's own consciousness.[4] What matters for the discerning Muslim is the underlying knowledge, the fundamental intuition, or deep sense, that, despite apparent contradictions between their forms, all the divine revelations are strictly equivalent as regards their essence; therefore, the communities engendered by these revelations are to be spiritually respected and not just legally tolerated. The spirit of tolerance in Islam is inseparable in essence from the spirit of respect and, more fundamentally, the sense of the inviolable sanctity of the religious forms flowing from divine revelation.

The spirit of tolerance is ideally buttressed by a host of kindred virtues, such as kindness, compassion, forbearance, generosity—in short, all those ethical qualities comprised in the key prophetic virtue of *ḥilm*, to be discussed below. In such a context of spiritual and moral values, the practice of tolerance is much more than just a religio–political rule, arising out of an injunction of the revealed Law; it will emerge, rather, as an ethical imperative, rooted in the very heart of Muslim conscience. The legal injunction to tolerate the religious Other will then be seen as an outward expression of the voice of this inner conscience; it is not the case that the spirit of tolerance, still less the Muslim conscience as such, are mere concomitants of obedience to the Law.

Tolerance cannot therefore be separated from revealed knowledge, which in turn presupposes a spiritual and intellectual culture within which the pursuit of knowledge *per se* is enshrined as a key value, a permanent orientation, a supreme goal. In his seminal study, *Knowledge Triumphant: The Concept of Knowledge in Medieval Islam*, Franz Rosenthal draws attention to the extraordinary extent to which knowledge (*'ilm*) defines the essence of Islamic civilisation:

> Arabic *'ilm* is fairly well rendered by our 'knowledge'. However, 'knowledge' falls short of expressing all the factual and emotional

> contents of *'ilm*. For *'ilm* is one of those concepts that have dominated Islam and given Muslim civilization its distinctive shape and complexion. In fact, there is no other concept that has been as operative a determinant of Muslim civilization in all its aspects to the same extent as *'ilm* . . . There is no branch of Muslim intellectual life, of Muslim religious and political life, and of the daily life of the average Muslim, that remained untouched by the all-pervasive attitude toward 'knowledge' as something of supreme value for Muslim being. *'Ilm* is Islam . . . [5]

Rosenthal in fact makes the radical claim, which he substantiates with impressive evidence, that 'in Islam, the concept of knowledge enjoyed an importance unparalleled in other civilizations.' While admitting that knowledge held a privileged place in such cultures as ancient Greece, he insists that 'nobody would wish to argue that the attitude toward knowledge in the Ancient World as a whole or in any particular region or epoch of it was inspired and sustained by the same single-minded devotion that existed in medieval Islam.'[6]

The Islamic revelation was inaugurated by the following verse: 'Read: in the Name of your Lord who created; created man from a clot. Read: and your Lord is most bounteous. He who teaches by the Pen; teaches man what he knows not' (96:1–5). We have here a prefiguration of what was to become one of the most literate and philosophically articulate societies on earth, a prophetic prefiguration given to an illiterate man living in a predominantly oral culture in Arabia in the seventh century, which no one would have dreamed could become the nucleus for a world civilisation based on 'the Pen'. As noted by Rosenthal, there was nothing in the culture of Arabia that could be regarded as providing a foundation for the elevation of knowledge as a definitive feature of religious life: ' . . . native Arabian stimuli by themselves could hardly have provoked a development such as we find in the Qur'ān with respect to knowledge'. He adds that we would not be justified in assuming that in pre-Islamic Arabia 'knowledge was a concept that possessed religious urgency and was ready to play a prominent role in a new religious movement.'[7]

According to the very first verse which was revealed to the Prophet, then, the primary act of the Lord, after creating man, is to impart knowledge: man is taught by God what he was ignorant of—or rather, what he had forgotten. For, in many other verses, the Qur'an describes itself as a 'reminder' (*dhikrā*), or a 'remembrance' (*dhikr*): it reminds those who possess inner 'substance' (*lubb*) (39:21); those who have 'a heart' (50:37); the Prophet is told to remind people, 'for you are only one who reminds' (88:21); and again, he is told: 'So remind; truly the reminder is of benefit' (87:9).

The reminder can only be of benefit if one already knows, but has forgotten, what one is being reminded of. The revelation is a metaphysical 'aide-memoire', it induces a 're-cognition' of what is known in one's depths, but has been forgotten on the surface of one's consciousness. The reminder is of benefit because man by nature is forgetful; what has been forgotten is the truth inscribed in man's God-given original nature, the *fiṭra* to which we made reference earlier: 'So set your purpose for religion as one by nature upright (*ḥanīfan*): the *fiṭra* of God, that according to which He created man. There is no changing the creation of God. That is the right religion, but most people know not' (30:30).

The primordial or immutable nature of the human being is at one with the quality expressed by the word *ḥanīf*, the root meaning of which is to swerve or incline continuously towards something. The *ḥanīf* is therefore one who is by nature and disposition permanently oriented to the oneness of ultimate reality on all levels—doctrinal, spiritual and ethical; he is a 'monotheist' in the most profound sense of the term. In the Qur'ān, the *ḥanīf* par excellence is the prophet Abraham, with whom the cycle of Semitic monotheism was inaugurated. But this is only one of the cycles of revelation, pertaining to one of the 'sectors' of humanity; the Qur'ānic perspective has in view all the cycles of revelation which pass through all sectors of humanity. Seyyed Hossein Nasr elucidates the way in which this universal view of revelation enters into the articulation of the 'spiritual anthropology' of the Qur'ān, and how this anthropology is closely related to the claim that Islam does nothing more than re-establish, in a fresh idiom, the primordial or immutable religion. The terminality of Islam rejoins the primordiality of 'Adamic', not just 'Abrahamic', faith; the terminal and the primordial bear witness to what is immutable in the human spirit:

> The spiritual anthropology depicted in the Quran makes of prophecy a necessary element of the human condition. Man is truly man only

> by virtue of his participation in a tradition . . . Human history consists of cycles of prophecy, with each new prophecy beginning a new cycle of humanity. Islam also considers itself to be the reassertion of the original religion, of the doctrine of Unity, which always was and always will be. That is why it is called the primordial religion (*al-dīn al-ḥanīf*); it comes at the end of this human cycle to reassert the essential truth of the primordial tradition.[8]

The *ḥanīf* is often defined, in polemical fashion, as one who is neither Jew nor Christian. This point of view is based on the following verse: 'Abraham was neither a Jew nor a Christian; rather, he was a *ḥanīf*, one who had surrendered [or: 'a Muslim'], and was not one of the idolators' (3:67). Narrowly interpreted, this verse appears to contrast negatively the state of the *ḥanīf* with the confessions of Judaism and Christianity, and to stress Abraham's status as a Muslim, one who had 'submitted' to God as a true monotheist. But the verse can also be read as an allusion to the primordial state, the *fiṭra*, which is both 'pre-religious' (symbolised chronologically within the Semitic world by the fact that Abraham comes before the Jewish prophets and before Jesus), and 'supra-religious', in that the *fiṭra* goes beyond all formal or institutional religions and by that very token comprises them all.

The fact that the quality of the *ḥanīf* is coupled with that of the *fiṭra* is clear from Q 30:30. The *ḥanīf* is one who is faithful to the *fiṭra*, being oriented to the fundamental nature of absolute reality, such as this reality fashions the entirety of the creation, including, crucially, the nature of the human soul. That is, the *ḥanīf* is permanently disposed in view of the *Fāṭir*, the Creator: 'Indeed, I have turned my face towards Him who created (*faṭara*) the heavens and the earth as one by nature upright (*ḥanīfan*); and I am not one of the idolators' (6:79).

The *ḥanīf* is one who inclines permanently to the *fiṭra*, the natural 'stamp' impressed on the soul by *al-Fāṭir*. This 'impression' made by the divine substance upon human nature is indelible, whatever be the religion or lack thereof imposed upon the soul by its environment: 'Every baby is born according to the *fiṭra*; its parents make him a Jew, a Christian or a Zoroastrian', the Prophet said,[9] indicating that all formal religion is something of a secondary 'superstructure': the immutable infrastructure of the soul is the *fiṭra*, and this is primordial religion, or religion as such. The success of Islam or any other religion depends on the degree to which this *fiṭra* is cultivated and brought to fruition. In light of this view of the human soul, it should be clear why we stated earlier that the kind of wholesale barbarism inflicted in the name of 'civilisation' upon indigenous people deemed 'savage' by European conquerors in the Americas has no parallel in Islamic history. One recalls Imam 'Alī's exhortation to Mālik al-Ashtar, cited in the previous chapter: 'Infuse your heart with mercy for the people in your charge, have love for them and be kind to them. Be not like a ravenous beast of prey above them, seeking to devour them. For they are of two types: either your brother in religion or your equal in creation.' Similarly, the second caliph, 'Umar b. al-Khaṭṭāb, upon hearing of the mistreatment of a Christian by the son of 'Amr b. al-'Āṣ, conqueror of Egypt, severely rebuked him in a letter, saying: 'O 'Amr, would you enslave a human being born to be free?'.[10]

Islam sees itself as the restoration of the *dīn al-fiṭra*, or as Seyyed Hossein Nasr put it in the above citation, *al-dīn al-ḥanīf*. This primordial faith cannot be confined to Islam, understood as a historically conditioned confession; nor can it be restricted to the sphere of Semitic monotheism, despite the fact that Abraham is the supreme exemplar of the *ḥanīf*. As Bosnian scholar Nevad Kahteran explains: 'What the *ḥanīfiyya* model in fact denotes is the Abrahamic wisdom bestowed [by God] on the eternal heritage for the life of the world, and permanently entrenched in the foundations of the Judaeo–Christian–Islamic tradition'.[11] The universal and primordial wisdom of Abraham which unites the three branches of Semitic monotheism is to be seen as embracing all faiths, because it is one with faith as such: it cannot then be restrictively identifiable with such and such a faith.

This primordial faith defines the essential nature of the human being as such: it cannot be the monopoly of such and such a human being. Triumphalism, and the intolerance and pride it generates, cannot easily find a home in a climate dominated by such a perspective on the fundamental nature of each human being. Rather, tolerance on the religious plane is the outcome of the fundamental respect due to the human soul as such, as fashioned by the Creator. Again, we observe the way in which tolerance emerges as a basic corollary of Muslim faith: respect for what God has implanted in the soul of each human being—and which thereby comes to constitute its immutable and inalienable substance—generates tolerance at all levels.

The spiritual quality of the *ḥanīf* is central to the ethic of generous tolerance (*samḥa*); and it is the presence of this tolerance within religion—any religion—that renders it 'lovable to God'. As noted at the outset of this essay, when asked which religion was most beloved to God, the Prophet replied: 'The primordial, generously tolerant faith (*al-ḥanīfiyya al-samḥa*)'.[12] We shall return to this saying below. For the present context we wish to stress that this generous tolerance cannot be fully appreciated apart from the sacred knowledge proper to the *ḥanīf*, that is, to one who is fully attuned to the *fiṭra*. For the *fiṭra* comprises the potentiality of spiritual perfection, and this in turn implies that the seeds of all knowledge are contained within the human soul. Knowledge of all things is contained, in undifferentiated synthetic unity, within the very spirit of God 'breathed' into Adam at his creation: 'Then He fashioned [man] and breathed into him of His Spirit' (32:9).

The following verse expresses the complementary aspect of this innate knowledge, that is, the principles of the differentiated sciences which outwardly deploy the unitive Spirit: 'And He taught Adam the names, all of them . . . ' (2:31). It is because of this Spirit and the knowledge it comprises, that the angels are commanded to bow down to Adam: 'And when your Lord said unto the angels: Verily I am creating a mortal from clay of black mud, altered. So, when I have made him and have breathed into him of My Spirit, fall down, prostrating yourselves before him (15:28–29).'[13]

Such verses as these mark the specifically sapiential or intellective character of the Islamic revelation. It is to be noted that the 'Forbidden Tree' in the Qur'ānic account is not referred to as the 'Tree of the knowledge of good and evil' as it is in Genesis, 2:17; it is simply referred to as a tree which one must not approach. This important difference between the two narratives underscores the extent to which knowledge is enshrined as a supreme value at the very core of the Islamic revelation. In his penetrating exposition of the metaphysical dimensions of Islam, *Understanding Islam*, Frithjof Schuon makes this point well by contrasting the basic perspectives of Islam and Christianity as regards the role of the intellect:

> For Christianity, man is *a priori* will, or more exactly, he is will corrupted; clearly the intelligence is not denied, but it is taken into

> consideration only as an aspect of will; man is will and in man will is intelligent; when the will is corrupted, so also is the intelligence corrupted in the sense that in no way could it redress the will. Therefore a divine intervention is needed: the sacrament. In the case of Islam, where man is considered as the intelligence and intelligence comes 'before' the will, it is the content or direction of the intelligence which has sacramental efficacy: whoever accepts that the transcendent Absolute alone is absolute and transcendent, and draws from this the consequences for the will, is saved.[14]

In the Qur'ān the Prophet himself is told to supplicate as follows: 'My Lord, increase me in knowledge' (20:114). If this is incumbent upon the Prophet, it is even more so upon his followers. Indeed, to the Qur'ānic exhortation to engage in intellectual endeavour must be added the immense number of sayings of the Prophet Muḥammad in which the quest for knowledge is stressed. These sayings are given pride of place in both the Sunni and Shi'i compilations of *ḥadīth*.[15] In the immensely influential 'Book of Knowledge' in his monumental *Iḥyā' 'ulūm al-dīn* ('Revival of religious sciences'), al-Ghazāli cites, among others, the following important sayings of the Prophet as regards the primacy of the quest for knowledge:

> Seeking knowledge is incumbent on every Muslim.
> Seek knowledge, even as far as China.
> The knowers are the heirs of the prophets.
> The knower is the trustee of God on earth.
> The pre-eminence of the knower in relation to the worshipper is like my pre-eminence in relation to the lowest of my companions.
> God is not worshipped with anything more excellent than a profound understanding [of the principles] of religion (*fiqh fī al-dīn*).[16]

The answer given by the Prophet to the question, 'Which works are best?' is particularly illuminating. He replied: 'Your knowledge of God.' His companions said: 'We enquire about works and you reply concerning knowledge!' The Prophet then explained: 'A few works, accompanied by knowledge of God, will be of benefit; but many works, accompanied by ignorance of God, will be of no benefit.'[17] Works are valued according to their intention, and this intention is in turn fashioned by one's knowledge of the higher truths and deeper realities to which one aspires. In this perspective there is a 'virtuous circle' between knowledge, virtue and worship, each reinforcing the other; but it is knowledge that has primacy, as the sayings above make clear. One seeks knowledge (*'ilm*, or, with a stress on the spiritual aspects of knowledge, *ma'rifa*) with the intellect, *al-'aql*; and the meaning of the intellect, in Islamic terms, cannot be dissociated either from revelation or from virtue—the intellect is the medium by which the substance of divine revelation penetrates the soul, illuminates the heart and elevates the character.

This mediating role of the intellect—its operative valorisation of both virtue and revelation—is referred to by Imam 'Alī in terms of 'translation' or 'interpretation', *tarjumān*: 'The messenger [or prophet] of a man is the interpreter of his intellect (*rasūl al-rajul tarjumān 'aqlihi*).'[18] He also makes explicit the correspondence between the intellect and the 'inner' messenger: the intellect is 'the messenger of the Real'.[19] The scope of the intellect goes far beyond the mind, and is intimately related to the heart; the Qur'ān indicates the connection between the capacity to use the intellect and the spiritual quality of the heart—that deeper seat of consciousness upon which the mind depends—by referring to those who 'have hearts with which they understand not (*lā ya'qilūna bihā*)' (7:179; see also 22:46 which poses the question: 'do they not have hearts by which to understand?'). It is the heart, therefore, and not simply the mind, which must be engaged by intellection.

In the depth of one's heart lies that immense potentiality of consciousness 'breathed' into the human soul at its creation—this breath, in essence, being nothing other than the very Spirit of God. To realise the knowledge latent in this spiritual consciousness, however, requires divine revelation. According to Imam 'Alī, one of the main reasons why God sent prophets to the world was to unearth for people 'the buried treasures of the intellects (*dafā'in al-'uqūl*)'. He also said: 'There is no religion for one who has no intellect'; and stressed that the intellect cannot acquire true knowledge without the participation of such qualities as kindness and contentment, courtesy, generosity, modesty, wise forbearance (*ḥilm*), as well as love and a sense of beauty, both outward and inward.[20] Divine revelation awakens the hidden depths of human intelligence; but intelligence, in turn, requires the perfection of character for its full realisation; and all the virtues are required for perfection of character—including, needless to say, such virtues as forbearance, kindness, generosity and tolerance.

* * *

Given the centrality of the Qur'ānic verse 5:48 to the principle of religious plurality in Islam, it may be profitable to reflect upon its content in some detail. Earlier we cited the second part of the verse. The verse in full reads as follows:

> We have revealed unto you the Scripture with the Truth, as a confirmer (*muṣaddiq*) of whatever [revealed] Scripture came before it, and a protector (*muhaymin*) thereof. So judge between them according to that which God has revealed, and follow not their desires away from the Truth which has come to you. For each We have appointed a Law and a Way. And had God willed, He could have made you one community. But in order that He might try you by that which He has given you [He has made you as you are]. So compete with one another in good works. Unto God you will all return, He will disclose to you [the truth] of that about which you had different opinions (5:48).

From the theological point of view, this verse is important not only on account of its unequivocal affirmation of the divine root of the different religious traditions preceding the Qur'ānic revelation; it is also deemed to be an affirmation of the Qur'ānic abrogation or supersession (*naskh*) of these revelations. Whence the injunction: 'So judge between them [the different religious communities] according to that which God has revealed, and follow not their desires away from the Truth which has come to you.' The implication here is that earlier religious communities have allowed their 'desires' to cause them to deviate from the Truth that was revealed through their scriptures. Muslims are warned not to do the same, and to adhere rigorously to the Qur'ānic revelation which has a divine guarantee of immunity from distortion (*taḥrīf*): 'Falsehood cannot come at it from in front of it or from behind it. [It is] a revelation from the Wise, the Praised' (41:42).

Nonetheless, the supersession in question here is not one which renders null and void the religious traditions being superseded. Earlier, we made reference to Tim Winter's apt theological designation of this type of abrogation. He defines it as 'non-categoric supersession', according to which the religions deemed to have been superseded by Islam retain, in different degrees, their salvific efficacy on account of the revelation at the source of their tradition. Winter stresses that such a view of other religions does not necessarily entail a sense of Muslim triumphalism or pride, for salvation is the preserve of no religious community to the exclusion of others; rather, salvation depends on the imponderables of faith, virtue and grace.

The rest of 5:48, in which the divine ordainment of religious plurality is presented, can thus be viewed as reinforcing the humility, respect and objectivity vis-à-vis other religious communities that the Muslim is expected to maintain alongside the belief that the Qur'ān is God's final, and most complete, revelation to mankind. Part of this completeness entails, precisely, its unique embrace of all revelations, its unique perspective on the plurality of the religious phenomenon, and thus its concomitant emphasis on tolerance of, and respect for, believers in all communities founded by an authentic revelation of God. Ibn al-'Arabī's view of *naskh* is most instructive in this connection, reconciling the fact that Islam supersedes all religions with the continuing validity of these religions:

> All the revealed religions are lights. Among these religions, the revealed religion of Muhammad is like the light of the sun among the lights of the stars. When the sun appears, the lights of the stars are hidden, and their lights are included in the light of the sun. Their being hidden is like the abrogation of the other revealed religions that takes place through Muhammad's revealed religion. Nevertheless, they do in fact exist, just as the existence of the lights of the stars is actualized. This explains why we have been required in our all-inclusive religion to have faith in the truth of all the messengers and all the revealed religions. They are not rendered null (*bāṭil*) by abrogation—that is the opinion of the ignorant.[21]

Verse 5:48 contains several key principles; for our purposes, it suffices to draw attention to the following four:

(1) The Qurʾān confirms and protects *all* divine revelations preceding it: 'We have revealed unto you the Scripture with the Truth, as a confirmer of whatever [revealed] Scripture came before it, and a protector thereof.'
(2) The plurality of revelations, like the diversity of human communities, is divinely-willed: 'For each We have appointed a Law and a Way. And had God willed, He could have made you one community.'
(3) The diversity of revelations and plurality of communities is intended to stimulate a healthy 'competition' or mutual enrichment in the domain of 'good works': 'But in order that He might try you by that which He has given you [He has made you as you are]. So compete with one another in good works.'
(4) Differences of dogma, doctrine, perspective and opinion are inevitable consequences of the polyvalent meaning embodied in diverse revelations; these differences, and even the disagreements they might engender, are to be tolerated on the human plane, and will be finally resolved in the Hereafter: 'Unto God you will all return, He will disclose to you [the truth] of that about which you had different opinions.'

Let us take a closer look at each of these principles in turn.

Confirmation and Protection

As already noted, the Qurʾān is unique among the scriptures of the world for explicitly confirming the validity of all scriptures revealed before it. It is indeed one of the remarkable facts about the Qurʾānic revelation that in its very 'letter', and not just its spirit, other scriptures, prophets and religious traditions are granted formal recognition and profound respect. In other scriptural traditions, it is necessary to engage in subtle hermeneutical strategies in order to arrive at any kind of confirmation of the validity of other religious traditions; in other words, one has to move from the exoteric letter to the esoteric spirit of the scripture in order to be universalist in one's embrace of other traditions. Ironically, in Islam, the exoteric or formalistic theologian has the very opposite problem: the literal meaning of so many verses has to be explained away—through strategies of abrogation, specification, circumscription, etc.[22]—in order to minimise or deny their clear universalist implications.

However, when it comes to the basic postulate of belief in *all* scriptures revealed by God, and *all* prophets sent by God, there is no disagreement between the theologians and the mystics—for the Qur'ān is too categorical about this for there to be any room for doubt. As noted above, the verses which begin and end Chapter 2, *al-Baqara*, express something of a Muslim *credo*. Belief in the spiritual equivalence of all scriptural revelations is an essential part of Muslim belief in God, in the divine provenance of the Qur'ān, and in the finality of the prophethood of Muḥammad. The necessity of belief in all scriptural revelations and all prophets prior to the Qur'ān is given a greater degree of explicit affirmation in the following verses, which refer by name to several of the prophets:

> Say: We believe in God and that which is revealed unto us, and that which is revealed unto Abraham and Ishmael and Isaac and Jacob and the tribes, and that which was given unto Moses and Jesus and the prophets from their Lord. We make no distinction between any of them, and unto Him we have submitted (3:84).

Although the Qur'ān mentions twenty-four prophets by name, the scope of prophetic guidance extends far beyond them, for, as noted earlier: 'Truly, We sent Messengers before you; among them are those about whom We have told you, and those about whom We have not told you' (40:78). The unrestricted scope of prophetic guidance means that no human community is left without a guide: 'For every community (*umma*) there is a Messenger' (10:47). The outward variety of modes of revelation imparted through the different prophets, together with their underlying unity of essence, is linked in the following verses with the idea that all of the revealed messages together constitute an 'argument' against which there is no appeal:

> Truly We have revealed unto you as We have revealed to Noah and the prophets after him, as We revealed to Abraham and Ishmael and Isaac and the tribes, and Jesus and Job and Jonah and Aaron and Solomon, and as We bestowed upon David the Psalms, and Messengers We have mentioned to you before and Messengers We

> have not mentioned to you—and God spoke directly to Moses—Messengers giving good tidings and [also] warnings, so that mankind might have no argument against God after the Messengers. God is ever Mighty, Wise (4:163–165).

The idea of the totality of divinely-inspired Messengers constituting a self-evident argument or an irrefutable proof (*ḥujja*) of divine guidance takes us to the very heart of the *knowledge* called for by the Islamic revelation. To know that God is one is only a single aspect of this knowledge, the most fundamental aspect, expressed in the doctrine of *tawḥīd*, 'declaring the Oneness of God' or, in more spiritual terms, 'realising the Oneness of Reality'.[23] This knowledge also implies consciousness of the fact that God has sent Messengers to mankind with the same essential message: 'And We sent no Messenger before you but We inspired him [saying]: There is no God save Me, so worship Me' (21:25). And: 'Nothing is said to you [Muḥammad] other than what was said to the Messengers before you' (41:43).

God's reality and unity is proclaimed by all the Messengers, who were sent to every community on earth, with modes of guidance which differed outwardly according to the diverse needs of the different communities: 'And We never sent a Messenger save with the language of his people, so that he might make [Our message] clear to them' (14:4). The tolerance which emerges out of these and other verses is based not on personal whim, subjective conjecture or merely sentimental desire: it is based on knowledge of the universality of divine revelation; knowledge that it is nothing but the one divinity which lies at the source of the great world religions; knowledge that tolerance of those of different faiths is a compelling expression of the universal truth and the comprehensive finality of Islam itself. This knowledge acquires an irresistible divine logic, an objective, self-evident status, because it has been revealed as the ultimate proof, or *ḥujja*, in the face of which all human arguments are silenced.

As for the other function mentioned in this part of the verse, that of the Qur'ān's role as 'protector' of all previous scriptures and, implicitly, those who believe in them, this role is nowhere more clearly enacted, ironically, than in the domain of warfare. Despite the media stereotypes fashioned by modern Islamophobic propaganda and Muslim extremists alike, there is no place in Islam for any kind of 'holy war' for the spread of the faith: the simple words 'there is no compulsion in religion' renders absurd any effort to force people to become Muslims.[24] We shall explore this further in relation to point number 4, below. At this point, though, let us stress that one of the central purposes or justifications of warfare in Islam is to ensure that *all* faiths are protected, and that the adherents of *all* faiths be permitted to practise their faith unmolested. Again, the key theme here is universality.

This altogether fundamental principle is unequivocally expressed in the following verse, regarded by most commentators as the first to be revealed in relation to warfare,[25] granting Muslims the right to fight back in self-defence:

> Permission [to fight] is given to those who are being fought, for they have been wronged . . . Had God not driven back some by means of others, then indeed monasteries, churches, synagogues and mosques—wherein the name of God is oft-invoked—would assuredly have been destroyed (22:39–40).

We saw earlier how this principle of protecting all believers, and their places of worship, was implemented in dramatic fashion by the Emir 'Abd al-Qādir, whose heroic action in Damascus in 1860, though exceptional, must be seen as stemming from the Qur'ānic ethos, and, based thereupon, the authentic Muslim tradition with which the Emir explicitly identified. In other words, the Emir's heroism was not an exception to the Islamic rule, but rather, a spectacular way of upholding the rule.

It is interesting to look at the way the Emir comments on one of the many verses affirming the all-embracing Qur'ānic perspective on religion. This will help show the complete congruence in Islam between sublime metaphysics and eminently practical action. The Emir was both chivalric hero and spiritual master, a rare latter-day embodiment of the unique configuration of qualities manifested to perfection by Imam 'Alī b. Abī Ṭālib. The verse in question is Q 29:46: 'Say: we believe in that which has been revealed to us and in that which has been revealed to you; your God and our God are but one God, and unto Him we surrender.' In his esoteric masterpiece, *al-Mawāqif*, the Emir comments as follows:

> God commands Muhammadans to say to all the communities who belong to the 'People of the Book'—Christians, Jews, Sabeans and others—'we believe in that which was revealed to us': that is, in that which epiphanizes itself to us, namely the God exempt from all limitation, transcendent in His very immanence, and, even more, transcendent in His very transcendence, who, in all that, still remains immanent; 'and in that which was revealed to you': that is, in that which epiphanizes itself to you in conditioned, immanent and limited form. It is He whom His theophanies manifest to you, as to us.[26]

This highly mystical view of the principles of transcendence and immanence in relation to the modes of manifestation of different qualities of God to different religious traditions is, of course, only going to make sense to a minority of like-minded Sufis. The point here is that the highest metaphysical interpretations of Sufis such as the Emir are rooted in the same vision—that of a spiritual unity at the heart of confessional multiplicity—which is revealed to all Muslims by such verses as 29:46. Moreover, the Emir's tolerance, magnanimity and heroism cannot be divorced from his metaphysical knowledge, nor, *a fortiori*, from the Qur'ānic revelation and the prophetic paradigm upon which that knowledge is based.

It is important here to address the following objection: one of the first acts of the new Muslim state in Medina was to launch raids (*ghazawāt*) on the caravans of the Meccans; can this be called 'self-defence'? We would reply as follows: the verses cited above make it clear that permission to fight is being given 'to those who are being fought', thus it is undeniable that self-defence is the primary reason for permission being granted. The context in which this verse was revealed was one in which the Muslims at Medina were indeed being 'fought against', insofar as they had been subjected, first, to persecution, then to a trade boycott, and finally, after a foiled attempt to murder the Prophet, the Muslims were forced to flee their homes as exiles. According to the tribal customs then prevailing, when two tribes or confederations were not formally established in a state of peace, ratified by some kind of treaty, then the default state was one of war.

One can therefore argue that verses 22:39–40 were revealed to the Prophet in the context of a *de facto* state of war, one which could only be brought to an end by the promulgation of a *de jure* state of peace—

such as was in fact brought into being by the treaty of Ḥudaybiyya, several years later. But at the time of the revelation of these verses, the Muslims at Medina were *de facto* at war with the Meccans. In this state of war, the launching of a raid by one tribe against another was not regarded as having violated any implicit code of honour. In the words of Karen Armstrong: 'The *ghazu* [*ghazwa*] or raid . . . had long been a sort of national sport in Arabia, and an accepted way of making ends meet when times were hard . . . The *ghazu* had been a rough and ready way of securing a fair calculation of the available wealth during the nomadic period.'[27]

In her subsequent biography, aptly entitled *Muhammad: Prophet For Our Time*, Armstrong reinforces this point: 'Their aim was not to shed blood, but to secure an income by capturing camels, merchandise and prisoners, who could be held for ransom. Nobody would have been particularly shocked by this development. The *ghazu* was a normal expedient in times of hardship, though some of the Arabs would have been surprised by the Muslims' temerity in taking on the mighty Quraysh.'[28]

Therefore the early raids launched by the Muslims in no way amounted to an act of aggression, a violation of some pre-existing peace agreement. Such aggression is explicitly prohibited in the following verse, which more clearly perhaps than any other, enshrines the principle of defensive warfare in Islam: 'And fight in the way of God those who fight you, but do not commit aggression. God loves not the aggressors' (2:190). This principle forms the core argument of one of the most important treatises on the subject of warfare in the Qur'ān written in recent times, *al-Qur'ān wa'l-qitāl* ('The Qur'ān and Fighting'); the fact that it was written by Maḥmūd Shalṭūṭ, Shaykh of al-Azhar from 1958 to 1963—thus, the most authoritative scholar of Sunni Islam in his day—lends considerable weight to the argument made therein: that the Qur'ān only allows warfare to be waged in self-defence.[29] Verses such as the following figured prominently in Shalṭūṭ's treatise:

> And if they incline to peace, then you should also incline to it, and place your trust in God (8:61).
>
> As regards those who do not fight you on account of religion, nor drive you forth from your homes, God does not forbid you

> from showing them kindness and dealing with them justly. Surely God loves the just. God only forbids you from affiliating yourselves with those who fight you for religion, and drive you forth from your homes, and help [others] in your expulsion. Whoever takes them as affiliates, they are the wrongdoers (60:8–9).

These verses, together with 2:190 and 22:39–40, uphold the principle that Muslims are only permitted to fight in self-defence. All too often, extremists cite out of context verses or parts of a verse in which Muslims are urged to fight; all such citations are to be understood in the context of warfare which has already been commenced, and not as an encouragement to initiate hostilities. Acts of aggression violate the principle of self-defence unequivocally stated by 2:190: 'And fight in the way of God those who fight you, but do not commit aggression. God loves not the aggressors'.[30]

Another objection should be addressed here. Verse 3:85 states: 'And whoever seeks a religion other than Islam, it will not be accepted from him, and he will be a loser in the Hereafter.' How can this be reconciled with the claim that Islam confirms and protects all religions? One answer is to look at what the word 'Islam' means here: is it the specific religion heralded by the Qurʾān and conveyed by the Prophet Muḥammad, or is it universal 'submission', the literal meaning of the word, that same submission spoken of in relation to all previous prophets and their faithful followers? Abraham, for example, as we saw earlier, is referred to as both a *ḥanīf* and a *muslim*. The religion, 'Islam', is therefore not to be identified exclusively with the final manifestation of the principle defined by the Arabic word, *islām*. Rather, this final manifestation is to be integrated into its universal principle, whence the common designation of Islam as 'the religion of primordial nature' (*dīn al-fiṭra*) synonymous with *al-dīn al-ḥanīf* or *al-dīn al-ḥanīfī*.

This interpretation of the meaning of 3:85 is reinforced when one reads it in context, for the preceding verse, 3:84, as noted above, reads: 'Say: We believe in God and that which is revealed unto us, and that which is revealed unto Abraham and Ishmael and Isaac and Jacob and the tribes, and that which was given unto Moses and Jesus and the prophets from their Lord. We make no distinction between any of them, and unto Him we have submitted.' Verse 3:85 can therefore be read as a confirmation of the validity of all the revelations brought by all the prophets mentioned in 3:84. From the inclusive point of view, *islām* encompasses all revelations, which can thus be seen as so many different facets of the same principle of submission. Rather than simply designating a specific religion, *islām* can be appreciated as indicating a fundamental disposition of soul toward the guidance bestowed by divine revelation.[31]

Plurality of Faiths

As we have seen, according to the Qur'ān, both the plurality of faiths and the diversity of the human race are expressions of divine wisdom. Appreciation of this fundamental fact leads to a knowledge which cannot but generate tolerant attitudes towards the religions of the Other—even, as we shall see, those not specifically mentioned in the Qur'ān. They are also signs indicating something about the infinitude of the divine nature itself: 'And among His signs is the creation of the heavens and the earth, and the differences of your languages and colours. Indeed, herein are signs for those who know' (30:22). Again, it is *knowledge* that is stressed here: the very existence of human diversity is a 'sign' *for those who know*. The sign therefore can also generate this knowledge, and this is precisely what the Qur'ān repeatedly calls out for: meditation upon the 'signs' of God, pondering and reflecting upon them, in order to arrive at a deeper, contemplative knowledge of the mysteries of God's creation. In respect of the creation of man, we might see the 'sign' of the sheer diversity of races, languages, colours and ethnicities as being a reflection of the infinite nature of divine creativity, itself a 'sign' of the infinitude of God *per se*. Just as God is both absolutely one yet immeasurably infinite, so the human race is one in its essence, yet marvellously variegated in its forms.

We have discussed the way in which the *fiṭra* is conceived as the inalienable substance of each human being; and this essence of human identity takes priority over all external forms of identity such as race and nation, culture or even religion, for according to the saying of the Prophet cited earlier, this *fiṭra* precedes and underlies all subsequent religious affiliations: every baby is born in accordance with the *fiṭra*; his parents superimpose a particular religion upon him. The only criterion by which hierarchical distinction can be established among human beings is *taqwā*, piety or righteousness, as we are told at 49:13: 'O mankind, We have created you male and female, and We have made you into tribes and nations in order that you might come to know one another. Truly, in the sight of God, the most honoured amongst you is the most pious amongst you.' Intolerance is fed by an unwarranted sense of superiority; a pious standard of excellence, by contrast, calls not only for tolerance of other 'tribes and nations', but also respect for adherents of other religions, and indeed humility towards them in the very measure of their superiority to oneself as regards the only criterion of honour in the sight of God: piety and, *a fortiori*, sanctity.

As regards the diversity of religious rites, the fact that this, too, is derived directly from God is further affirmed in the following verse: 'Unto each community We have given sacred rites (*mansakan*) which they are to perform; so let them not dispute with you about the matter, but summon them unto your Lord' (22:67). This kind of verse helps explain how it is that, when faced with such alien religious rites and beliefs as those of the Buddhists and Hindus, the considered response of Ḥajjāj's scholars was to have a 'good opinion' (*ḥusn al-ẓann*), and advise that they be treated with respect as being akin to the 'People of the Book'.

The Prophet is instructed in the Qur'ān: 'Say: I am not a novelty among the Messengers' (46:9). He transmits nothing 'new', he merely brings, freshly minted, the one primordial message of revelation, a message which comprises diverse modes and facets, but which remains always one and the same in its essence. One of the glories of the Qur'ān is the fact that it constitutes the consummation of the revelations preceding it, a kind of crystallisation of the quintessence of all possible revelation; a proper consciousness of this universal aspect of Islam allows tolerant Muslims to respect and admire all previous revelations, together with the traditions of holiness, beauty and virtue springing therefrom, without any fear of diluting, still less betraying, the essence of one's faith. On the contrary, this non-dogmatic approach to religious diversity bears witness to the unique comprehensiveness of the Qur'ānic perspective.

It also makes possible a more subtle perception that these 'other' traditions are indeed radically different, but not necessarily 'alien'.

Rather they can be seen as 'Islamic' in the supra-confessional, trans-historical sense; they can be appreciated as being, at their origins, so many modes of 'submission' to God. Not just Hinduism and Buddhism, but also such traditions as Confucianism, Taoism, Shintoism, together with the primal shamanistic traditions of the Americas, Africa and Australasia—all of these expressions of the spiritual heritage of mankind can be approached with a 'good opinion'. They can be seen as originating in authentic divine revelation, even if they may have undergone varying degrees of degeneration over time; for, on the one hand: 'We never sent a Messenger save with the language of his people, so that he might make [Our message] clear to them' (14:4); and on the other, 'For every community there is a Messenger' (10:47). According to tradition, God has sent 124,000 prophets to mankind; the Qur'ān tells us, as noted earlier, that not all of the prophets have been mentioned by name in the Qur'ān itself (40:78). In this light it becomes reasonable to suppose that the primal traditions were indeed inaugurated by prophets, whose message or 'book' was constituted by the phenomena of virgin nature—the 'verses' which are also 'signs', the Arabic *āya* comprising both meanings.[32]

Those Muslims sensitive to the Qur'ānic view of the sanctity of the cosmos will observe, moreover, that these traditions are, at their best, particularly instructive in regard to primordial—that is, pre-dogmatic—modes of thought and worship, and may reveal something profound about the nature of the *fiṭra* and, by extension, the nature of pre-lapsarian Edenic perfection. Their intimacy with the rhythms of virgin nature, allied to a profound sense of symbolism, evokes such verses as the following, which draw attention to the signs, symbols and similitudes of which the whole of the natural world is woven:

- We shall show them our signs [or: verses, *āyāt*] on the horizons and within themselves until it be clear to them that He is the Real (41:53).
- Unto God belong the East and the West; to whichever direction you turn, there is the Face of God (2:115).
- Do you not see how God strikes similitudes? A good word is as a good tree: its root firm, its branches in heaven, giving

forth its fruits in every season, by the leave of its Lord. And God strikes similitudes for mankind in order that they might remember (14:25).

- God does not disdain from citing as a similitude even a gnat or something smaller. So as for the faithful, they know it is the truth from their Lord; and as for the disbelievers, they say: What does God intend by this similitude? (2:26).
- God is the light of the heavens and the earth. A similitude of His light is a niche wherein is a lamp; the lamp is enclosed in a glass; the glass is as it were a shining star. [The lamp] is lit [by the oil of] a blessed olive tree, neither of the East nor of the West. The oil well-nigh shines forth, though fire touch it not. Light upon light! God guides to His light whom He will; and God strikes similitudes for mankind; and God knows all things (24:35).
- And Solomon was the heir of David. He said: O people, we have indeed been taught the language of the birds . . . (27:16).[33]
- Then your hearts hardened after that, so that they became as stones, or even harder. For indeed there are some stones from which streams gush forth, and indeed there are some which split, so that water issues from them, and indeed there are some which fall in awe of God (2:74).
- And your Lord inspired the bee [saying]: Make your home in the mountains, and on the trees, and the trellises they erect (16:68).
- All that is in the heavens and the earth glorifies God; and He is the Mighty, the Wise (57:1).
- The seven heavens and the earth and all that is therein praise Him; and there is not a thing but it hymns His praise, but you do not understand their praise (17:44).
- Have you not seen that God—He it is Whom all who are in the heavens and the earth praise—and the birds in flight: indeed, each knows its prayer and its form of glorification (24:41).[34]
- The sun and the moon are made punctual; the stars and the trees prostrate; and the sky He has uplifted, and He has

established the measure that you exceed not the measure; but observe the measure with justice, do not fall short thereof. And the earth He has appointed for the creatures; wherein are fruit and sheathed palm-trees, husked grain and scented herb. Which, then, of the favours of your Lord, will you deny? (55:5–13).

- The slaves of the Compassionate (*'ibād al-Raḥmān*) are those who walk upon the earth gently, and when the arrogantly ignorant ones (*al-jāhilūn*)[35] address them, they answer: Peace! (25:63).[36]

Given the fact that the entire creation is constituted by 'signs' which are 'verses', Sufi exegetes distinguished between *al-Qur'ān al-takwīnī*, 'the creational Qur'ān' and *al-Qur'ān al-tadwīnī*, 'the written Qur'ān'. For example, the fourteenth century Sufi, 'Azīz al-Dīn Nasafī, writes: 'Each day, destiny and the passage of time set this book before you, *sūrah* for *sūrah*, verse for verse, letter for letter and read it to you . . .'[37] Such a view is clearly in harmony with the cosmological spirit underlying the shamanistic traditions. In this contemplative perspective the Qur'ānic phrase 'People of the Book' goes well beyond the narrow category defined by the jurists and theologians, and can be understood as an allusion to all those who uphold, to some degree at least, the founding revelation of their tradition, whether this revelation comes in the form of a historically verifiable scripture or in the form of 'verses' of the cosmic script.

The Qur'ānic vision of religious plurality thus transcends the world of Semitic monotheism, and invites one not just to tolerate followers of other faiths, but also to investigate with respect the sources and the manifestations of their beliefs and practices. Ibn al-'Arabī sums up well the open-minded spirit of inquiry fostered by the essentially pluralistic message of the Qur'ān, linking one's respectful investigation of all religious creeds and doctrines to two key verses: on the one hand 'they do not rate God at His true worth' (6:91); and on the other, 'My mercy embraces all things' (7:156). If we are to give God His due, we must make an effort to see how the all-embracing scope of His mercy is also expressed in the form of revealed guidance to all:

> He who counsels his own soul should investigate, during his life in this world, all doctrines concerning God. He should learn from whence each possessor of a doctrine affirms the validity of his doctrine. Once its validity has been affirmed for him in the specific mode in which it is correct for him who upholds it, then he should support it in the case of him who believes in it. He should not deny it or reject it, for he will gather its fruit on the Day of Visitation . . . So turn your attention to what we have mentioned and put it into practice! Then you will give the Divinity its due . . . For God is exalted high above entering under delimitation. He cannot be tied down by one form rather than another. From here you will come to know the all-inclusiveness of felicity for God's creatures and the all-embracingness of the 'mercy which covers everything' [7:156].[38]

The following word of warning from the *Fuṣūṣ*, cited earlier, follows logically both from the above passage and from 2:115, which tells that the Face of God is to be found wherever we may look:

> Beware of being bound up by a particular creed and rejecting others as unbelief! Try to make yourself a prime matter for all forms of religious belief. God is greater and wider than to be confined to one particular creed to the exclusion of others. For He says 'To whichever direction you turn, there is the Face of God [2:115].'[39]

Healthy Competition

'So compete with one another in good works.' The ultimate goal in such a competition between religious believers is, of course, salvation in the Hereafter and sanctification here below. The performance of 'good works' (*khayrāt*) is intended not only to establish moral conduct on earth but also to make one less unworthy of receiving the grace by which, alone, one attains salvation in the Hereafter. The Prophet said that nobody enters Paradise on account of their deeds. His companions asked him: 'Not even you, O Messenger of God?' 'Not even I', he replied, 'it is only if God whelms me with his bounty and mercy [that I can enter Paradise].'[40] If even the deeds of the Messenger of God are insufficient to warrant salvation, the exclusivist notion that one's religion alone grants access to salvation—all others being false religions leading nowhere—is all the more illogical. The kind of exclusivism summed up in the Roman Catholic formula *extra ecclesiam nulla salus*: 'there is no salvation outside of the Church', can only find a place in Islamic thought with great difficulty. The necessary—but insufficient—conditions for salvation according to the Qur'ān are stated in various places, such as the following key verse:

> Truly those who believe, and the Jews, and the Christians, and the Sabeans—whoever believes in God and the Last Day and performs virtuous deeds—surely their reward is with their Lord, and no fear shall come upon them, neither shall they grieve (2:62; repeated almost verbatim at 5:69).

According to this verse, what is required, above all else, for salvation is belief in the Absolute, belief in accountability to that Absolute, and virtuous conduct in consequence of these beliefs. Given this clear expression of the supra-confessional approach to the question of salvation, any lapse into the kind of religious chauvinism which feeds intolerance is impermissible. So the kind of 'competition' in good deeds enjoined by the Qur'ān has nothing to do with proving the superiority of one's religion, which thus becomes an extension of one's egotism rather than the means of overcoming it. Such sanctimonious boasting is a sign of pride and worldliness; boasting in general is mentioned as one of the sins of worldliness: 'Know that the life of the world is only play, and idle talk, and pageantry, and boasting among you, and rivalry in respect of wealth and children' (57:20). Similarly, in the words of advice given by the sage Luqmān to his son, we are made to see the ugliness of pride and boastfulness, together with the beauty of humility:

> Establish worship and enjoin kindness and forbid iniquity, and bear with patience whatever may befall you. Truly, that is of the steadfast heart of things. Do not turn your nose up in scorn toward folk, nor walk exultantly in the land. Truly, God does not love any arrogant boaster. Be modest in your bearing and lower your voice. Verily, the most repugnant of all sounds is the braying of the ass (31:17–19).

Boasting about one's religion being superior to other religions, such as is indulged by some triumphalist Muslims behind the mask of piety, is thus far from the kind of wholesome 'competition' enjoined in 5:48. It also directly contravenes the Qur'ānic guidance on how to engage in debate or discourse with followers of other faiths: 'Call unto the way of your Lord with wisdom (*ḥikma*) and beautiful exhortation (*mawʿiẓa ḥasana*), and hold discourse with them [the People of the Book] in the most beautiful manner (16:125).' It is neither wise nor beautiful to engage in mutual recrimination and religious polemics. This is made clear in the following verses, which explicitly mention forms of religious exclusivism which the Muslims had encountered among various communities of the 'People of the Book':

> And they say: 'None enters Paradise unless he be a Jew or a Christian'. These are their vain desires. Say: 'Bring your proof if you are truthful.' Rather, whosoever submits (*aslama*) his purpose to God, and he is virtuous, his reward is with his Lord. No fear shall come upon them, neither shall they grieve (2:111–112).

In other words, the Muslim is not allowed to play the game of religious polemics. The verses here are not accusing all Jews and Christians of playing this game; they are simply warning believers not to fall into the attitude of religious arrogance, an attitude unfortunately to be found in every religious community. Instead of responding in kind to any sort of chauvinistic claims or 'vain desires' aimed at monopolising Paradise, the Muslim is instructed to raise the dialogue to a higher level, and to call for reasoned debate, asking one's partners in dialogue: 'bring your proof'. The Qur'ānic position is to affirm the universal salvific criteria of piety, accessible to all human beings, whatever be their religious affiliation. This position is further affirmed in the following verses:

> It will not be in accordance with your desires, nor with the desires of the People of the Book. He who does wrong will have its recompense . . .
>
> And whoso performs good works, whether male or female, and is a believer, such will enter Paradise, and will not be wronged the dint of a date-stone (4:123–124).

If Muslims indulge their own 'desires' that salvation be restricted to Muslims in the specific, communal sense, then they are making exactly the same error as those Christians and Jews who assert that they, alone, are the 'chosen people'. So the word 'submits', *aslama*, in 2:112, should be read in the lexical and not communitarian sense. The response to religious chauvinism is to assert that what is necessary for salvation is wholehearted submission to God—whatever be the religious medium by which this submission is articulated. Certain Jews and Christians fall into the trap of mutual recrimination:

> The Jews say: 'The Christians stand on nothing.' And the Christians say: 'The Jews stand on nothing'—though they [both] read the Book. Such words are spoken by those who have no knowledge. God will judge between them on the Day of Resurrection concerning that about which they had differences [of opinion] (2:113).

The logic of such verses as 2:111–113 and 4:123–124 leads one to assert that one form of religious prejudice must not be confronted with an alternative form of religious prejudice; rather, all forms of prejudice must be transcended through an objective recognition of the inexorable and universal law of divine justice. This objectivity presupposes discernment as regards the variety of types and attitudes manifested within all religions, including one's own. Hence, in regard to the 'People of the Book', the Qur'ān warns against making simplistic generalisations:

> They are not all alike. Of the People of the Book there is an upright community who recite the revelations of God in the watches of the night, falling prostrate. They believe in God and the Last Day, and enjoin right conduct and forbid indecency, and compete with one another in good works. These are of the righteous. And whatever good they do, they will not be denied it; and God knows the pious (3:113–114).

The Qur'ān also draws attention to two fundamental qualities—intensity of worship and depth of humility—that will bring about 'affection' between believers of different faiths:

> You will find the nearest of them [the People of the Book] in affection to those who believe to be those who say: Verily, we are Christians. That is because there are among them priests and monks, and they are not proud (5:82).

The humble adoration personified by sincere priests and monks in Christianity is to be found in all communities, as is its opposite: heedlessness of God combined with contempt for people of other faiths. Muslims are enjoined in these and other verses to maintain a lively sense of discernment and to avoid making simplistic generalisations and reifications in regard to different religious communities. Such discernment and impartiality are reflections of God's justice and wisdom. A proper sense of divine justice renders absurd the shrill claims of religious tribalism (*ʿaṣabiyya*). This tribalist mentality of the *jāhiliyya*, together with the intolerant fanaticism (*taʿaṣṣub*) it feeds, is precisely what Islam intended to abolish, as we shall see in more detail below, in our discussion of the cardinal prophetic virtue of wise forbearance, or *ḥilm*.[42]

The qualities of fanaticism and pride come together in a particularly striking way in the disobedience of Iblis, the devil, as Imam ʿAlī reveals. He refers to Iblis as 'the leader of the fanatics and the forerunner of the proud (*imām al-mutaʿaṣṣibīn wa salaf al-mustakbirīn*)'.[43] It was his sense of superiority over Adam, his consciousness of being made of fire rather than clay, that prevented Iblis from prostrating to Adam in obedience to God's command. The Muslim sensitive to the deeper meaning of this story cannot allow himself to engage in the 'disgrace' of egotism, vanity, pride—which can all too easily lead to a fanatical intolerance of those deemed inferior to oneself. This, in turn, results in an inability to maintain objectivity, to see things as they are truly are, and instead to identify the truth with one's own opinions, which are then articulated as ideology. Al-Ghazālī makes this clear in his description of *taʿṣṣub*, fanaticism. He writes that it 'usually comes together with a man's disregard of his neighbor, and of his opinions, and the taking root in his heart of certain ideas which become so much a part of him that he fails to distinguish between right and wrong'.[44]

The Prophet alerted his followers to the dangers of this kind of fanaticism and egotism in the guise of piety. He also warned against falling into conceit through exaggerated claims in the apparent service of Islam: 'Do not make me better than Moses', he said.[45] Boasting, pride, arrogance—the very stuff of intolerance, and the very opposite of *ḥilm*—was clearly anathema to the Prophet. We are reminded here of the Prophet's refusal to name a specific religion when asked which was most loved by God; his very answer, 'the primordial, generously tolerant faith', indicates the reason why one should refrain from trumpeting triumphalist claims for one's religion. That religion is best which most successfully instils into the substance of faith the qualities of the *ḥanīf*, particularly nobility, generosity and tolerance—the traits expressed by the word *samḥa*. Conversely, religion is ruined by those who lack these qualities, and instead give full rein to all the vices produced by unrestrained egotism, in particular, intolerance, fanaticism and tyranny. 'Avoid extremism (*al-ghuluww*), for people have been led to destruction by extremism', the Prophet said, as cited earlier.[46]

Rather than engage in hierarchical classification of religions, the Prophet stressed the need to perceive the oneness of the prophetic message, and the unity of the spiritual family of the prophets, saying that all the prophets were born of the same father but had different mothers, sharing the same religion.[47] This principle is particularly accentuated in one of the most fundamental practical expressions of piety and spirituality in Islam, the invocation of blessings on the Prophet. This invocation is enjoined in the following verse: 'Truly, God and His angels bless the Prophet. O you who believe, bless him and greet him with peace' (33:56). Upon the revelation of this verse, the Prophet was asked how one was to perform this blessing, and he replied that the blessings were to be invoked upon him as follows: 'O God, bless Muḥammad and the progeny of Muḥammad, as You have blessed Abraham and the progeny of Abraham. Truly, You are the Praised, the Glorious . . .'[48] The fact that pious Muslims repeat this invocation several times each day in their formal prayers is full of spiritual as well as ritual significance. It is an expression of the inclusive intentionality of Islam, the incorporation of the Prophet of Islam within the cycle of Abrahamic revelation, thus reinforcing, on a daily ritual basis, the essential unity of the prophets of a single Judaeo–Christian–Islamic family. And, as noted above, this family is part of the larger Adamic family, incorporating all the 124,000 prophets sent to mankind by God.

Finally, it is of interest to note that in our own times, the Dalai Lama echoes the Qurʾānic call for wholesome and salutary 'competition' between followers of different religious traditions. In a speech entitled 'Harmony, Dialogue and Meditation' delivered at the famous 'Gethsemani Encounter', which brought Christian and Buddhist monks together in dialogue during July, 1996 in Gethsemani, Kentucky, he issued a warning: the participants in the dialogue should avoid the temptation to engage in 'advertisement' for their own tradition, and to guard against a certain kind of unhealthy competition. He then added: 'But I think we should have one kind of constructive competition. The Buddhists should implement what we believe in daily life; and our Christian brothers and sisters should also implement their teachings in daily life.' Implementation of belief is central to the Dalai Lama's vision of the transformative power of 'practice'; it is insofar as 'each side would like to be better practitioners' that the competition between them is constructive and not destructive.[49]

Inevitability of Difference

Allied to the idea of healthy competition is that of the inevitability and legitimacy of differences of opinion; these are to be seen as logical consequences of the very plurality of meanings embodied in diverse revelations, the different doctrinal means of conceptualising the Absolute, and the different rites and rituals giving outward form to those doctrines; all such differences are to be tolerated on the human plane, and will be finally resolved in the Hereafter: 'Unto God you will all return, He will disclose to you [the truth] of that about which you had different opinions'.

The verse which tells us that 'there is no compulsion in religion' (2:256) logically implies that differences of opinion on that most contentious and potentially explosive of all subjects, religion, must be tolerated and not suppressed. A *ḥadīth* states: 'Differences of opinion within my *umma* constitute a mercy (*raḥma*).'[50] Even in regard to the disbelievers, the Muslim is enjoined to let them go their way unmolested, to let them believe in their own 'religion':

> Say: O you who disbelieve, I worship not that which you worship, nor do you worship that which I worship. And I shall not worship

> that which you worship, nor will you worship that which I worship. For you your religion, for me, mine (109:1–6).

The Muslim who emulates the Prophet only has the duty to deliver the message, and not to impose it, nor to refuse to engage in peaceful discourse. As regards this latter principle, the following verse, already cited above, is altogether definitive: 'Call unto the way of your Lord with wisdom and fair exhortation, and hold discourse with them [the People of the Book] in the finest manner' (16:125). The Prophet carried out this injunction to perfection in his engagement with the Christians of Najrān, as noted above: on the one hand, he expressed 'fair exhortation' in the manner of his debate with the Christians over points of dogmatic contention; but he complemented this level of doctrinal engagement with the 'wisdom' that comes from something transcending the plane of dogma; hence his gracious allowance of Christian worship to be enacted in his mosque. Tolerance was manifested in the very teeth of dogmatic difference.

The invitation (*da'wa*) to embrace Islam is by no means obviated by the universal perspective of the Qur'ān which logically entails the legitimacy of diversity; the Muslim is called upon to bear witness to his faith, certainly, but the manner of doing so should be in conformity with beauty and wisdom: the Qur'ān calls for bearing witness through wise discourse and not polemical diatribe. This kind of peaceful dialogue goes hand in hand with tolerant acceptance of the right of the Other to disagree. Paradoxically, as noted above in various places, this expression of tolerance was itself often one of the most effective means by which non-Muslims came to embrace Islam. Demonstrating the utter falsity of the claim that Islam was 'spread by the sword', Thomas Arnold asserts that it was the manifestation of tolerance, among other factors, that made the religion of Islam so attractive to non-Muslims. He cites a great mass of contemporaneous documents illustrating this principle, of which the following will suffice for our purposes. The Christians of the Persian province of Khurasan embraced Islam en masse within the first century of Muslim rule over Persia. This elicited a bitter complaint from the Nestorian Patriarch, Isho-yabh III to Simeon, Metropolitan of Rev-Ardashir, Primate of Persia:

> Alas, alas! Out of so many thousands who bore the name of Christians, not even one single victim was consecrated unto God by the shedding of his blood for the true faith . . . (the Arabs) attack not the Christian faith, but on the contrary, they favour our religion, do honour to our priests and the saints of our Lord and confer benefits on churches and monasteries. Why, then, have your people of Merv abandoned their faith for the sake of these Arabs?[51]

Returning to the duty of the believer only to deliver the message, there are a number of verses to note; for example:

> 'If they submit, they are rightly guided, but if they turn away, you have no duty other than conveying the message . . .' (3:20).
> 'If they are averse, We have not sent you as a guardian over them: your duty is but to convey the message' (42:48).

Tolerating the expression of opinions contrary to one's own raises the question of freedom of speech. In our times, the intolerance of Muslims extends not only to non-Muslims but also, and above all, to Muslims themselves—witness the oppression meted out by Muslim regimes to their political opponents, driving them further into militant opposition. That this violation of the right of freedom of speech contradicts fundamental Islamic norms should be clear from what has been said thus far; but the principle of freedom of speech is brought into particularly sharp focus by the conduct of Imam 'Alī towards his political opponents, the Kharijites, during his caliphate (656–661). He gave these opponents full rights to express their dissenting opinions, and even when they anathematised him, calling him a *kāfir*, he did not violate their right to express their opinions: 'If they oppose me through speech, I will hold discourse and argue with them'; and 'I will only resort to arms when they fight me.'[52]

Even when Kharijite opposition to him was clear and intense, he never ceased paying them their salaries from the public treasury. Only when vociferous opposition turned to open warfare was this payment stopped. The Imam addressed the Kharijites on several occasions with these or similar words: 'You have three prerogatives in regard to us: we shall not prevent you from praying in the mosques; nor shall we stop payment of the *fay'* due to you from the treasury; nor shall we initiate hostilities against you until you fight us.'[53] In other words, the socio-economic rights and the political liberties of the Kharijites were in no way compromised by their vehement religious opposition to the caliph, for as long as this opposition remained non-violent. This tolerant policy of the Imam is all the more remarkable for being applied at a time of nearly constant warfare—a time, in other words, when various 'emergency measures' are normally invoked by the state in order to justify the curtailment of the rights and freedoms of its citizens.

Finally, returning to the principle of the divinely-willed diversity of faiths, let it be noted that this phenomenon is, like the diversity of races, languages, and cultures within humanity, something to be respected and, at a higher level, contemplated as a sign of divine creativity. Any attempt at homogenisation of this divinely-willed diversity—any tendency to reduce the complexity of the spectrum of the faiths to some uniform, putatively quintessential form of supra-confessional spirituality or 'new age consciousness'—is to violate the irreducible uniqueness of each of the faiths, a uniqueness willed by God: 'for each We have established a law and a path'. One divine dispensation is not another, and is not to be merged with another or reduced to another. Each has its own formal law and spiritual path, the two dimensions complementing each other within a unique configuration of divinely revealed elements. The dazzling beauty of the multi-faceted phenomenon of religion is in large part predicated upon the contrasts between the different religions, contrasts which in turn are based on irreducible differences. These differences are, from the spiritual point of view, the results of different combinations of the specific divine qualities which lie at the roots of each of the religions. These qualities are no doubt at one with each other within the Oneness of the Divine Essence; but the distinctive properties of each of the qualities paradoxically manifest both the uniqueness of their source and its infinite possibilities. For the Essence is both absolutely One and infinitely variegated. The irreducible differences between the divine qualities are thus a vital expression of the infinite inner riches of the one reality they reveal in their unique way.

Analogously, the irreducible differences between the revealed religions of the world are vital expressions of the infinite creativity of their unique source. The religions are one in essence, stemming from the unicity of the One; and they are diverse in form, this diversity stemming from the infinity of the One. The following image can be interpreted as alluding to the way in which this formal diversity on the plane of revelation mysteriously manifests the essential unity of the divine source of revelation:

> And in the earth are neighbouring tracts, and gardens of vines, and fields sown, and palms in pairs, and palms single, watered with one water. And we have made some of them to excel others in fruit. Surely herein are signs for a people who understand (13:4).

The Prophetic Paradigm: Compassionate Forbearance

To speak about the intellectual search for knowledge, therefore, is also, and inescapably, to speak about the pursuit of virtue, and it is here that the paradigm of prophetic perfection is of the utmost importance: 'I was raised up as a Prophet to perfect the most noble traits of character (*makārim al-akhlāq*)',[55] the Prophet said, in an allusion to the principle that understanding the message of Divine Oneness—the conveyance of which was the chief reason for his being 'raised up' as a prophet—both requires and produces nobility of character. In other words, there can be no authentic assimilation of the mysteries of divine revelation, the meaning of prophetic guidance, or the depths of authentic knowledge, without the full participation of the whole personality,[56] or rather, the personality made whole through perfect nobility of soul, or magnanimity.

Such magnanimity is defined according to the prophetic model of perfection, and the Prophet's soul is described precisely in terms of qualities, at once human and divine, of kindness and loving mercy. In the following verse, he is referred to as *ra'ūf* (kind) and *raḥīm* (merciful), both of which are also names of God, *al-Ra'ūf, al-Raḥīm*: 'There has indeed come unto you a Prophet from amongst you; whatever harms you is grievous to him; he is ever-caring in your regard; unto the believers, kind (*ra'ūf*) and merciful (*raḥīm*)' (9:128). The importance of this gentle predisposition of the prophetic character for the very success of the Islamic religion can hardly be over-estimated. The Qur'ān itself bears testimony to its key role in attracting people to the religion. Had the Prophet been intolerant and hard-hearted, people would have been repelled both from him and from the religion he was representing and conveying: 'It was a mercy from God that you are gently disposed to them (*linta lahum*); had you been fierce and hard-hearted, they would have fled from you' (3:159).

The Prophet is told in the Qur'ān to say to people: 'If you love God, follow me; God will love you' (3:31). In the light of the preceding points it should be clear that 'following the Prophet' does not simply mean obeying the law he conveys; it means, in addition and more fundamentally, that one must make an effort to emulate his 'beautiful example' (*uswa ḥasana*): 'Indeed there is for you in the Messenger of God a beautiful example' (33:21). The prophetic character is also described as 'tremendous' (*'aẓīm*): 'And indeed your character is of a tremendous nature' (68:4). If we ask which are the actual virtues to be emulated in this 'beautiful example', what is the concrete, identifiable and thus imitable content of this 'tremendous character', the answer we are given in the Qur'ān is remarkable: for the Prophet's character is described, almost invariably, in terms of gentleness and kindness, concern and compassion; and it is these qualities which must be emulated by all Muslims who wish to 'follow the Prophet', and thus become lovable to God. In other words, the cardinal prophetic virtues to be emulated are those gentle and forbearing ones comprised within the quality of *ḥilm*. The Prophet went so far in his exhortation to emulate his own quality of *ḥilm* as to say: 'The *ḥalīm* is almost a prophet (*kāda'l-ḥalīm an yakūna nabiyyan*)'.[57] He himself is described in the traditional sources as *aḥlam al-nās:*[58] 'the most forbearing of people'—the one with the greatest plenitude of *ḥilm*.

Scholars of Islam have routinely been struck by this aspect of the Prophet's character. For example, in his renowned work *Muḥammad at Medina*, Montgomery Watt draws a touching portrait of the Prophet as a gentle, loving, and compassionate person, stressing his love for children, his gentleness with all, especially women, and even manifesting an extraordinary concern for the welfare of animals: 'His kindness extended even to animals, and this is something remarkable for Muḥammad's century and his part of the world. As his men marched towards Mecca just before the conquest they passed a bitch with puppies, and Muḥammad not merely gave orders that they were not to be disturbed, but posted a man to see that the orders were carried out.' It is not surprising that he states: 'Of all the world's great men none has been so much maligned as Muḥammad'.[59]

The above is not to be seen simply as a quaint anecdote. The Prophet's attitude to animals manifested the scope of his compassionate concern for all God's creatures, and was nothing short of revolutionary for his times. The Arabs were accustomed to torturing their animals; such practices, together with organised fights between animals, were abolished, as was the customary overloading of beasts of burden. The Prophet is reported to have said in this connection: 'If you behold three mounting an animal, stone them until one of them descends.'[60] Similarly, he forbade hunting for sport, going so far as to warn that a sparrow that was hunted for sport and not eaten will complain about its killer on the Day of Judgement. He is reported as also saying: 'No one will kill a sparrow or anything larger, without just cause, without God asking him about it on the Day of Judgement.' When asked what was a just cause, he replied: 'That you slaughter it and eat it.'[61]

This is not to say that the strength of the Prophet's character, his resolve, determination, courage, and other rigorous virtues are to be ignored. Rather, it is to see that, by nature, the Prophet was of a gentle and generous disposition, and would manifest the complementary virtues of courage and strength only when circumstances objectively required it. As we shall see in more detail below, all of the Prophet's battles were of a defensive nature. Among Western scholars, Karen Armstrong offers an objective evaluation of Muslim conduct in this regard, putting into proper context the Prophet's reasons for resorting to warfare: 'In the West we often imagine Muḥammad as a warlord, brandishing his sword in order to impose Islam on a reluctant world by force of arms. The reality was quite different. Muḥammad and the first Muslims were fighting for their lives.'[62] In this context, the following verse is of particular pertinence: 'Warfare is enjoined upon you, though it is hateful to you' (2:216). For the Prophet and those true to his example, warfare is neither glorified, nor is it deemed an end in itself, nor is it a means of spreading Islam: one fights because, and insofar as, one is fought against.

The quality of *ḥilm* entails avoiding conflict, and seeking instead peace, reconciliation and justice. It calls for wisdom, an objective view of what is required in each situation, an ability to be detached from self-interest, as well from one's own anger, sentiment or desire. It is the quality which therefore enables one to resist the pressures of tribalism, nationalism, or any other prejudice which might distort one's perception of justice and propriety. Possibly the most graphic illustration of the Prophet's resistance to such 'populist' pressures and prejudices is provided by his magnanimity and mercy towards the Quraysh at the peaceful conquest of Mecca in 630. Instead of taking revenge upon his erstwhile persecutors, his attitude was summed up in his citing of the words of Joseph to his brothers, as given in the Qur'ān: 'There is no reproach against you this day; may God forgive you. He is the most merciful of the merciful' (12:92). According to Stanley Lane-Poole, the Prophet's conduct at this triumphant climax to his prophetic mission manifested an unsurpassable degree of maganimity:

> He freely forgave the Quraish all the years of sorrow and cruel scorn in which they had afflicted him, and gave an amnesty to the whole population of Mekka. Four criminals whom justice condemned made up Muhammad's proscription list when he entered as a conqueror to the city of his bitterest enemies. The army followed his example, and entered quietly and peaceably; no house was robbed, no woman insulted . . . Through all the annals of conquest there is no triumphant entry comparable to this one.[63]

A correct understanding of *ḥilm* takes us to the very heart of Islamic virtue, and one cannot fully appreciate the roots of tolerance in Islam without understanding the meaning, the influence, and the radiance of this key prophetic virtue. Toshihiko Izutsu claims, in his pioneering work on key Qur'ānic terms, that it is not just the Prophet's character, but also the Qur'ān 'as a whole', which 'is dominated by the very spirit of *ḥilm*.'[64] In making this claim, he is echoing a basic postulate of Islamic faith, namely, belief in the fundamental affinity between the Message and the Messenger. When asked about the character of the Prophet, his wife 'Ā'isha replied: 'His character was the Qur'ān (*kāna khuluquhu al-Qur'ān*)'.[65] Both the Qur'ān and the soul of the Prophet were alike suffused with the quality of *ḥilm*.

It is impossible to render the word *ḥilm* accurately into English by just a single word. It comprises the following meanings: forbearance, wisdom, patience, composure, self-mastery, imperturbability, together with the qualities of kindness, mildness and gentleness. The divine Name, *al-Ḥalīm*, is often, though inadequately, translated into English as 'the Gentle' or 'the Mild'. In order to make the word 'gentle' less inappropriate a translation for *ḥalīm*, one would need to revert to the original meaning of the word, bearing in mind its relationship to nobility of soul, which is evoked still today by the term 'gentleman'. To be a gentleman is to be courteous and kind, certainly, but it also implied originally the sense of nobility or aristocracy, which itself must be understood not in any restrictively social sense but in the original, Greek meaning, 'rule of the best': aristocrats, according to Plato, are those in whom the best part of the soul governs the other elements—that is, their intellectual element governs the passional and the irascible elements of the soul.[66] So if the word 'gentle' be used in the sense of nobility and aristocracy—thus, with the meaning of perfect self-mastery, together with the sense of love—thus with the meaning of tenderness, compassion and kindness—then it comes close to connoting the range of meanings implied by the single word *ḥilm*. The relationship between *ḥilm* and tolerance is clear; for there can be no tolerance in the integral sense—that is, tolerance based on sincere respect—if *ḥilm* and its associated qualities be absent. Tolerance can be seen as a natural concomitant of the attitudes of forbearance and patience towards the Other, attitudes that in turn presuppose at least a degree of self-dominion, together with the graciousness and serenity which flow from true wisdom. All of these attitudes are implied and evoked by the quality of *ḥilm*.

The vice which is most completely opposed to *ḥilm* is, surprisingly perhaps, *jahl*, a term all too often simply translated as 'ignorance', but which is much more than a simple absence of knowledge. It is true that both *'ilm* and *ḥilm* are antonyms of *jahl*, but what this shows us is that *'ilm* is at root inseparable from the forbearance, patience, kindness and self-dominion proper to *ḥilm*, on the one hand; and that, on the other, *jahl* is, at root, inseparable from egocentricity, impetuosity, fanaticism, rashness and capriciousness—in short, the range of vices unleashed by the absence of self-control; all of these vices stand in direct opposition to the qualities inherent in *ḥilm*.[67] One observes a symbiosis between *ḥilm and 'ilm*, so that one might define *ḥilm* as that forbearance which stems from knowledge, and *'ilm* as that knowledge which generates forbearance. As Imam 'Alī put it: '*Ḥilm* is the completion of the intellect'.[68] The so-called 'age of ignorance', *al-jāhiliyya*, which preceded Islam was an age in which no norm of behaviour or conduct transcended the rules of the tribe: one supported with zeal one's tribesmen, whether they were right or wrong. Or rather, the very notion of 'right' was identified exclusively with one's tribe. Such tribalism clearly stands at the antipodes of universal justice and objective reality; in this communalistic extension of the ego, there was little place for any compassionate tolerance of the Other, or any authentic code of ethics. Whence Islam's uncompromising rejection of the tribalist mentality, and its championing of the virtue of *ḥilm*.

The opposition between the qualities of the *ḥalīm* and the *jāhil* is well brought out in the following couplet, cited by Izutsu:

> Many the large black cooking pots which our maidservants take good care of, once their belly becomes *jāhil* [i.e., 'boil up'] it will never become *ḥalīm* [i.e., 'calm down'].[69]

As Izutsu rightly stresses, *ḥilm* is far from being a passive quality of simple patience or forbearance in the face of provocation, although it definitely comprises these virtues; *ḥilm* must also be understood as 'a positive and active power of the soul that is strong enough to curb her [i.e., the soul's] own impetuosity . . . calm it down to patience and forbearance. It is a sign of the power and superiority of the mind'. He quotes another poet, Sālim b. Wābiṣa, to illustrate this:

> Verily, to take the attitude of humility consciously is a kind of *ḥilm*,
> And in fact *ḥilm* based on power is a virtue characteristic of the nobleness of the soul (*faḍl min al-karam*).[70]

Izutsu also makes the important point that, as a divine attribute, *ḥilm* is that particular kind of mildness and gentleness which emerges as the surface expression of underlying power: 'God forgives sins committed by men and is gentle, but it is not a simple gentleness; it is a gentleness based on power, a forbearance based on calm wisdom, which is possible only because it is coupled with infinite power.'[71] So if *al-Ḥalīm*, on the divine level, describes one whose gentle forbearance is based on infinite power, *al-ḥalīm*, on the human level, describes one whose forbearance is based, not on infinite power, but on total self-mastery; such self-mastery being the primary reflection, on the human plane, of the infinite power of God, for there is no power greater than that required to completely dominate one's own soul. Success in the quest for self-mastery is victory in what the Prophet famously described as the 'greatest of all struggles', *al-jihād al-akbar*. The following sayings of Imam ʿAlī help us to see the way in which neither *ʿilm* nor *ḥilm* can be separated from the quest for self-mastery in this most challenging of all struggles:

- Struggling against the soul through knowledge—such is the mark of the intellect.
- The strongest people are those who are strongest against their own souls.
- The ultimate battle is that of a man against his own soul.
- He who knows his soul fights it.[72]

In another important saying, Imam ʿAlī refers to the forces which are engaged in this battle for the soul: the intellect commands the forces of *al-Raḥmān* (the Compassionate), while caprice (*hawā*) commands those of *al-Shayṭān* (the devil). The soul itself vacillates between these two poles, susceptible to the attraction of both (*mutajādhiba baynahumā*) and enters into 'the domain of whichever of the two will triumph.'[73] The attainment of self-mastery, then, cannot be realized without that grace constituted by the *raḥma* or loving compassion of God.[74]

Ḥilm is therefore closely related to compassion and peace as well as the power necessary for self-dominion. *Jahl*, on the contrary, is associated with ruthlessness and agitation, along with the moral weakness of vainglory and self-aggrandisement. The contrast between the two qualities is brought out in the following verse of the Qurʾān, revealed on the occasion of the conclusion of the Treaty of Ḥudaybiyya (628):

> When the disbelievers had set up in their hearts zealotry (*ḥamiyya*), the zealotry of *jāhiliyya*; then God sent down His spirit of peace (*sakīna*) upon His Messenger and upon the believers, and caused them to abide by the word of God-consciousness; and they were most worthy and deserving of it . . . (48:26).

Traditional exegesis explains the 'zealotry' mentioned in this verse with reference to the stubborn insistence of the Quraysh, when they drew up terms of a ten-year truce that were, on the surface, unfavourable to the Muslims. Among other things, it was agreed that any Muslim wishing to leave Mecca and join the Prophet against the will of his or her guardian would be sent back to Mecca by the Prophet; whilst any Muslim wishing to leave the Prophet and rejoin the Meccans would be allowed to do so unconditionally. The Prophet accepted this and other stringent conditions, however, realising that the political environment formalised by the ten-year truce would be congenial to the peaceful spread of the message of Islam. He was proved right. As Ibn Isḥāq says, in his classical biography of the Prophet, commenting on the fact that the chapter entitled 'The Victory' (*al-Fatḥ*), number 48, was revealed on this occasion:

> No previous victory in Islam was greater than this. [Prior to Ḥudaybiyya] There was nothing but battle when men met; but when there was an armistice and war was abolished, and men met in safety and consulted together, none talked about Islam intelligently without entering it. In those two years [subsequent to the signing of the treaty] double as many, or more than double as many, entered Islam as ever before.[75]

Martin Lings describes well the way in which Islam spread in the period following the truce. In addition to political and economic motivations, he draws attention to the magnetism exerted by the serenity of the believers, a serenity born of the 'spirit of peace', *sakīna*, referred to in 48:26 and also earlier in the same chapter, at 48:4 ('He it is who has sent down the spirit of peace into the hearts of the believers'):

> In many cases the political and religious motives [for embracing Islam] were inextricably connected; but there was also a factor, slow-working yet powerful and profound, which had nothing whatsoever to do with politics, and which was also largely independent of the deliberate efforts made by the believers to spread the message of Islam. This was the remarkable serenity which characterised those who practised the new religion. The Koran, the Book of God's Oneness, was also the Book of Mercy and the Book of Paradise.

> The recitation of its verses, combined with the teaching of the Messenger, imbued the believers with the certainty that they had within easy reach, that is through the fulfilment of certain conditions well within their capacity, the eternal satisfaction of every possible desire. The resulting happiness was a criterion of faith. The Prophet insisted: 'All is well with the faithful, whatever the circumstances.'[76]

When, two years after Ḥudaybiyya, the Quraysh broke the terms of the treaty, Islam had spread, peacefully, to such an extent that the army summoned by the Prophet to confront the Quraysh was irresistible, hence the submission of the Quraysh to the Prophet in 630, mentioned above. The Prophet's magnanimity and compassion at the conquest of Mecca must be seen as flowing from the same quality, *ḥilm*, which was manifested at Ḥudaybiyya, and which is indeed referred to as the 'victory' (*fatḥ*) after which Chapter 48 is named: 'Indeed, We have given you (O Prophet) a signal victory' (48:1). The conquest of Mecca was but a political consequence of this spiritual 'victory' of *ḥilm* over *jahl*, of imperturbable serenity (*sakīna*) over arrogant agitation (*ḥamiyya*), that was effected at Ḥudaybiyya and referred to in 48:26.[77] We should also note in this verse the importance of the relationship between the 'spirit of peace' and the 'word of God-consciousness (*kalimat al-taqwā*)': 'then God sent down His spirit of peace (*sakīna*) upon His Messenger and upon the believers, and caused them to abide by the word of God-consciousness'. The imperturbable serenity that allows one to retain one's composure in the face of unreasonable zealotry can only come about through the grace of God; and this grace is expressed, in part, by the ability to 'abide by the word of God-consciousness', that is to abide within a state dominated by the remembrance of God, this remembrance being the best safeguard against obsession with oneself, one's presumed rights and one's egocentric idolatry.

Imam 'Alī expresses this principle in the following piece of advice to Mālik al-Ashtar, which not only helps to disclose the way to ensure that *ḥilm* prevails over *jahl*; it also reveals that the true power of *ḥilm* is derived from the graces bestowed through—and as—the remembrance of God, *dhikru'Llāh*, or God-consciousness, *taqwā*:

> Dominate the zeal of your pride, the vehemence of your castigation, the power of your hand, and the sharpness of your tongue. Guard against these vices by restraining all impulsiveness, and putting off all resort to force until your anger subsides, and you regain self-control. But you cannot attain such self-domination without increasing your pre-occupation with remembrance of your return to your Lord.[78]

The difference between the self-control that inheres in *ḥilm* and the self-indulgence which is entailed by *jahl* is implicitly expressed by the words uttered by Joseph when he was being subjected to the seductive wiles of Zulaykhā and her guests: 'O my Lord! Prison is dearer to me than that which they are urging me to do; and if You do fend not off their wiles from me I might incline unto them and become of the ignorant (*min al-jāhilīn*)' (12:33). Joseph's capacity to resist temptation is, likewise, predicated on what Imam 'Alī refers to as 'pre-occupation with remembrance' of God, for, on the one hand, we are told earlier in the narrative: 'She desired him and he would have desired her, had he not seen the evidence of his Lord' (12:24); and on the other, when he is exonerated in the presence of Pharoah, Joseph says: 'I do not exculpate myself: the soul ever incites to evil, except for one upon whom my Lord has mercy' (12:53).

Finally, on the theme of *ḥilm*, it should be noted that the Prophet manifested this quality to perfection at the peaceful conquest of Mecca. His *ḥilm* at this crowning moment of his earthly mission converted his erstwhile persecutors into staunch allies. His magnanimity and its consequences bore eloquent testimony to the principle expressed in the following verse:

> The good deed and the evil deed are not equal. Repel [evil] with that which is most fine, and behold: your enemy will become as a dear friend. But none is granted [such a capacity to respond to evil] except those who are patient; and none is granted it except those who have been blessed with immense good fortune (41:34–35).

Mention was made above of the quality of *raḥma* as being a definitive feature of the prophetic paradigm. It is important to stress the relationship between *raḥma* and the benevolent disposition of soul presupposed by tolerance. The crucial role played by the divine quality of *raḥma* in regard to both the ethical and intellectual dimensions of the human soul is asserted by many verses of the Qur'ān. For example, we are told that it is specifically *al-Raḥmān* who is responsible for both the creation and the illumination of the human spirit: '*Al-Raḥmān*—has taught the Qur'ān, created man, taught him articulation' (55:1–4). It is thus not surprising that *al-Raḥmān* should furnish the ultimate model of man's ethical comportment: through compassion, mercy and love, the intellect acquires the strength to overcome all one's whims, passions, and vain desires, and thereby to succeed in the quest for self-mastery—as noted in the sayings of Imam 'Alī above. And it is through this self-mastery, combined with wisdom, patience and forbearance, that one becomes imbued with a fundamentally benign disposition of soul. Tolerance of the Other is a key manifestation of this ideal state of soul; and, at a lower level, it will emerge as a concomitant of the struggle to attain this ideal state, a struggle incumbent on all those who claim to be 'following' the Prophet.

The Prophet, perfect embodiment of the benevolent predisposition proper to *ḥilm*, is not just *'abd Allāh*, 'slave of God', he is also, and pre-eminently, one of the 'slaves of the All-Compassionate (*'ibād al-Raḥmān*)', described in the Qur'ān as follows: 'The slaves of the All-Compassionate are those who walk gently upon the earth, and when addressed by the arrogantly ignorant, reply: Peace!' (25:63). As we saw above, Imam Shamīl stressed that what the Emir 'Abd al-Qādir did in his heroic defence of the Christians in Damascus in 1860 was to remind all people of this fundamental aspect of the prophetic mission: 'In reality, you have put into practice the words of the great apostle of God Most High, bearing witness to compassion for His humble creatures, and you have set up a barrier against those who would reject his great example.' It is important to note that compassion is here related to *all* of God's creatures; for the Prophet is described in the Qur'ān not just as a Messenger to the Arabs, but as a *raḥma* to the totality of creation: 'And we did not send you forth except as a *raḥma* to all the worlds' (21:107).

Raḥma is the quality that most faithfully evokes the ultimate nature of God: 'Call upon *Allāh* or call upon *al-Raḥmān*—whichever you call upon, His are the most beautiful Names' (17:110); 'He [God] has inscribed upon Himself *raḥma*' (6:12, almost verbatim at 6:54); 'My *raḥma* encompasses all things' (7:156). This *raḥma*, pulsating from the very heart of divinity, radiates through the soul of the Prophet to all beings. This universal radiance of love and compassion does not simply describe, objectively, the cosmic scope of the Messenger's concern; it also enters into the soul of each and every Muslim bent on following the Messenger's noble example, doing so as the goal towards which one aspires. Even if such universal compassion be realised to perfection exclusively by the Messenger, it nonetheless exerts a real spiritual influence upon the souls of those making the attempt to conform to the prophetic paradigm of perfection. In other words, the intention to be a source of compassion, mercy and love to all beings must be the defining feature of the souls of all those who 'follow' the Prophet. To truly 'follow' the Prophet is to realise and to radiate—at least to some degree—that quality of loving mercy which sustains and nurtures *ḥilm* and the qualities associated with it, such as the spirit of tolerance.

* * *

At this point one might object: is this analysis not hopelessly naïve and excessively idealistic? Have Muslims throughout the centuries really been so spiritually sensitive to these sublime prophetic ideals? Tolerance there may have been in Islamic history, but surely this is more the expression of *realpolitik* on the part of the holders of power than an expression of the spirit of tolerance comprised within the *raḥma* and the *ḥilm* of the Prophet?

One can reply to this objection on two levels, one principial, the other pragmatic. As regards the latter, the practice of tolerance on the level of statecraft cannot be divorced from either the precedents established on this plane by the Prophet himself, nor from the radiance of the Prophet's virtues, one of which is, precisely, benevolent—hence tolerant—governance. As head of state, the Prophet turned to political account all of his extraordinary virtues; the realm of politics was, as much as any other aspect of his life, to be fashioned by Islamic principles. As Martin Lings notes, the Prophet was a role model in many ways, being 'shepherd, merchant, hermit, exile, soldier, lawgiver and prophet-priest-king'. Just as the scope of the guidance given by the Qur'ān is all-encompassing, 'so it was the destiny of Muḥammad to penetrate with exceptional versatility into the domain of human experience, both public and private'.[79]

Students of political science need only make a cursory examination of the life and deeds of the Prophet to be inspired by his application of the most noble principles to the various exigencies of political life. Founder of the Arab League, and its first Secretary-General (1945–1952), ʿAbd al-Raḥmān ʿAzzām Pasha, is a case in point. In his biography of the Prophet he shows how the highest ideals of the faith were brought to bear upon the political, diplomatic and military spheres of life, and how these ideals can serve to inspire those who have political responsibilities in the contemporary world. One perhaps unexpected outcome of his reflections on the Prophet's conduct in the political domain concerns mercy, which, he says, is not only 'one of the basic principles of Muḥammad's message'; it also constitutes 'the cornerstone of the organized state ... A religion or state shorn of mercy turns to deceit and oppression.'[80]

Likewise, as regards the principle of tolerance, ʿAzzam's definition of the obligations and the respect owed by the Muslim to non-Muslims in their state is not simply based on legal precepts, but on a vision clearly inspired by the spiritual ethos of the prophetic paradigm. As regards the principle of *dhimma*, he draws attention to the fact that it does not imply 'second-class citizenship'; rather, 'originally, it signified superior merit, for the title came from the *dhimmat Allāh* (God's custody). It constituted the greatest possible affirmation of the protected one's right to enjoy complete religious, administrative and political freedom.' The *dhimmī* is defined as 'the neighbour of the Muslim, who befriends and associates with him ... Unlike the treaty commitments of many secular states, the *dhimmī* commitment in Muslim law is based on the principle of human brotherhood and the sanctity of the faith.'[81]

One clearly needs to probe the source of this perception of the link between the legal precept of tolerance and such ideals as 'human brotherhood' and the 'sanctity of faith'. These ideals are by no means logically presupposed by legal tolerance; whereas, conversely, legal tolerance is an inevitable outcome of the noble ideals inherent in the spiritual ethos of Islam. As we argued in the previous chapter, traditionally tolerance assumed the institutional form of the *dhimma* in Islamic contexts, but the spirit of tolerance is by no means exhausted by this particular institutional form: in the contemporary, post-imperial context, what matters is to follow the trajectory established by the deepest currents of this spirit and pay attention to the principial—hence trans-historical—ideals, rather than be bound by the institutional structures that were intended to implement these ideals in the medieval political environment.

As regards the medieval context, though, it should be noted that what propelled Muslim rulers and jurists alike into the religious tolerance observed in Islamic history, and noted in the previous chapter, was more than just political prudence or religious scruple.[82] Rather, such factors should themselves be seen as arising out of a deeper set of ethical and spiritual currents which are generated ever anew by the enduring power of the prophetic example. To appreciate the impact of this example on Muslim society one must take cognisance of the fundamental role played by veneration of the Prophet in all forms of Muslim piety. The very notion of piety (*taqwā*) cannot be understood without a profound appreciation of how the inaccessible transcendence (*tanzīh*) of God is compensated in Muslim piety by the concrete and eminently accessible example of human perfection constituted by the Prophet, who is 'closer to the believers than their own selves' (33:6). To venerate the Prophet is to emulate his 'noble example'—whence the inestimable importance of the popular recounting of stories from the *sīra* (biographies of the Prophet) literature and the immense wealth of the poetry in all Muslim languages, extolling the qualities of the Prophet.[83] Love of the Prophet is regarded as an indispensable aspect of faith in God: 'None of you will have [complete] faith until I am dearer to him than his own soul', the Prophet said.[84]

It is no coincidence that devotional practices connected to the Prophet, together with popular pilgrimages to shrines of local saints where one of the key celebrations is the *mawlid* (popular celebration of the birthday of the Prophet),[85] are among the chief targets of extremist Muslim iconoclasts in our times: negation of remembrance of the *ḥilm* and the *raḥma* characterizing the prophetic personality is essential for those who wish to portray Islam as a militant ideology.[86] Be that as it may, what Shabbir Akhtar refers to quite appropriately as 'the posthumous authority of Muḥammad' cannot so easily be dislodged from the hearts and minds of Muslims. We do not believe that Akhtar exaggerates in what he claims about this authority:

> The influence of the Arabian Prophet on the lives of millions, through the patterns of his biography daily imitated, is without parallel in the whole of history, religious or secular. The imitation of Muḥammad is, unlike the imitation of Christ, an accepted obligation, a routine occurrence. It is the ideal not only for the saints, but for all Muslims: from the beggars in the slums of India to the spectacularly wealthy sheikhs of Saudi Arabia, from the illiterate peasants of Pakistan to the erudite scholars of al-Azhar, from the village women of the Third World to the sophisticates of Western female society ... Muḥammad is dead. But he is dead only in the least significant sense ... The fact is that the Prophet of Islam is resurrected daily in what must be the greatest triumph over the limitations of physical extinction.[87]

Frithjof Schuon takes us a step further, explaining the depth of the spiritual power generated by emulation of the Prophet:

> Love of the Prophet constitutes a fundamental element in Islamic spirituality ... It arises because Muslims see in the Prophet the prototype and model of the virtues which constitute the theomorphism of man and the beauty and equilibrium of the Universe, and which are so many keys or paths toward liberating Unity—this is why they love him and imitate him even in the very smallest details of daily life. The Prophet, like Islam as a whole, is as it were a heavenly mold ready to receive the influx of the intelligence and will of the believer and one wherein even effort becomes a kind of supernatural repose.[88]

* * *

If *raḥma* generates tolerance, knowledge of God can be seen as a key for entering into and being penetrated by *raḥma*. For a concrete consciousness of the true nature of Reality effectively generates *raḥma* in the soul, inasmuch as Reality is, essentially, *raḥma*. As noted above, God is said to have 'inscribed' *raḥma* upon Himself. As opposed to those attributes which, in theological parlance, are called 'attributes of essence' (*ṣifāt al-dhāt*), such as life, knowledge, power, will, speech, sight and hearing, the divine attribute of *raḥma* is the most fully revealing of the quality of the divine nature as such, as is attested by this statement, said to be written on the divine Throne: 'My *raḥma* overcomes My anger.'[89] Imam 'Alī makes clear the relationship between knowledge and *raḥma* in the following important saying. Here he is describing the true *faqīh*, 'the one who understands', not just 'the jurist', the primary meaning of *fiqh* being 'understanding' or 'comprehension', and only later coming to acquire the specific idea of legal comprehension: 'The true *faqīh* is he who does not make people ever despair of the loving mercy of God.'[90]

Another clear demonstration of the relationship between knowledge and tolerance is given to us in one of the most oft-cited verses in relation to religious tolerance in Islam: 'There is no compulsion in religion' (2:256).[91] The relationship between knowledge and this prohibition of compulsion in all matter religious, however, will be overlooked if the next part of the verse is not also cited: 'Indeed, the right way has become distinct from error.' The word *tabayyana*, to become distinct, clear, evident, relates this imperative of tolerance directly to *knowledge*, to the correct exercise of human capacity to distinguish the true from the false, that capacity which has been given to man alone by *al-Raḥmān*, as we noted above: '*Al-Raḥmān*—has taught the Qur'ān, created man, taught him articulation (*'allamahu'l-bayān*)' (55:1–4). The word *bayān*, related to the verb *tabayyana*, can be translated simply as speech, but means more than simply speaking; it refers implicitly to the entire apparatus of rational thought of which speech is but the outward expression. Speech is thus the articulation of thought, that which renders clear, that which distinguishes man from all other creatures, namely, intelligence. In turn, intelligence consists essentially in the capacity to distinguish the true from the false, to separate rectitude from error, and this is what the word 'discernment' means: the Latin root *discerner* means 'to separate'.[92]

The point we wish to stress here is that the prohibition on compulsion in religion, together with its implicit corollary, the necessity of tolerance in all matters pertaining to religious faith and individual conscience, is not so much a simple injunction arbitrarily plucked out of the air by the inscrutable will of God, and which man must simply implement in unquestioning obedience to that will. Rather, it is an injunction that presupposes a degree of discernment, and in turn contributes to the full realization of that initial discernment. In the light of the knowledge revealed by the Qur'ān and assimilated by the intelligence, the ethical 'illogicality' of intolerance will appear as repulsive as the logic of tolerance is attractive. Correct discernment, in other words, leads to knowledge, and knowledge produces tolerance, which in turn opens one up to further knowledge, this time knowledge of the Other as Other: such mutual knowledge, *ta'āruf*, being precisely the divine *raison d'être* of diversity, as we noted above: 'O mankind, We have created you male and female, and We have made you into tribes and nations in order that you might come to know one another. Truly, in the sight of God, the most honoured amongst you is the most pious amongst you' (49:13).

In his famous 'farewell sermon', at the performance of his last Ḥajj (632), the Prophet is said to have cited this verse and said: 'You are all brothers, and you are all equal. None of you can claim any privilege or any superiority over any other. An Arab is not to be preferred to a non-Arab, nor is a non-Arab to be preferred to an Arab.'[93]

This explicit rejection of racial prejudice expresses, among other things, the divine wisdom underlying the diversity of human types, races, cultures, languages, and so on. This wisdom is expressed in terms of mutual knowledge: 'that you might come to know one another' (*li-ta'ārafū*)—the benefits that accrue from the deepening of mutual knowledge are here given as the divine purpose underlying the creation of diverse human communities. As seen above, understanding this divine cause of human diversity generates a tolerant attitude towards the Other. And the resulting tolerance, combined with intellectual inquiry, itself generates not just enhanced knowledge of the Other and a deeper respect for the Other: mutual knowledge also results in a deepening of knowledge *per se*, which is inseparable from knowledge of oneself, and thus of God: for 'he who knows himself knows his Lord' according to the famous prophetic maxim. In this way, knowledge of the Other, as Other, enhances one's receptivity to the knowledge and the remembrance of God.

Let us focus on the words in the final part of this important verse, 'the most honoured amongst you is the most pious of you', and note that the Prophet's reply to the question, 'Which religion is most loved by God?' can be read as a comment on this verse. Instead of referring to such and such a religion, he highlights the key *characteristic* which should be infused into the soul by all religions, or by religion as such—

whichever religion is most successful in producing this trait becomes 'the most beloved' religion to God: 'The primordial, generously tolerant faith (*al-ḥanīfiyya al-samḥa*)'.

In this strongly authenticated saying, the Prophet highlights the centrality of tolerance to the *raison d'être* of religion as such, and not just the religion of Islam. It also implies, as does verse 49:13, the absolute equality of all believers, the sole permissible hierarchy within humanity being that based on intrinsic piety, not on such extrinsic factors as gender, tribe, nation, race or religion. Given this view of equality on the human plane, coupled with the Islamic doctrine of universal and cyclical revelation—according to which no community is deprived of authentic divine revelation and guidance—intolerance of the Other is reprehensible on both the moral and spiritual planes, and is not just prohibited on the legal plane. Intolerance feeds on ignorance, while tolerance thrives on knowledge; and religion itself is only true to its God-given purpose when it generates the spirit of generous tolerance in the souls of its adherents.

When one knows through revelation that religious diversity is divinely willed, such knowledge inspires tolerance as a spiritual, and not just an ethical imperative. Followers of other faiths are granted respectful tolerance, and the source of their faith is granted reverence, in the measure that one knows or simply believes that God alone is the source of the revelations inaugurating the religious traditions of the non-Muslim Other. One cannot but grant respectful tolerance to fellow-believers when one knows or believes that what these non-Muslim fellow-believers worship is nothing other than the one and only absolute Reality.[94] With regard to those of lesser degrees of spiritual sensitivity, such knowledge, even on the merely factual level, will at least instil a sense of legal and moral obligation towards the rights of those of other faiths—formal tolerance will thus be granted on the outward plane because the sacred Law, expressing the will of God, demands it, and it is this attitude which, on the plane of practical politics and statecraft, ensured that tolerance would not simply be demonstrated by spiritual elites sensitive to the wisdom and holiness in the religions of the Other. It led to the practice of political and religious tolerance even by those who may have only partially assimilated the sacred knowledge on the basis of which the Other is both respectfully tolerated and spiritually appreciated.

A graphic expression of what this sacred knowledge entails in practice is given to us in the well-attested episode in the life of the Prophet reference to which has been made in the preceding pages. In the ninth year after the Hijra (631), a prominent Christian delegation from Najrān, an important centre of Christianity in the Yemen, came to Medina to negotiate a treaty and engage the Prophet in theological debate. The main point of contention was the nature of Christ: was he one of the messengers of God or the unique Son of God? What is of importance for our purposes is not the disagreements voiced, but the worship conducted by the Christians in the midst of these disagreements. When the Christians expressed their desire to pray—presumably to perform some form of congregational liturgy—the Prophet invited them to accomplish their rites in his own mosque. According to Ibn Isḥāq, who gives the standard account of this remarkable event, the Christians in question were 'Malikī', that is, they were affiliated to the 'Emperor', in other words, to the Byzantine church.[95] This means that they were enacting some form of the rites which incorporated the fully-developed trinitarian theology of the Orthodox councils, emphasising the definitive creed of the divine sonship of Christ—a doctrine explicitly criticised in the Qur'ān. Nonetheless, the Prophet allowed the Christians to perform their rites in his own mosque. Disagreement on the plane of dogma is one thing, tolerance of the enactment of that dogma is another.

Now it might be argued that the Prophet's allowance of the Christians to pray in his mosque was not so much an act of religious tolerance; rather, it was an act of political courtesy, a diplomatic gesture to the delegation of Najrānīs who were being encouraged to make obeisance to the then rapidly expanding Islamic state. This argument, however, only serves to heighten our appreciation of the extent to which the spirit of tolerance determines political praxis as well as religious principle in Islam. For it shows how religious tolerance—in the very teeth of dogmatic disagreement—dovetails with political wisdom according to the prophetic paradigm. It should be stressed that the Prophet did not propose any kind of compromise over the dogmas of the Incarnation or the Trinity. The debates he held with the Christians of Najrān yielded no fruit as regards the fundamental point in dispute—whether Jesus was the incarnate Son of God, or simply a fully human Messenger of God.

The point which must be stressed here is that, despite fundamentally disagreeing with some of the definitive dogmas of Christianity, the Prophet allowed the Christians to perform their prayers in his most sacred spot, the inviolable space of his mosque, thereby indicating at least two principles to his followers: however much we may disagree with the theological tenets of Christians—or any other member of the broadly definable category, 'People of the Book'—we are duty-bound to uphold their right to worship according to those tenets; we have no right to interfere with that worship, to undermine it, or to subject it to restrictive conditions. Secondly, we are being instructed that tolerance of the religious Other is an inherent principle of political propriety in Islam, and any deviation from that principle is a violation on both the religious and the political planes.

This act of the Prophet should not be seen in isolation but rather as one in a series of such symbolic acts which, more powerfully than words, uphold the inviolability of the religious rights of the Other and the necessity of exercising generosity and not just tolerance in regard to the Other—of exercising *samḥa*, precisely. Another such act was the protection by the Prophet of the icon of the Virgin and Child in the Ka'ba. He instructed all idols within the holy house to be destroyed, but, according to at least two early historians, Wāqidī and Azraqī, he himself protected this icon, not allowing it to be destroyed.[96] Also of relevance here is the charter, said to be sealed by the Prophet himself, granting protection to the monastery of St Catherine in Sinai. The charter states that wherever monks or hermits are to be found '. . . on any mountain, hill, village, or other habitable place, on the sea or in the deserts or in any convent, church or house of prayer, I shall be watching over them as their protector, with all my soul, together with all my *umma*; because they [the monks and hermits] are a part of my own people, and part of those protected by me.' Also, most significantly, the charter makes it incumbent on the Muslims not only to protect the monks, but also, in regard to Christians generally, to 'consolidate (*tamkīn*) their worship in their churches'.[97] The well-attested invitation by the Prophet to the Najrānī Christians to pray in his mosque is disputed by none in the tradition, and this lends considerable plausibility to the Prophet's charter to the monks and to his protection of the icon all of which can be viewed as eloquent expressions of the spirit of tolerance in Islam.

Epilogue

At the beginning of this essay we referred to the unhealthy symbiosis between intolerant Muslims and prejudiced Islamophobes. We hope that both the principles presented here and the historical examples illustrating them will help to debunk the pernicious stereotype generated by this unhealthy symbiosis. The anti-Muslim prejudice animating much of Western mass media feeds upon the all too frequent manifestations of Muslim fanaticism and intolerance, while, alas, ignoring the traditional Islamic norm of tolerance and moderation from which these outbursts of intolerance are evident deviations. One should also take note that, despite these deviations, the norm or the spirit of tolerance still characterises the 'silent majority'—indeed the overwhelming majority—of Muslims worldwide. We would like to draw attention here to one immensely positive movement which is representative of this silent majority, and which revives and builds upon some of the finest aspects of the rich tradition of Islamic tolerance we have sketched out here.

This movement is twofold: one dimension concerns tolerance within Islam, and the second pertains to tolerance in the context of dialogue and reconciliation in the interfaith domain. As regards the first, in July 2005, King Abdullah II of Jordan convened an international Islamic conference of 200 of the world's leading Islamic scholars from 50 countries in Amman. The scholars unanimously issued a ruling on three fundamental principles:

(1) They specifically recognised the validity of eight schools of law within Islam: the four principal schools of Sunni jurisprudence (Shāfiʿī, Ḥanafī, Mālikī and Ḥanbalī); the two principal Shiʿi schools (the Jaʿfarī *madhhab*, with which the Ismaili school was affiliated, and the Zaydī *madhhab*); the ʿIbādhī school; and the Ẓāhirī school.

(2) Based upon this all-embracing definition of who is a Muslim,

> they forbade the practice of *takfir*, that is, declaring infidel anyone who is included in the above mentioned schools of law.
> (3) The scholars then affirmed that only those fatwas issued by experts trained in the above schools of law are to be recognised as valid.

In one stroke, therefore, this declaration affirmed the paramount imperative of mutual tolerance within a broadly redefined Muslim *umma*, at the same time as robustly rejecting the validity of so-called fatwas issued by illegitimate, self-styled leaders motivated by political aims. Thus, such 'fatwas' which declare certain Muslims to be *kāfirs*, and legitimise the use of violence against civilians both Muslims and non-Muslims alike, were stripped of their veneer of religious authority. An article in *The Economist* summed up well the significance of this event. First, as regards the rejection of intolerant and violent versions of Islam:

> In several ways, the muftis and professors agreed to minimise their own (previously sharp) differences and work together to promote what they regard as 'good theology' over some superficial, violence-promoting interpretations of Islam that have circulated, electronically and in print, all over the world. Among the scholars' main conclusions is that nobody who accepts Islam's basic beliefs should be denied the label of Muslim. A statement of the obvious? Far from it, because a hallmark of virtually all the shrillest voices in Islam is that they reject the Muslim credentials of anybody who disagrees with them.

Second, as regards the historic significance of the broadening of the definition of Islamic 'orthodoxy', and the mutual tolerance it presupposes: 'At least in theory, this implies a degree of mutual respect between rival versions of Islam that has not been seen since the Fatimid empire a millennium ago.'[1]

Turning now to the second initiative within this courageous attempt to revive and build upon the tolerant traditions of Islam: 'A Common Word between us and you'[2] is the title of the interfaith initiative, launched by the Royal Aal al-Bayt Institute in Amman, Jordan, on October 13 2007, when an open letter was sent by 138 Muslim scholars, representing every major school of thought, to the leaders of all Christian churches. The letter invited these leaders to enter into friendly dialogue with Muslims on the basis of 'the two great commandments' enunciated by Jesus, love of God and love of neighbour.[3] This invitation met with an immediate and overwhelmingly positive response, such that 'A Common Word' rapidly became referred to as the most successful interfaith initiative between Christians and Muslims to date. Nearly all the leaders of the major Christian denominations responded favourably to the invitation.[4] The following response, from Dr Rowan Williams, Archbishop of Canterbury, describes well the value of the initiative:

> We find in it a hospitable and friendly spirit, expressed in its focus on love of God and love of neighbour—a focus which draws together the languages of Christianity and Islam, and of Judaism also ... Our belief is that only through a commitment to that transcendent perspective to which your letter points, and to which we also look, shall we find the resources for radical, transforming, non-violent engagement with the deepest needs of our world and our common humanity.[5]

* * *

As noted at the outset, and throughout this essay, the Prophet of Islam taught that tolerance is a universal ethical imperative. What renders a religion lovable to God is the presence within it of souls dominated by what the Prophet called *al-ḥanīfiyya al-samḥa*: primordial, generously tolerant faith in the One. The tolerance proper to the *ḥanīf*, perfectly embodied by Abraham, must be infused into the moral fibre of each human being, such that faith in one God translates, on the plane of human virtue, into tolerance of all those who believe in that unique Reality, whatever it be called. The Prophet's teachings on tolerance are rooted in the sacred knowledge revealed in the Qur'ān; in particular, the knowledge that human society is characterised by a divinely-willed diversity of religions and cultures. If this human diversity is an expression of the divine will and wisdom, then tolerance of the differences which will perforce accompany that diversity becomes not just an ethical obligation to our fellow creatures, but also a mode of engaging with and reflecting the wisdom of the Creator. That wisdom is at one with mercy, for God encompasses all things 'in mercy and knowledge' (40:7). From the point of view of the sacred vision of Islam, then, tolerance is not just a noble human ethic, it is also the outward expression of an uplifting spiritual ideal: a reflection of, and a participation in, the compassionate wisdom of God.

Notes

Introduction: The Trajectory of Tolerance

1 Muḥammad b. Ismāʿīl al-Bukhārī, *Ṣaḥīḥ al-Bukhārī: Arabic-English*, tr. Muhammad Muhsin Khan (Chicago, 1976), vol. 1, p. 34 (translation modified). See Hamza Yusuf, 'Generous Tolerance in Islam,' in *Seasons: Semiannual Journal of Zaytuna Institute*, 2 (2005), p.27.

2 H. A. R. Gibb, ed., *Whither Islam? A Survey of Modern Movements in the Moslem World* (New York and London, 2000, reprint of 1932 ed.), p. 379. He makes this point in the context of his belief that Islam could render an important service 'to the cause of humanity'. It comes in his own essay, after which the volume of collected essays edited by him is named, 'Whither Islam?', pp. 315–379. Another prominent scholar of Islam, Montgomery Watt, takes to its logical conclusion the testimony to Islam's authenticity which is provided by the record of Islamic civilisation: 'I consider that Muḥammad was truly a prophet, and think that we Christians should admit this on the basis of the Christian principle that "by their fruits you will know them", since, through the centuries, Islam has produced many upright and saintly people. If he is a prophet, too, then in accordance with the Christian doctrine that the Holy Spirit spoke by the prophets, the Qur'ān may be accepted as of divine origin.' M. Montgomery Watt, *Muḥammad's Mecca: History in the Qur'ān* (Edinburgh, 1988), p. 1.

3 Thomas Arnold, *The Preaching of Islam* (London, 1935), pp. 420–421.

4 Wilfred Cantwell Smith, *The Meaning and End of Religion: A Revolutionary Approach to the Great Religious Traditions* (London, 1978), chapter four, 'The Special Case of Islam' pp. 80–118.

5 Bernard Lewis, *The Multiple Identities of the Middle East* (New York, 1998), p. 120.

6 Ibid, p. 129.

7 John Locke, 'A Letter Concerning Toleration', in John Horton and Susan Mendus, ed., *A Letter Concerning Toleration: In Focus* (London and New York, 1991), p. 24. See for discussion Nabil Matar, 'John Locke and the Turbanned Nations', *Journal of Islamic Studies*, 2 (1991), p. 72.

8 Locke, 'A Letter Concerning Toleration', p. 51. Tim Winter, citing Ahmed Gunny, *Images of Islam in Eighteenth-Century Writings* (London, 1996), p. 132, writes that Locke's utopian work, *Reasonableness of Christianity*, made the ideal form of Christianity look very much like Islam, and was criticised for this very reason. See, for this and several important points concerning the relationship between Western 'Enlightenment' philosophers and Islam,

Tim Winter's fine essay, 'Ishmael and the Enlightenment *Crise de Coeur*', in Basit Koshul and Steven Kepnes, ed., *Scripture, Reason and the Contemporary Islam-West Encounter: Studying the 'Other', Understanding the 'Self'* (New York, 2007), pp. 149–175.

9 Norman Daniel, *Islam, Europe and Empire* (Edinburgh, 1966), p. 12.

10 Mohammed Sharafuddin, *Islam and Romantic Orientalism* (London and New York, 1996), p. ix. This idea is an elaboration of Edward Said's famous thesis *Orientalism* (London and New York, repr. 2003).

11 Winter, 'Ishmael and the Enlightenment', p. 170, n. 10; Winter is referring here to J. G. A. Pocock, *Barbarism and Religion* (Cambridge, 1999), vol. 2, p. 109. However, the *philosophes* of the Enlightenment also used Islam and the Turks as symbols of tyranny: Voltaire's play *Mahomet* used the figure of the Prophet to ridicule religion as a source of corrupt power and beguiling superstition. Such thinkers as Herder and Goethe, however, had nothing but praise for Islam and the Prophet. It is interesting to note that Goethe expressed deep regret at having been forced to translate Voltaire's play into German, upon the orders of his prince at Weimar; see Fred Dallmayr, 'West-Eastern Divan: Goethe and Hafiz in Dialogue', Chapter 8 of his *Dialogue Among Civilizations: Some Exemplary Voices* (New York and Basingstoke, 2002), p. 151. Dallmayr cites (p. 258, n. 4) the work of Katharina Mommsen, *Goethe und der Islam* (Stuttgart, 1964), and *Goethe und die arabische Welt* (Frankfurt-Main, 1988), according to whom Goethe found most attractive such doctrines of Islam as the following: 'the idea of the unity of God; the conviction of God's manifestness in nature; the notion that God has spoken to humankind through different messengers'.

12 See for a concise discussion of this vast topic, De Lacy O'Leary, *Islamic Thought and its Place in History* (New Delhi 2001; reprint of London, 1939 edition, originally entitled *Arabic Thought and its Place in History*); and S. E. Al-Djazairi, *The Hidden Debt to Islamic Civilisation* (Oxford, 2005).

13 This dilution of religious exclusivism can also have a negative impact on the commitment to one's own faith, as many committed Christians have noted in our times of religious relativism. In his *The Meeting of Religions and the Trinity* (Edinburgh, 2000), Catholic scholar and theologian Gavin D'Costa criticises the kind of religious pluralism associated with John Hick, and argues that an approach to other religions based on trinitarian theology can achieve more successfully the goals of pluralism—openness, tolerance, equality, etc.—than pluralist approaches themselves. He argues: 'Within a Roman Catholic trinitarian orientation the other is always interesting in their difference, and may be the possible face of God ... Furthermore, the other may teach Christians to know and worship their own trinitarian God more truthfully and richly. Trinitarian theology provides the context for a critical, reverent and open engagement with otherness, without any predictable outcome' (p. 9).

14 Eugene A. Myers, *Arabic Thought and the Western World in the Golden Age of Islam* (New York, 1964), pp. 133–134.

15 Hammond demonstrated, by painstaking comparative analysis, the extent to which such theologians as Aquinas borrowed from—in today's terms, 'plagia-

rised'—philosophers like al-Fārābī and Ibn Sīnā. Juxtaposing passages from the former and Aquinas, one sees almost verbatim translations from Arabic into Latin. See Robert Hammond, *The Philosophy of Al-Fārābī and its Influence on Medieval Thought* (New York, 1947), as cited in Myers, *Arabic Thought*, p. 23; and also A. M. Goichon, *The Philosophy of Avicenna and its Influence on Medieval Europe* (Delhi, 1969).

16 Myers, *Arabic Thought*, pp. 132–133.

17 Robert Briffault, *The Making of Humanity* (Lahore, 1980), p. 192. See also Osman Bakar, *Tawḥīd and Science* (Lahore, 1998), especially chapter 7, 'The Influence of Islamic Science on Medieval Christian Conceptions of Nature', pp. 131–155; and D. M. Dunlop, *Arabic Science and the West* (Karachi, 1958).

18 Giorgio de Santillana, *The Age of Adventure: The Renaissance Philosophers* (New York, 1970), p. 11 (emphasis added).

19 Charles Glenn Wallis, in the introduction to his translation of Giovanni Pico della Mirandola, *On the Dignity of Man* (Indianapolis, 1998), pp. vii–x.

20 Quoted by George Makdisi, *The Rise of Humanism in Classical Islam and the Christian West: With Special Reference to Scholasticism* (Edinburgh, 1990), pp. 307–308.

21 Wallis, *On the Dignity of Man*, p. vii.

22 Makdisi, *The Rise of Humanism.*, p. 301 ff. See the slightly different translation of this key sentence by Wallis, *On the Dignity of Man*, p. 3.

23 See the translation of *On the Dignity of Man* by Elizabeth Livermore Forbes, in Ernst Cassirer, Paul Oskar Kristeller, John Herman Randall, ed., *The Renaissance Philosophy of Man* (Chicago, 1948), p. 243. In their general introduction to this volume the editors remark that Pico was 'familiar with many of the original sources of medieval Arabic and Jewish philosophy' (p. 8).

24 George Makdisi, 'Interaction Between Islam and the West,' *Revue des Études Islamiques*, 44 (1976), pp. 287–309.

25 For a summary of his position as regards both Western scholasticism and humanism, see George Makdisi, 'Scholasticism and Humanism in Classical Islam and the Christian West', in *Journal of the Americal Oriental Society*, 109 (1989), pp. 175–182. Makdisi also claims that Western academia derived the notion of a 'chair' in a particular field of study from 'the traditional Islamic pattern of teaching where the professor sits on a chair (*kursī*) and the students sit around him'; whence also the term 'academic circle' (*ḥalqa*). For discussion see Hugh Goddard, *A History of Christian-Muslim Relations* (Edinburgh, 2000), p. 100.

26 Sir John Glubb, *The Life and Times of Muhammad* (New York, 1971), p. 244. Titus Burckhardt shows that this Muslim influence extended into the domain of chivalric love, and demonstrates that 'the [Christian] knightly attitude towards woman is Islamic in origin'. Titus Burckhardt, *Moorish Culture in Spain*, tr. Alisa Jaffa (London, 1970), p. 93. Similarly, Roger Boase argues that the principle and practice of courtly love must have been passed from Islamic Spain to the Christian world by word of mouth, in a process of cultural diffusion, given the numerous points of contact between Moorish Spain and the Christian world—trade, diplomacy, war, inter-marriage, migration, etc. All of these resulted in a flow of ideas from the more refined

and noble to the less sophisticated culture. Roger Boase, *The Origin and Meaning of Courtly Love* (Manchester, 1977), p. 68.

27 Seyyed Hossein Nasr, *Religion and the Order of Nature* (New York and Oxford, 1996), p. 163. Dallmayr brings home the shocking reality of this 'culture of conquest': 'the conquest of the Americas by European powers resulted in the course of less than a century in the deaths by killing, starvation, and disease of some 70 million native inhabitants', that is, 90 per cent of the population of the time. Dallmayr, *Beyond Orientalism: Essays on Cross-Cultural Encounter* (Albany, NY, 1996), pp. 1–2.

28 Dallmayr, *Beyond Orientalism*, pp. 12–13.

29 The translations of Qur'ānic verses given here are substantially based on M. M. Pickthall's *The Meanings of the Glorious Qur'an* (London, 1976); the following translations were also consulted: M. A. S. Abdel Haleem (Oxford, 2005), 'Alī Quli Qara'i (London, 2004), Muhammad Asad (Bristol, 2003), A. J. Arberry (London, 1964), The Royal Aal al-Bayt Institute Translation (www.altafsir.com).

30 A typical interpretation of this verse cited by Kamili is that of al-Alūsī (d. 1270/1854): ' . . . all members of the human race, including the pious and the sinner, are endowed with dignity, nobility and honour'. See Mohammad Hashim Kamali, *The Dignity of Man: An Islamic Perspective* (Cambridge, 2002), p. 1.

31 This is clearly an echo of Q. 49:13: 'O mankind, We have created you male and female, and We have made you into tribes and nations in order that you might come to know one another. Truly, in the sight of God, the most honoured amongst you is the most pious amongst you.'

32 Kamali, *Dignity of Man*, pp. 1–8; 70.

33 See Reza Shah-Kazemi, *Justice and Remembrance: Introducing the Spirituality of Imam 'Alī* (London, 2006), Chapter 2, pp. 73–133, for an analysis of the letter of Imam 'Alī to Mālik; and Appendix 2, pp. 219–234 for a complete translation of the letter.

34 Tzvetan Todorov, *The Conquest of America: The Question of the Other*, tr. Richard Howard (New York, 1984), p. 50; as cited in Dallmayr, *Beyond Orientalism*, p. 227, n. 9.

35 John L. Phelan, *The Hispanization of the Philippines*, as cited in Dallmayr, *Beyond Orientalism*, p. 9.

36 Although the blatant religious discrimination against Muslims, in the name of 'laïcité', in France is a notable exception. Also, there are worrying signs of growing Islamophobia in many countries of Europe. For example, in 2009, following a referendum, the Swiss constitution was amended to prohibit the construction of minarets. See Norman Doe, *Law and Religion in Europe: A Comparative Introduction* (Oxford, 2011), p. 167.

37 Ashis Nandy, 'The Politics of Secularism and the Recovery of Religious Tolerance': *Alternatives*, 13 (1988), p. 189 as cited in Dallmayr, *Beyond Orientalism*, p. 27.

38 Tim Winter, 'Islam and the Threat of Europe', in *World Faiths Encounter*, 29 (2001), p. 11.

39 Abdal Hakim Murad [Tim Winter], 'Faith in the Future: Islam after the

Enlightenment'. This is from a transcript of the First Annual Altaf Gauhar Memorial Lecture, Islamabad (23 December, 2002). Published online at http://www.masud.co.uk/ISLAM/ahm/postEnlight.htm.

Part 1: A Glance at the Historical Record

1 The only Muslim 'inquisition' that can compare with Christian inquisitions, albeit still much milder in form, is the *miḥna* (literally 'examination') conducted by the Abbasid state, which attempted to impose a Mu'tazilite-inspired 'orthodoxy' on all Muslims. Its reversal by the caliph al-Mutawakkil in 849 signified the victory of the religious scholars (*al-'ulamā'*), as a group, over the court in regard not just to the main point of doctrine at issue—the Mu'tazilite thesis that the Qur'ān is created and not eternal, upheld by the caliphs al-Ma'mūn, al-Mu'taṣim and al-Wāthiq—but also in regard to the claims of the state to be the ultimate source of authority in religious belief.

2 Benjamin Braude and Bernard Lewis, ed., *Christians and Jews in the Ottoman Empire: The Functioning of a Plural Society*, vol. 1: *The Central Lands* (New York, 1982), p. 1.

3 Stanford Shaw, *History of the Ottoman Empire and Modern Turkey*, vol. 1: *Empire of the Gazis: The Rise and Decline of the Ottoman Empire 1280–1808* (Cambridge, 1976), p. 59.

4 Arnold, *The Preaching of Islam*, p. 155.

5 Arnold, *The Preaching of Islam*, pp. 156–157.

6 A. L. Maycock, *The Papacy* (London, 1927), p. 48. When the Pope was told about the outrage, he excommunicated the entire army.

7 Shaw stresses the irony that Christian religious leaders were given far greater authority over their communities 'in secular as well as religious matters, than was possible in Christian states.' Stanford Shaw, *History of the Ottoman Empire*, p. 164.

8 Braude and Lewis, *Christians and Jews*, pp. 3–4.

9 We shall return to this point in our discussion of the status of the *dhimmī* at the end of part one of this essay.

10 Shaw, *History of the Ottoman Empire*, p. 165.

11 Yusuf Ibish, 'Traditional Guilds in the Ottoman Empire' in R. Shah-Kazemi, ed., *Turkey: The Pendulum Swings Back* (London, 1996), p. 22.

12 Shaw, *History of the Ottoman Empire*, p. 164.

13 Cited in Braude and Lewis, *Christians and Jews*, pp. 16–17.

14 It is interesting to note that the 'Mozarabs', Arabic-speaking Christians in Spain, also felt that their religion had been protected by the Arabs; in this context, they felt protected against inappropriate innovations taking root in Latin Christendom during the eighth to the eleventh centuries. When they were confronted by their co-religionists from northern Europe in Toledo after 1085 (the year in which Toledo was conquered by the Christians under Alfonso VI, who established it as the new archiepiscopal see of the Church) these 'Romanised' Christians were seen by the Mozarabs as having lost touch with their origins. 'The new Christians, who from the outset occupied the

most powerful ecclesiological positions, were a community whose reformed liturgy was, in the eyes of the Mozarabs, corrupted by new-fangled notions, while their own rite, kept pristine in its Arabic wrapping and thus unchanged since the eighth century, was far more traditional.' Maria Rosa Menocal, *Ornament of the World: How Muslims, Jews and Christians Created a Culture of Tolerance in Medieval Spain* (New York, 2002), p. 144.

15 Arnold, *Preaching of Islam*, pp. 201–204.

16 Ibid, p. 172.

17 Susan Ritchie, 'The Islamic Ottoman Influence on the Development of Religious Toleration in Reformation Transylvania', in *Seasons: Semiannual Journal of Zaytuna Institute*, 2 (2004), p. 62.

18 Ibid, p. 59.

19 Daniel, *Islam, Europe and Empire*, p. 12.

20 Quoted in S.A. Schleifer, 'Jews and Muslims: A Hidden History', in Karen Armstrong et al, ed., *The Spirit of Palestine* (Barcelona, 1994), p. 8.

21 Tim Winter, 'Spiritual Life in Ottoman Turkey', in R. Shah-Kazemi, ed., *Turkey: The Pendulum Swings Back*, pp. 32–41.

22 Marshall G. H. Hodgson, *The Venture of Islam: Conscience and History in a World Civilization* (Chicago and London, 1974), vol. 2: *The Expansion of Islam in the Middle Periods*, p. 125.

23 By the fifteenth century, it had also become closely associated with the Janissary corps, so crucial a part of the military structure of the Empire. See Halil Inalcık, *The Ottoman Empire: The Classical Age, 1300–1600*, tr. Norman Itzkowitz and Colin Imber (London, 1973), p. 194.

24 This accolade comes in Arberry's introduction to his translation of Rūmī's *Kitāb fīhi mā fīhi*, entitled *Discourses of Rūmī* (London, 1961), p. 9.

25 Halil Inalcık, *The Ottoman Empire*, p. 201. See for discussion of the role of the Sufi orders in the Ottoman empire, Chapter 19, 'Popular Culture and the Tarīkats: Mystical Orders', pp. 186–202; and for a succinct account of the role of Islam in the Ottoman world, Şerif Mardin, 'Islam in the Ottoman Empire and Turkey' in Shah-Kazemi, ed., *Turkey: The Pendulum Swings Back*, pp. 10–11.

26 Winter, 'Spiritual Life in Ottoman Turkey', p. 37.

27 *The Mathnawī of Jalāl ud-Dīn Rūmī*, tr. R. A. Nicholson (London, 1930), Book 2, line 1770.

28 R. A. Nicholson, *Selected Poems from the Dīvāni Shamsi Tabrīz* (Cambridge, 1976), pp. 126–127. The final line is an Arabic paraphrase of Q. 57:6.

29 *The Discourses of Rūmī*, p. 109.

30 Ibid, pp. 108–109 (translation modified). Hodgson refers to the importance of informal Sufi sessions in respect of the process of conversion to Islam. While the more formal institutions of exoteric Islam were largely inaccessible to would-be converts from other religions, the Sufi sessions were by and large open to all, as implied in the passage just cited. 'Hence it was only in more informal preaching sessions, and especially at Sufi *khāniqāhs* where the concern was not the public order and dignity of Islam, but the welfare of the individual soul, that the inquiring infidel could begin to participate enough in Islam to be moved to commit himself to it.' Hodgson, *The Venture of Islam*, p. 536.

31 As Henry Corbin notes, the *Mathnawī* is 'meditated and practised as the "Persian Qur'an" (*Qur'an-i Fārsī*)'. *En Islam iranien* (Paris, 1971), vol. 3, pp. 216–217.
32 S. H. Nasr, *Islamic Art and Spirituality* (Cambridge, 1987), p. 145, n.5, referring to an unpublished work of Hādī Ḥā'irī in which this calculation was made.
33 Dallmayr, *Beyond Orientalism*, p. 35.
34 See for further details, Iqtidar Alam Khan, 'The Nobility under Akbar and the Development of his Religious Policy', in *Journal of the Royal Asiatic Society*, 1 (1968), pp. 29–32; and M. Athar Ali, 'Towards an Interpretation of the Mughal Empire', in *Journal of the Royal Asiatic Society*, 1 (1978), pp. 38–49. Also, more generally, see S. A. A. Rizvi, *Religious and Intellectual History of the Muslims in Akbar's Reign* (New Delhi, 1975).
35 Sri Ram Sharma, *Mughal Government and Administration* (Bombay, 1965), p. 175.
36 S. Chandra, *Mughal Religious Policies, the Rajputs, and the Deccan* (New Delhi, 1993), pp. 22–24.
37 Sharma, *Mughal Government*, p. 173.
38 Aziz Ahmad, *Studies in Islamic Culture in the Indian Environment* (Oxford, 1964), pp. 80–81.
39 Sri Ram Sharma, *Religious Policy of the Mughal Empire* (London, 1962), p. 20.
40 Sharma, *Mughal Government*, pp. 174–175.
41 S. M. Ikram, *Muslim Civilization in India* (New York, 1964), p. 164.
42 Annemarie Schimmel, *Islam in the Indian Subcontinent* (Leiden, 1980), p. 77.
43 Annemarie Schimmel, *Islam in India and Pakistan* (Leiden, 1982), p. 10.
44 Sharma, *Religious Policy*, p. 21.
45 Rizvi, *Religious and Intellectual History*. p. 222.
46 Abu'l-Faḍl 'deftly wove Akbar's "unspoken wishes" into the matrix of a philosophical system', according to K. A. Nizami, *On History and Historians of Medieval India* (New Delhi, 1982), p. 142.
47 Rizvi, *Religious and Intellectual History*, p. 340.
48 Ibid, p. 140.
49 Muḥyī al-Dīn Ibn al-'Arabī, *Fuṣūṣ al-ḥikam* (Cairo, 1903), pp. 135–136. See Caner Dagli's annotated translation of the chapter in which this passage is found, 'The Ringstone of the Wisdom of Unity in the Word of Hūd', in *The Ringstones of Wisdom* (Fuṣūṣ al-ḥikam), tr. Caner K. Dagli (Chicago, 2004), pp. 105–117; also, see Toshihiko Izutsu, *Sufism and Taoism: A Comparative Study of Key Philosophical Concepts* (Berkeley, CA, 1983), pp. 254–261, for a fine discussion of this aspect of Ibn al-'Arabī's teachings.
50 Cited by Michel Chodkiewicz, *Un Océan Sans Rivage: Ibn 'Arabī, le Livre et la Loi* (Paris, 1992), p. 40. Chodkiewicz, one of the foremost authorities on Ibn al-'Arabī in the West, poses the question: Is this claim not merely a prudent concession to majoritarian, exoteric norms; is the Qur'ān not being used here as pretext rather than as text? He answers in the negative, drawing attention to the scrupulous fidelity of Ibn al-'Arabī not simply to the inner

meaning of the Qur'ān, but also to its literal wording, and also to the very structure of its composition, which is reflected in a subtle manner in the structure of his own voluminous work, *al-Futūḥāt al-Makkiyya*. See Chodkiewicz, pp. 43–54. For a clear and concise exposition of Ibn al-ʿArabī's universal approach to the religious phenomenon, see William C. Chittick, *Imaginal Worlds: Ibn al-ʿArabī and the Problem of Religious Diversity* (Albany, 1994).

51 Awrangzeb is described as having actively taken up the 'programme' of restoration formulated by Sirhindī. For this and other similar opinions from several Indian historians, see S. A. A. Rizvi, *Muslim Revivalist Movements in Northern India in the Sixteenth and Seventeenth Centuries* (Agra, 1965), pp. 414–416; and K. A. Nizami, *Akbar and Religion* (Delhi, 1989), p. 261.

52 Ibid, pp. 100–160. The three phases correspond to the periods 1557–74, 1574–80 and 1580–1605.

53 I. M. Qureshi, *Ulema in Politics* (Karachi, 1972), pp. 65–68.

54 Cited in Annemarie Schimmel, *The Empire of the Great Mughals*, tr. Corinne Atwood (London, 2004), p. 93.

55 See Heinz Halm, *The Empire of the Mahdi*, tr. Michael Bonner (Leiden, 1996), pp. 412–413, for discussion of various clauses in the *amān* document. And for a full translation and analysis of the document itself, see Shainool Jiwa, 'Inclusive Governance: A Fatimid Illustration', in Amyn Sajoo, ed., *A Companion to the Muslim World* (London, 2010), pp. 157–175.

56 As will be explained below, the term *dhimma* is a noun meaning 'protection', while the term *dhimmī* is an adjective, meaning 'one who is protected'.

57 Jiwa, 'Inclusive Governance', p. 166.

58 This is referred to by al-Qāḍī al-Nuʿmān in his *Daʿāʾim al-Islām*, as cited by Michael Brett in *The Rise of the Fatimids: The World of the Mediterranean and the Middle East in the Tenth Century CE* (Leiden, 2001), pp. 302–303. Brett notes (p. 303) that the first Abbasid caliph, al-Saffāḥ also referred to this wider notion of *dhimma* in his inaugural speech in 132/749.

59 Farhad Daftary, *A Short History of the Ismailis* (Edinburgh, 1998), p. 80.

60 Heinz Halm, *The Fatimids and their Traditions of Learning* (London, 1997), p. 31.

61 Ibid, p. 2.

62 Farhad Daftary, *The Ismāʿīlīs: Their History and Doctrines* (2nd ed., Cambridge, 2007), p. 159.

63 S. D. Goitein, *A Mediterranean Society: The Jewish Communities of the World as Portrayed in the Documents of the Cairo Geniza* (Berkeley, CA, 1967), vol. 1, p. 19.

64 S. D. Goitein, *A Mediterranean Society: An Abridgement in One Volume*, ed. Jacob Lassner (Berkeley and Los Angeles, CA, 1999), p. 300.

65 Goitein, *A Mediterranean Society*, vol. 1, p. 31.

66 Bernard Lewis, *Origins of Ismāʿīlism: A Study of the Historical Background of the Fāṭimid Caliphate* (Cambridge, 1940), pp. 93–94.

67 Ibid, p. 96. The citation is from Jaʿfar al-Yaman's work, *al-Shawāhid*.

68 Samuel M. Stern, *Studies in Early Ismāʿīlism* (Leiden, 1983), p. 86.

69 Ibid, p. 86.

70 As has been amply demonstrated in the writings of Seyyed Hossein Nasr,

who stresses throughout his works the ways in which the principle of *tawḥīd* generated a spirit of intellectual and philosophical openness to knowledge *per se*, no matter what its cultural, philosophical or religious origin. See for example his *Science and Civilization in Islam* (Cambridge, 1987); *An Introduction to Islamic Cosmological Doctrines* (London, 1978); and *Islamic Philosophy from its Origins to the Present* (Albany, 2006).

71 Wilferd Madelung and Paul. E. Walker, tr. and ed., *The Advent of the Fatimids: A Contemporary Shiʿi Witness: Ibn Haytham's* Kitāb al-Munāẓarāt (London, 2000), p. 140.

72 Seyyed Hossein Nasr, 'Introduction' to Abū Ḥātim al-Rāzī, *Aʿlām al-nubuwwa*, ed. Salah al-Sawy and Gholam-Reza Aavani (Tehran, 1381 Sh./2002), p. 3. See also H. Daiber, 'Abū Ḥātim ar–Rāzī (tenth century A.D.) on the Unity and Diversity of Religions', in J. Gort et al., ed., *Dialogue and Syncretism: An Interdisciplinary Approach* (Grand Rapids, MI, 1989), pp. 87–104.

73 Goitein, *A Mediterranean Society*, vol. 1, p. 296.

74 Ibid, p. 295.

75 See Daftary, *The Ismāʿīlīs,* pp. 180–181, for an overview of the policies implemented during the rule of al-Ḥākim.

76 Halm, *The Fatimids*, pp. 37–38.

77 Ibid, p. 37.

78 Yaacov Lev, *State and Society in Fatimid Egypt* (Leiden, 1991), p. 190.

79 Ibid, p. 195.

80 Cited in Schleifer, 'Jews and Muslims', p. 5.

81 Samuel D. Goitein, *Jews and Arabs: Their Contacts Through the Ages* (New York, 1964), p. 130.

82 Bernard Lewis, *The Jews of Islam* (Princeton, NJ, 1984), p. 8. This claim is further substantiated by his *Semites and Anti-Semites: An Inquiry into Conflict and Prejudice* (London, 1986), pp. 117–39, 164–259.

83 Mark R. Cohen, 'Islam and the Jews: Myth, Counter-Myth, History', in *Jerusalem Quarterly*, 38 (1986), p. 136.

84 Burckhardt, *Moorish Culture in Spain*, pp. 27–28.

85 Roger Collins, *Early Medieval Spain: Unity in Diversity, 400–1000* (London, 1995), p. 200.

86 Maria Rosa Menocal, *Ornament of the World;* see note 14 above.

87 Ibid, p. 21.

88 Together, the three subjects of the trivium and the four of the quadrivium made up what came to be known as 'the seven liberal arts'. The trivium consisted of grammar, dialectic and rhetoric; the quadrivium consisted of arithmetic, music, geometry and astronomy. See Angus MacNab, *Spain under the Crescent Moon* (Louisville, 1999), p. 180.

89 Menocal, *Ornament of the World*, pp. 32–34.

90 Ibid, p. 25.

91 Ibid, p. 30.

92 Maria Rosa Menocal, 'Culture in the Time of Tolerance: Al-Andalus as a model for our own time', in *Palestine-Israel Journal of Politics, Economics and Culture*, 8 (2001), pp. 173–174.

93 Thomas F. Glick, *Islamic and Christian Spain in the Early Middle Ages* (Leiden, 2005), p. 211.
94 Hanna Kassis, 'The Arabicization and Islamicization of the Christians of al-Andalus: Evidence of their Scriptures' in Ross Brann, ed., *Languages of Power in Islamic Spain* (Bethesda, MD, 1997), p. 139.
95 Menocal, 'Culture in the Time of Tolerance', p. 178.
96 We shall be focusing upon these verses, and especially 5:48, in Part 2 of this monograph.
97 E. Lévi-Provençal, *Histoire de l'Espagne musulmane: La Conquête et l'émirat hispano-umaiyade (710–912)* (Paris and Leiden, 1950), p. 272.
98 Richard Fletcher, *The Cross and the Crescent: Christianity and Islam from Muhammad to the Reformation* (New York and London, 2004), p. 48; citing Colin Smith, *Christians and Moors in Spain* (Warminster, 1988), vol. 1, pp. 65–67.
99 Collins, *Early Medieval Spain*, p. 213.
100 Ibid, p. 216.
101 Ibid, p. 215. This report is found in Alvar's *Vita Eulogii* ('Life of Eulogius'). Collins sounds a note of caution about these reports, however, in that they bear such close resemblance to the early accounts of Christian martyrs in Rome.
102 Kassis, 'Arabicization and Islamicization', p. 141.
103 Jessica A. Coope, *The Martyrs of Cordoba: Community and Family Conflict in an Age of Mass Conversion* (Lincoln and London, 1995), p. 11.
104 Ibid, p. 15.
105 Thomas F. Glick, *Islamic and Christian Spain in the Early Middle Ages* (Leiden, 2005), p. 188.
106 Ibid, p. 197.
107 Collins, *Early Medieval Spain*, p. 201.
108 Eliahu Klein, *Kabbalah of Creation: The Mysticism of Isaac Luria, Founder of Modern Kabbalah* (Berkeley, 2005), p. xvi.
109 See Daniel Chanan Matt, *Zohar: The Book of Enlightenment* (New Jersey, 1983).
110 Ibn al-ʿArabī, *The Tarjumān al-Ashwāq: A Collection of Mystical Odes*, tr. R. A. Nicholson, (London, 1978), p. 52.
111 James W. Morris, 'Ibn al-ʿArabī's Spiritual Ascension', in Michel Chodkiewicz et al, ed., *Les Illuminations de La Mecque* (Paris, 1988), p. 379.
112 E. W. Lane, *Arabic–English Lexicon* (Cambridge, 1984), vol. 1, p. 976.
113 The Zoroastrians are mentioned in the Qur'ān, but the jurists debated the question of whether they are to be included in the category of the *ahl al-kitāb*. Decisive in this regard was the opinion of Shāfiʿī, who maintained that Zoroastrians were not just to be regarded as *dhimmīs*, but also as *ahl al-kitāb*. See for discussion Yohannan Friedmann, *Tolerance and Coercion in Islam: Interfaith Relation in the Muslim Tradition* (Cambridge, 2003), p. 81.
114 Gobind Khushalani, *Chachnamah Retold: An Account of the Arab Conquest of Sindh* (New Delhi, 2006), p. 156.
115 Aḥmad al-Balādhurī, *Futūḥ al-buldān* (Beirut, 1988), pp. 422–423.

116 Ibid, p. 424. For further discussion, see S. M. Ikram, *History of Muslim Civilization in India and Pakistan* (Lahore, 1989).

117 According to the Buddhist scholar, Dr Alexander Berzin: 'The destruction at Valabhi ... was an exception to the general religious trends and official policies of the early Abbasid period. There are two plausible explanations for it. It was either the work of a militant fanatic general acting on his own, or a mistaken operation ordered because of the Arabs' confusing the local "white-clad" Jains with supporters of Abu Muslim and then not differentiating the Buddhists from the Jains. It was not part of a *jihad* specifically against Buddhism.' See his 'The Historical Interaction between the Buddhist and Islamic Cultures before the Mongol Empire', in 'The Berzin Archives: The Buddhist Archives of Dr Alexander Berzin', http://www.berzinarchives.com/web/en/archives/e-books/unpublished_manuscripts/historical_interaction/pt2/history_cultures_10.html). The other acts of unprincipled violence by rogue Muslim generals, such as the destruction of the temple of Nalanda by Bakhtiyar Khalji in 1193, are to be seen, likewise, as contrary to 'the general religious trends and official policies' of Muslim states acting in accordance with the Islamic precepts that the religious rights of Hindus and Buddhists, as *dhimmīs*, were to be respected.

118 For discussion of the spiritual affinities between Buddhism and Islam, see R. Shah-Kazemi, *Common Ground between Islam and Buddhism* (Louisville, 2010); and Hamza Yusuf's remarkable essay, in the same book, 'Buddha in the Qur'ān?', pp. 113–136.

119 We say 'apparently polytheistic' because the quintessence of Hinduism is Advaita, 'non-duality'. The 'gods' of the Hindu pantheon are to be interpreted in the light of Advaita, not according to popular Hindu culture. They are thus akin to so many qualities of the one and only God (Brahma), or so many angelic or archangelic functions, according to the level of manifestation at which the gods are conceived. See the important works of René Guénon, *Introduction to the Study of the Hindu Doctrines*, tr. Marco Pallis (New York, 2001); and *Man and his Becoming according to the Vedanta*, tr. Richard C. Nicholson (New York, 2001).

120 Aḥmad al-Balādhurī, *Futūḥ al-buldān*, tr. Philip K. Hitti as *The Origins of the Islamic State* (New York, 1916), vol. 1, pp. 100–101.

121 See Bat Ye'or, *The Decline of Eastern Christianity Under Islam: From Jihad to Dhimmitude, Seventh-Twentieth Century*, tr. Miriam Kochan and David Littman (New Jersey and London, 1996), pp. 244–248, where she argues that 'dhimmitude' is a political form of oppression, and should not in any respect be identified with modern tolerance. The name 'Bat Ye'or' means 'daughter of the Nile', and is the pseudonym adopted by a Jewish woman expelled from Egypt in 1956, as noted by Mark Cohen, ('Islam and the Jews', p. 127), who refers to her work as part of a 'revisionist' effort to portray the tradition of Muslim–Jewish relations in wholly negative terms; Cohen refers to this view as a 'counter-myth' which is more serious an error than the 'myth' of a Muslim–Jewish egalitarian utopia which it was intended to rectify.

122 See Friedmann, *Tolerance and Coercion in Islam*.

123 'Abdul Ḥamīd Abū Sulaymān, *The Islamic Theory of International Relations: New Directions for Islamic Methodology and Thought* (Herndon, VA, 1987).

124 The work of Khaled Abou el-Fadl is also important in this contemporary reevaluation of Muslim juridical thought. He argues forcefully in favour of viewing jurisprudence not as an immutable relic of Islamic history, but as a dynamic methodology, the very success of which is gauged by its ability to creatively adapt immutable principles to ever-changing practical exigencies. He is opposed to 'authoritarian' modes of legal interpretation, by which he means 'a hermeneutic methodology that usurps and subjugates the mechanisms of producing meaning from a text to a highly subjective and selective reading'. Khaled Abou El Fadl, *Speaking in God's Name: Islamic Law, Authority and Women* (Oxford, 2001), p. 5. The works of Mohammad Hashim Kamali, cited in this monograph, are good examples of the kind of creative thought which is proving itself capable of adapting 'immutable principles to 'ever-changing practical exigencies'. See also his excellent monograph, *Moderation and Balance in Islam: The Qur'ānic Principle of Wasaṭiyyah* (Kuala Lumpur, 2010).

125 Abū Sulaymān, *The Islamic Theory of International Relations*, pp. 24, 40–41.

126 See Tim Winter, 'The Last Trump Card: Islam and the Supersession of Other Faiths', in *Studies in Interreligious Dialogue*, 9 (1999), p. 153.

127 Ibid, p. 134.

128 Ibid, p. 137.

129 Ramaḍān al-Būṭī, *al-Jihād fi'l-Islām* (Damascus, 2005), p. 133.

130 Ignaz Goldziher, *Introduction to Islamic Theology and Law* (New Jersey, 1981), p. 35.

131 Barnaby Rogerson, *The Heirs of the Prophet Muhammad* (London, 2006), p. 184.

132 Daniel J. Sahas, 'The Face to Face Encounter between Patriarch Sophronius of Jerusalem and the caliph 'Umar ibn al-Khaṭṭāb: Friends or Foes?', in Emmanouela Grypeou, Mark Swanson, and David Thomas, ed.,*The Encounter of Eastern Christianity with Early Islam* (Leiden, 2006), p. 39.

133 Norman Stillman, *The Jews of Arab Lands: A History and Source Book* (Philadelphia, PA, 1979), pp. 154–155.

134 *The History of al-Ṭabarī*, vol. 12, tr. Y. Friedmann (Albany, NY, 1985), p. 191.

135 Sidney Griffith, *The Church in the Shadow of the Mosque: Christians and Muslims in the World of Islam* (Princeton, NJ and Oxford, 2008), p. 4. William Dalrymple writes eloquently of the testimony to tolerance and co-existence provided by the living presence of ancient Christian communities in the Muslim world. See his *From the Holy Mountain: A Journey among the Christians of the Middle East* (New York, 1999). Note the remarkable description he gives of a visit he paid in 1994 to Seidnaya, a Greek Orthodox monastery outside of Damascus, where he witnessed Muslims and Christians praying together, each in accordance with their own tradition, but in complete harmony: 'It was a truly extraordinary sight, Christians and Muslims praying. Yet this was, of course, the old way: the Eastern Christians and the Muslims have lived side by side for nearly one-and-a-half millennia and have only

been able to do so due to a degree of mutual tolerance and shared customs unimaginable in the solidly Christian West.' William Dalrymple, 'Of Saints and Sufis in the Near East: Past and Present', in Roger Boase, ed., *Islam and Global Dialogue: Religious Pluralism and the Pursuit of Peace* (Aldershot, 2005), p. 98.

136 Muḥammad Ṭayy, 'Ru'yat al-Imām 'Alī wa muwaqqifuh min waḥdat al-umma wa ḥuqūq al-aqalliyyāt al-siyāsiyya wa al-dīniyya' ['The vision of Imam 'Alī and his way of establishing the unity of the Umma and the rights of political and religious minorities'], in Mehdi Golshani, ed., *Proceedings of the Congress on Imam Ali and Justice, Unity and Security* (Tehran, 1423/2002), vol. 2, p. 71.

137 In the perspective of the Imam 'Alī, the principle of tolerance also extended to the domain of socio-economic rights, both of which were to come within the purview of justice. The Imam had a strict policy of non-discrimination between Muslim and non-Muslim as regards the duty of the state to support those unable to provide for themselves. The Imam came across an old, blind beggar and inquired about him. He was told that the beggar was a Christian. He told those around him, 'You have employed him to the point where he is old and infirm, and now you refuse to help him. Give him maintenance from the public funds (*bayt al-māl*).' Cited by Muḥammad Ṭayy, 'Ru'yat al-Imām 'Alī', p. 72.

138 See the important recent biography by John W. Kiser, *Commander of the Faithful: The Life and Times of Emir Abd el-Kader* (Cambridge, 2008); and also R. Shah-Kazemi, 'From the Spirituality of Jihad to the Ideology of Jihadism', in *Seasons: Semiannual Journal of Zaytuna Institute*, 2 (2005), pp. 45–68. The following paragraphs are based on this article.

139 Charles Henry Churchill, *The Life of Abdel Kader* (London, 1867), p. 314.

140 This incident is recorded in Boualem Bessaïeh, 'Abdelkader à Damas et le sauvetage de douze mille chrétiens', in *Itinéraires: Revue semestrielle*, 6 (2003), p. 90.

141 Churchill, *The Life of Abdel Kader*, p. 318.

142 Cited by Mgr. Henri Teissier (Bishop of Algeria) in 'Le sens du dialogue inter–religions', *Itinéraires: Revue semestrielle*, 6 (2003), p. 47.

143 'Avoid extremism (*al-ghuluww*)', the Prophet said, 'for people have been led to destruction by extremism.' Cited by Hashim Kamali, *Dignity of Man*, p. 68.

144 Like the Emir, Imam Shamīl was regarded with awe not only by his own followers, but also by his opponents; when he was finally defeated and taken to Russia, he was fêted as a hero. Although occasionally embroidered with romanticism, Lesley Blanch's *Sabres of Paradise* (New York, 1960) conveys well the heroic aspect of Shamil's resistance. For a more scholarly account, see Moshe Gammer, *Muslim Resistance to the Tsar: Shamil and the Conquest of Chechnia and Daghestan* (London, 1994). See also R. Shah-Kazemi, *Crisis in Chechnia: Russian Imperialism, Chechen Nationalism and Militant Sufism* (London, 1995) offers for an overview of the Chechen quest for independence from the eigthteenth century through to the war of the mid-1990s, with a particular stress on the role of the Sufi brotherhoods in this quest. It is to

be noted that both the Emir and Shamīl were great Sufi masters; the Emir was the author of one of the most esoteric texts in recent times, *Kitāb al-mawāqif*. See Michel Chodkiewicz, *The Spiritual Writings of Amir 'Abd al-Kader*, tr. James Chrestensen and Tom Manning (Albany, NY, 1995).

145 Cited by Boualem Bessaïeh, 'Abdelkader à Damas', p. 91–92 (translation modified).

146 Quoted in Churchill, *The Life of Abdel Kader*, p. 323.

147 Cited by the Comte de Cirvy in his work, 'Napoleon III et Abd el-Kader'; see 'Document: Un portrait de l'Emir par le Comte de Cirvy (1853)' in *Itinéraires: Revue semestrielle*, 5 (2001), p. 11.

148 Abū Zakariyya al-Nawawī, *Rawḍat al-ṭālibīn*, ed. Zuhayr al-Shawish (Beirut, 1991), vol. 10, pp. 316–317; cited by Khaled Abou El Fadl, *The Place of Tolerance in Islam* (Boston, 2002), p. 22.

Part 2: The Spirit of Tolerance

1 Henri Corbin, *En Islam iranien*, vol. 1, p. 33.

2 See the exegesis on this verse by the classical commentator, Abū Ja'far al-Ṭabarī, *Jāmi' al-bayān* (Beirut, 2001), vol. 17, p. 100 in which this implication is expressed.

3 These are 'isolated letters' which begin certain chapters, interpretation of which varies from commentator to commentator, all of whom assert that their real meaning is known by God alone.

4 See the following important essays on this subject by Seyyed Hossein Nasr: 'One God, Many Prophets', in his *The Heart of Islam: Enduring Values for Humanity* (New York, 2002), pp. 1–54; and 'Metaphysics and Philosophy East and West: Necessary Conditions for Meaningful Comparative Study', in his *Islam and the Plight of Modern Man* (Lahore, 1988), pp. 27–36. For a profound metaphysical resolution of the apparent contradictions between different religious traditions, see Frithjof Schuon, *The Transcendent Unity of Religions*, tr. Peter Townsend (London, 1953).

5 Franz Rosenthal, *Knowledge Triumphant: The Concept of Knowledge in Medieval Islam* (Leiden, 2007), pp. 1–2.

6 Ibid, pp. 334, 336.

7 Ibid, pp. 22–23.

8 S.H. Nasr, *Sufi Essays* (London, 1972), p. 131.

9 *Ṣaḥīḥ al-Bukhārī*, tr. M. M. Khan (Chicago, 1977), vol. 2, pp. 247–248.

10 Cited by 'Abd al-Raḥmān 'Azzām, *The Eternal Message of Muḥammad*, tr. Caesar E. Farah (New York, 1964), p. 52.

11 Nevad Kahteran, 'Ḥanīf', in *The Qur'an: An Encyclopaedia*, ed. Oliver Leaman (Oxford, 2006).

12 *Ṣaḥīḥ al-Bukhārī*, vol. 1, p. 34. The word *ḥanīfiyya* can be translated also as 'original monotheism', the *ḥanīf* par excellence being the patriarch Abraham, who exemplifies primordial human nature, *al-fiṭra*, as noted earlier. As for the word *samḥa*, it connotes the notions of liberality, generosity, gentleness, easiness; it is thus closely related to *ḥilm*. The translation of the English word

'tolerance' in contemporary Arabic is *tasāmuḥ*, derived from the same root, s–m–ḥ. For a careful evaluation of the semantic field of this word, see Hamza Yusuf, 'Generous Tolerance in Islam,' especially pp. 26–35.

13 Almost identical to 38:71–2.

14 Frithjof Schuon, *Understanding Islam*, ed. Patrick Laude (Bloomington, IN, 2011), p. 2.

15 See for example the section on knowledge in *Ṣaḥīḥ al-Bukhārī*, vol. 1, pp. 50–100; and the section on knowledge in the primary Shiʿi compilation of *ḥadīth*, Muḥammad b. Yaʿqūb al-Kulaynī's *al-Uṣūl min al-kāfī* (Tehran, 1418/1997), vol. 1, pp. 45–91.

16 Abū Ḥāmid al-Ghazālī, *Book of Knowledge*, tr. Nabih Amin Faris (Lahore, 1970), pp. 11–18 (translation modified); *Iḥyā'*, vol. 1, pp. 12–16.

17 Ibid, vol. 1, p. 14 (translation modified); *Iḥyā'*, vol. 1, pp. 6–7.

18 Cited in ʿAbd al-Wāḥid Āmidī, *Ghurar al-ḥikam wa durar al-kalim*, published under the Persian title *Guftār-i Amīr al-mu'minīn ʿAlī*, ed. and tr. by Sayyid Ḥusayn Shaykhul–Islāmī (Qom, 2000), vol. 1, p. 595, no.2. The theme of the intellect as one's 'inner prophet' is thus closely connected with the esoteric idea of the '*imām* of one's own being', so fundamental to Shiʿi gnosis. See for discussion Henry Corbin, *Cyclical Time and Ismaili Gnosis*, tr. R. Manheim and J. Morris, (London, 1983), p. 128.

19 *Ghurar,* vol. 2, p. 954, no. 33.

20 See for further discussion our *Justice and Remembrance*, pp. 11–72.

21 Cited in William C. Chittick, *Imaginal Worlds*, (Albany, NY, 1994), p. 125.

22 Jane McAuliffe shows how these strategies work in relation to several of the key universalist verses, with particular stress on those which, in their literal meaning, are entirely positive in relation to Christians. She carefully studied what the exoteric commentators said about seven verse-groups 2:62, 3:55, 3:199, 5:66, 5:82–83, 28:52–55, 58:27, and concludes that 'ultimately, exegetical circumscription prevails. Within the commentary tradition on these seven verse groups, delimitation and specification clearly control the emerging depiction [of Christians]. The centuries-long testimony of commentary sunders the category of Christians, reserving to but a very limited number the application of divine approval and award . . . The commentators understand the Qur'an to make a clear distinction between true Christians, a tiny minority, and those who have appropriated and propagated a corrupted form of the religion of Jesus.' Jane D. McAuliffe, *Qur'anic Christians: An Analysis of Classical and Modern Exegesis* (Cambridge, 1991), p. 286.

23 The Oneness in question is not, however, of the numerical order. As is attested in most theological statements of belief (*ʿaqīda*), God's Oneness transcends the category of number, which pertains to the domain of relativity. Imam ʿAlī expresses the metaphysical unicity (the 'one-and-onliness') of God in the following words: 'That which has no second does not enter the category of number.' Cited in al-Shaykh al-Ṣadūq, *Kitāb al-tawḥīd* (Beirut, 1967), p. 83.

24 For juridical opinions on the inadmissibility of compelling non-Muslims to affirm belief in Islam see Mohammad Hashim Kamali, *Freedom of Expression in Islam* (Cambridge, 1997), pp. 88–93.

25 Most commentators refer to such early authorities as Ibn ʿAbbās, Mujāhid, Muqātil ibn Ḥayyān, etc., who made the assertion that this is the first verse revealed concerning warfare. See, for example, Ibn Kathīr, *Tafsīr al-Qur'an al-ʿaẓīm* (Riyadh, 1998), vol. 3, p. 103.

26 Chodkiwiecz, *The Spiritual Writings of Amir ʿAbd al-Kader*, p. 129.

27 Karen Armstrong, *Muhammad: A Western Attempt to Understand Islam* (London, 1991), p. 169.

28 Armstrong, *Muhammad: Prophet For Our Time* (London, 2006), pp. 126–127. Tor Andrae makes much the same point in his *Mohammed The Man and His Faith*, tr. Theophil Menzel (London, 1956), p. 140.

29 The treatise was published in Cairo in 1948, and translated by F. E. Peters under the title 'A Modernist Interpretation of Jihad: Mahmud Shaltut's Treatise, *Koran and Fighting*' in his book, *Jihad in Classical and Modern Islam* (Leiden, 1977), pp. 59–101. See also the excellent series of essays on Jihad by S. A. Schleifer. He mounts a compelling critique of the political reduction of Jihad, using as his basis 'traditional Islamic consciousness'. The series was published in the journal *Islamic Quarterly,* 23 (1979); Part 2 is in vol. 27, no. 4 (1983); Part 3 in vol. 28, no. 1 (1984); Part 4 in vol. 28, no. 2 (1984); and Part 5 in vol. 28, no. 3 (1984). For an important rebuttal of the false conception of Jihad as aggressive and perpetual warfare, see Zaid Shakir, 'Jihad is Not Perpetual Warfare', in *Seasons: Semiannual of Zaytuna Institute,* 1 (2003–2004), pp. 53–64.

30 See the useful comments by Muhammad Asad on these and related verses in the notes accompanying his translation of the Qur'ān, *The Message of the Qur'ān* (Bristol, 2003). Also see the important chapter by David Dakake, 'The Myth of a Militant Islam', in Joseph E. B. Lumbard, *Islam, Fundamentalism and the Betrayal of Tradition* (Bloomington, IN, 2009), pp. 3–38. Dakake focuses on the Qur'ānic verses most commonly cited by the extremists to justify their acts of terrorism; he effectively debunks their interpretations, doing so on the basis of the classical commentaries on these same verses.

31 See R. Shah-Kazemi, *The Other in the Light of the One: The Universality of the Qur'an and Interfaith Dialogue* (Cambridge, 2006), pp. 59–73 , for discussion of Ibn al-ʿArabī's hermeneutics, according to which the universalist interpretation of Qur'ānic verses need not be articulated in such a way as to exclude altogether the exclusivist interpretations. According to Ibn al-ʿArabī, no single interpretation can be put forward as right and true to the exclusion of all others. To exclude the exclusivist reading is to fall into a particular mode of exclusivism.

32 See the inspiring presentation of the traditional religion of the Oglala Sioux by the Medicine Man, Black Elk, in *The Sacred Pipe: Black Elk's Account of the Seven Rites of the Oglala Sioux*, recorded and edited by Joseph Epes Brown (Norman, OK, 1953); and the autobiographical classic *Black Elk Speaks*, recorded by John G. Neihardt (Lincoln, NE, 1979). It is clear from these, and many other similar works, that for the most profound representatives of the Native American traditions, the sense of the transcendence and unity of the Absolute is in no way compromised by the shamanistic perception of the Great Spirit within all things.

33 See René Guénon, 'The Language of the Birds' in his *Fundamental Symbols: The Universal Language of Sacred Science*, tr. Alvin Moore, Jnr (Cambridge, 1995), pp. 39–42, where he comments on the symbolism in question by reference to such mythical figures as Siegfried in the Nordic legend.

34 See further 13:13; 59:1; 61:1; 62:1; 64:1, et passim.

35 As will be discussed shortly, the *jāhil* is not just someone who is ignorant, he is also arrogant, impetuous and lacking in self-control.

36 One should note the remarkable affinity between the description of the slaves of the Compassionate here and the reference by Chief Seattle to 'our bare feet' being 'conscious of the sympathetic touch' of the earth, in his famous speech of 1855 to Governor Isaac Stevens in a place that was later to be named Seattle out of respect to the chief. See *In a Sacred Manner I Live: Native American Wisdom*, ed. Neil Philip (New York, 1997), p. 84.

37 Cited by Seyyed Hossein Nasr, 'The Cosmos and the Natural Order,' in *Islamic Spirituality: Foundations*, ed. S. H. Nasr (London, 1987), p. 355.

38 Cited in William C. Chittick, *The Sufi Path of Knowledge: Ibn al-ʿArabī and the Metaphysics of the Imagination* (Albany, NY, 1989), pp. 355–356.

39 See note 49 of Part 1 above.

40 *Ṣaḥīh al-Bukhārī-Summarised*, tr. M. M. Khan (Riyadh, 1994), p. 937.

41 This is one of the key themes stressed by Karen Armstrong in her second biography of the Prophet, *Muhammad: Prophet For Our Time*, referred to above. She rightly draws attention (p. 79) to the irascible arrogance that lay at the heart of the notion of *jahl*, hence the designation of the Prophet's most militant enemy, Abu'l-Ḥakam, as 'Abū Jahl', not because of his ignorance, but his arrogance.

42 *Nahj al-balāgha*, compiled by al-Sharīf al-Raḍī, ed. Shaykh ʿAzīzullāh al-ʿUṭārdī (Tehran, 1993), p. 288.

43 Cited by H. Lazarus-Yafeh, *Studies in Ghazzali* (Jerusalem, 1975), pp. 197–198.

44 Qadi 'Iyad Ibn Musa al-Yahsubi, *Muḥammad, Messenger of Allah: Ash-Shifa of Qadi 'Iyad*, tr. Aisha Abdarrahman Bewley (Inverness, 1991), p. 120.

45 This *ḥadīth* is found in the collections of Ibn Ḥanbal, al-Nasāʾī, Ibn Mājah, Ibn Abī Shayba, al-Ṭabarānī, and several others, according to Ibn Naasir al-ʿUbaykaan in 'The Khawaarij and their Renewed Ideology' (http://www.e-prism.org/images/neokhawaarij.pdf), p. 10, n. 43.

46 The *ḥadīth* reads as follows: *Al-anbiyāʾ ikhwa li-ʿallāt, ummahatuhum shattā, wa dīnuhum wāḥid*. See *Ṣaḥīḥ al-Bukhārī Summarised*, p. 680.

47 Al-Ḥākim al-Nīsābūrī, *al-Mustadrak ʿala'l-ṣaḥīḥayn* (Beirut, 2002), p. 943.

48 His Holiness the Dalai Lama, 'Harmony, Dialogue and Meditation', in D. W. Mitchell and J. Wiseman, ed., *The Gethsemani Encounter* (New York, 1999), p. 49.

49 Cited by Carl W. Ernst, *Following Muḥammad: Rethinking Islam in the Contemporary World* (Chapel Hill, 2003), p. 45.

50 Arnold, *Preaching of Islam*, pp. 81–82.

51 Muḥammad Ṭayy, 'Ru'yat al-Imam ʿAlī', pp. 63–64.

52 Ibid, p. 67.

53 This *ḥadīth* is found in the collections of Aḥmad b. Ḥanbal, Bayhaqī and

Ḥākim al-Nīsābūrī, as noted by al-Ḥāfiẓ al-ʿIrāqī in his gloss of 'verification' (*takhrīj*) upon al-Ghazālī's *Iḥyāʾ* vol. 3, p. 70, as found in the chapter devoted to the prophetic virtues, 'Kitāb ādāb al-maʿīsha wa akhlāq al-nubuwwa', vol. 3, pp. 69–109. See the translation by L. Zolondek, *Book XX of al-Ghazālī's Ihya Ulum al-Din* (Leiden, 1963).

54 Martin Lings points out that the words 'whole', 'holy' and 'health' share a single etymological root. All three are thus originally 'the same word and have merely been differentiated in form and in meaning through the fragmentation of language. The virtues of simplicity and sincerity are inseparable from this perfection, for each in its own way means undividedness of soul.' *Ancient Beliefs and Modern Superstitions* (Cambridge, 1996), p. 36. This, in its own way, demonstrates one of the meanings of *tawḥīd*, literally, 'realising one' or 'making one', thus, integration, and not merely 'affirming one' or 'declaring one'.

55 Cited in the compilation of Muḥammadī Rayshahrī, *Mīzān al-ḥikma*, tr. N. Virjee et al, *The Scale of Wisdom: A Compendium of Shiʿa Hadith* (London, 2009, p. 311).

56 This is how al-Ghazālī describes him in the sentence which begins the section on the Prophet's granting of pardon (*ʿafwu*), in Book 20 of the *Iḥyāʾ*, referred to above. See *Iḥyāʾ* vol. 3, p. 96; English trans., see Zolondek, *Book XX*, p. 35.

57 William Montgomery Watt, *Muhammad at Medina* (Oxford, 1956), pp. 321–324. Likewise, Karen Armstrong concludes her *Muhammad: Prophet For Our Time*, with a plea to Muslims and Westerners 'not merely to tolerate but to appreciate one another'. She adds: 'A good place to start is with the figure of Muhammad . . . who had profound genius and founded a religion and cultural tradition that was not based on the sword but whose name—"Islam"—signified peace and reconciliation' (p. 214).

58 Cited by ʿAzzām, *Eternal Message*, p. 61.

59 Cited by ʿAbdallāh Sirājuddīn al-Ḥusaynī, *Our Master Muhammad, the Messenger of Allah: His Sublime Character and Exalted Attributes*, tr. Khalid Williams (Amsterdam, 2009), p. 299. There are numerous sayings like the ones quoted, so much so that an entire section of Islamic law is devoted to the rights of animals. See part 5 of this work, entitled 'Our Master Muhammad, the Messenger of Mercy', pp. 264–303, for a comprehensive presentation of the sayings and incidents which express the mercy, compassion and *ḥilm* of the Prophet.

60 Karen Armstrong, *Muhammad: A Western Attempt to Understand Islam*, p. 168.

61 Stanley Lane-Poole, *The Speeches and Table Talk of the Prophet Muhammad* (Delhi, 1987), p. 29.

62 Toshihiko Izutsu, *God and Man in the Qur'an: Semantics of the Qur'anic Weltanschauung* (Kuala Lumpur, 2002), p. 236.

63 Qadi ʿIyad (already cited), *Muḥammad, Messenger of Allāh:*, p. 228; Arabic text: *Kitāb al-shifāʾ bi-taʿrīf ḥuqūq Sayyidinā al-Muṣṭafā* (Mecca, 1993), vol. 2, p. 23.

64 See *The Republic of Plato*, tr. Francis MacDonald Cornford (Oxford, 1969),

pp. 119–143. One better understands perhaps why Shakespeare speaks of the 'heavenly blessings' that are bestowed upon a 'gentle mind': 'You bear a gentle mind, and heavenly blessings follow such creatures', says the Lord Chamberlain in *Henry VIII* (Act 2, Scene 3). Likewise, Dante brings out the aspects of grace and nobility inherent in the Latin root of the word when he writes in his poem *Vita Nuova*: *Amore e'l cor gentil sono una cosa* ('Love and the gentle/noble/gracious heart are a single thing'). See Jay Ruud, *Dante: A Literary Reference to His Life and Work* (New York, 2008), p. 324.

65 The word *'aql*, intellect, is also regarded as a synonym of *ḥilm*, as Izutsu demonstrates; see *God and Man*, pp. 233–235.

66 Cited in Rayshahri, *Mīzān al-ḥikma*, p. 311.

67 Izutsu, *God and Man*, p. 223. This couplet was composed by 'Amr b. Aḥmar al-Bāhilī.

68 Ibid, p. 226.

69 Ibid, pp. 226–227.

70 Āmidī, *Ghurar*, vol. 1, pp. 208–211, nos. 20, 8, 23, 26.

71 Ibid, vol. 2, p. 951, no. 9.

72 The love which is inherent in the Arabic term, *raḥma*, is inadequately conveyed by the words 'compassion' or 'mercy'. *Raḥma* is that compassion or mercy which flows from the infinite love of God. This is clear from the Prophet's statement that God has more *raḥma* in relation to His creatures than a mother has in relation to her baby. Now, what the mother has for her baby is an organic, all-encompassing love, from which compassion and mercy flow naturally. It should also be noted that the word for 'womb' in Arabic is *raḥim*. See for further discussion, R. Shah-Kazemi, 'God "The Loving"' in *A Common Word: Muslims and Christians on Loving God and Neighbour*, ed. Miroslav Volf, Ghazi bin Muhammad, Melissa Yarrington (Grand Rapids and Cambridge, 2010), pp. 88–109.

73 A. Guillaume, *The Life of Muḥammad: A Translation of Ibn Isḥāq's Sīrat Rasūl Allāh* (Oxford, 1968), p. 507.

74 Martin Lings, *Muḥammad: His Life Based on the Earliest Sources* (Cambridge, 1984), p. 290.

75 The classical exegete, al-Zamakhsharī, defines *al-ḥamiyya* as *al-anafa*, that is, arrogant disdain; and *al-sakīna* as *al-waqār*, that is, sober dignity. Maḥmūd b. 'Umar al-Zamakhsharī, *Tafsīr al-Kashshāf* (Beirut, 1995), vol. 4, p. 335, on 48:26.

76 This is in the Imam's letter to Mālik al-Ashtar. Cited in Shah-Kazemi, *Justice and Remembrance*, p. 233.

77 Martin Lings, *What is Sufism?* (Cambridge, 1993), p. 34.

78 'Azzām, *Eternal Message*, p. 61. See also Tariq Ramadan *In the Footsteps of the Prophet: Lessons from the Life of Muhammad*, tr. Claude Dabbak (Oxford, 2007), for a biography which pays close attention to the ways in which a wide range of contemporary issues can be addressed by principles embodied and articulated by the Prophet's conduct.

79 'Azzām, *Eternal Message*, pp. 138–139.

80 One might also mention the economic motive: Muslim rulers benefited from the tax revenues yielded by the *jizya* levied on religious minorities, which

were normally higher than the revenues from the *zakāt* paid by Muslims. This was a far from insignificant factor inducing religious tolerance on the part of Muslim rulers; and, in its own way, it debunks the myth of Muslim conquerors imposing Islam on subject peoples at the point of the sword.

81 On this subject see the excellent study of the literature pertaining to popular devotion to the Prophet, Annemarie Schimmel, *And Muḥammad is His Messenger: The Veneration of the Prophet in Islamic Piety* (Chapel Hill and London, 1985), especially Chapter 2, 'Muhammad the Beautiful Model', pp. 24–55. See also the fine essay by Mostafa Badawi, 'The Muḥammadan Attributes', in *Seasons: Semiannual Journal of Zaytuna Institute*, 2 (2005), pp. 81–95.

82 Qadi 'Iyad, *Muḥammad, Messenger of Allāh*, p. 223.

83 See Julian Johansen, *Sufism and Islamic Reform in Egypt: The Battle for Islamic Tradition* (Oxford, 1996).

84 See the important critique of extremist, puritanical and fundamentalist interpretations of Islam presented in the numerous articles and books of Khaled Abou El-Fadl, especially *The Great Theft: Wrestling Islam From the Extremists* (New York, 2007); *The Place of Tolerance in Islam* (Boston, 2002); *Conference of the Books: The Search for Beauty in Islam* (Lanham, 2001).

85 Shabbir Akhtar, *Be Careful with Muḥammad! The Salman Rushdie Affair* (London, 1989), pp. 2–3.

86 Frithjof Schuon, *Understanding Islam*, p. 93.

87 *Ṣaḥīḥ al-Bukhārī*, vol. 4, p. 279. In some versions of this saying, one finds the word *sabaqat*, 'precedes', rather than *ghalabat*, 'overcomes'.

88 Āmidī, *Ghurar*, vol. 2, p. 1156.

89 The immediate context for the revelation of verse 2:256 was one in which certain Muslims wanted to insist that their children be converted from Judaism or Christianity to Islam. They are being reprimanded in this verse. Let us note here the incident in which the second caliph, 'Umar, received the request of an elderly Christian woman for help. After granting her what she had requested, he invited her to embrace Islam. She refused. The caliph sought the forgiveness of God lest he had exerted any undue pressure on her: 'O my Lord, I did not mean to compel her, as I know that there must be no compulsion in religion.' See Mohammad Hashim Kamali, *Freedom of Expression in Islam* (Cambridge, 1997), p. 92.

90 Both modes of knowledge, the rational, analytical and separative, on the one hand, and the contemplative, synthetic and unitive, on the other, are found in the very appellations ascribed to the Islamic revelation: on the one hand, the Qur'ān is called *al-Furqān*, 'that which separates', *faraqa* meaning to establish differentiation; while as *al-Qur'ān*, it is 'that which brings together', *qarana* meaning that which gathers disparate things together. This is one possible derivation of the word *Qur'an*, favoured by the Sufis; the other, more commonly given derivation is from *qara'a*, 'to recite'.

91 Aḥmad b. Ḥanbal, *Musnad*, vol. 5, p. 411, as cited by Mustafa Köylü, *Islam and its Quest for Peace: Jihad, Justice and Education* (Washington, DC, 2003), p. 78. There are various versions of this sermon; see for example Tariq Ramadan, *In the Footsteps of the Prophet*, p. 196; and Barnaby Rogerson, *The*

Prophet Muhammad: A Biography (London, 2003), p. 208. As Maxime Rodinson notes—even while questioning the authenticity of the ascription of these words to the Prophet on the occasion of the 'farewell sermon'—'this denunciation of racism . . . has provided a principle which has been more or less largely adhered to in Islamic practice'. See his *Muḥammad: Prophet of Islam*, tr. Anne Carter (London, 2002), p. 286.

92 See R. Shah-Kazemi, 'Do Muslims and Christians believe in the same God?' in *Dialogue in Depth: Selected Essays on Islamic Spirituality and Inter-religious Understanding* (forthcoming).

93 Guillaume, *The Life of Muḥammad*, pp. 270–277; see also Martin Lings, *Muḥammad*, pp. 324–325.

94 As cited by Lings, *Muḥammad*, p. 300. Although the historicity of this event is denied by other historians, the incident is not implausible. What is implausible is the idea that the icon would have been allowed to remain within the Ka'ba. One might conjecture that it was immediately given to a Christian Arab tribe for safe-keeping.

95 As viewed by this writer at St. Catherine's monastery, Sinai.

Epilogue

1 'The Men of Learning Against the Men of Violence', *The Economist*, 28 July, 2005.

2 This title is based on the Qur'ānic verse instructing Muslims to invite the People of the Book to worship the one and only divinity: 'Say: O People of the Book, come to a common word between us and you, that we shall worship God alone, and not take others as lords apart from God' (3:64).

3 See www.acommonword.com for the text itself, and the responses thereto.

4 Around 70 leading Christian figures responded to it in one form or another, including Pope Benedict XVI; the late Russian Orthodox Patriarch Alexi II of Russia; the Archbishop of Canterbury Dr. Rowan Williams; Presiding Bishop of the Lutheran World Federation, Bishop Mark Hanson; the President and General Secretary of the World Alliance of Reform Churches; the President of the World Baptist Alliance; Rev. Dr. Samuel Kobia; the President of the World Council of Churches; the Council of Bishops of Methodist Churches; the Head of the World Evangelical Alliance, to mention only some of the most important.

5 Apart from the dozens of conferences, symposia, lectures and talks based on the initiative, one measure of the success of 'A Common Word' is that the author of the document, Prince Ghazi bin Muhammad, was shortlisted for the 2009 Nobel Peace Prize. See http://www.acommonword.com/en/a-common-word/2-general/161-qa-common-wordq-accomplishments-2007-2009.html.

Select Bibliography

Abū Sulaymān, ʿAbdul Ḥamīd. *The Islamic Theory of International Relations: New Directions for Islamic Methodology and Thought*. Herndon, VA, 1987.

Ahmad, Aziz. *Studies in Islamic Culture in the Indian Environment*. Oxford, 1964.

Akhtar, Shabbir. *Be Careful with Muḥammad! The Salman Rushdie Affair*. London, 1989.

Ali, M. Athar. 'Towards an Interpretation of the Mughal Empire', in *Journal of the Royal Asiatic Society*, 1 (1978), pp. 38–49.

Armstrong, Karen. *Muhammad: A Western Attempt to Understand Islam*. London, 1991.

——*Muhammad: Prophet For Our Time*. London, 2006.

Arnold, Thomas. *The Preaching of Islam*. London, 1935.

Asad, Muhammad. *The Message of the Qurʾān*. Bristol, 2003.

Aziz, Zahid. *Islam, Peace and Tolerance*. Lahore, 2007.

ʿAzzām, ʿAbd al-Raḥmān. *The Eternal Message of Muḥammad*, tr. Caesar E. Farah. New York, 1964.

Badawi, Mostafa. 'The Muḥammadan Attributes', in *Seasons: Semiannual Journal of Zaytuna Institute*, 2 (2005), pp. 81–95.

al-Balādhurī, Aḥmad. *Futūḥ al-buldān*. Beirut, 1988; tr. by Philip K. Hitti as *The Origins of the Islamic State*. New York, 1916.

Bakar, Osman. *Tawḥīd and Science*. Lahore, 1998.

Beneke, Chris. *Beyond Toleration: The Religious Origins of American Pluralism*. Oxford, 2006.

Black Elk. *Black Elk Speaks*. Recorded by John G. Neihardt. Lincoln, NE, 1979.

——*The Sacred Pipe: Black Elk's Account of the Seven Rites of the Oglala Sioux*, recorded and edited by Joseph Epes Brown. Norman, OK, 1953.

Blanch, Lesley. *Sabres of Paradise*. New York, 1960.

Boase, Roger. *The Origin and Meaning of Courtly Love*. Manchester, 1977.

Braude, Benjamin and Bernard Lewis, ed. *Christians and Jews in the Ottoman Empire: The Functioning of a Plural Society*, vol. 1: The Central Lands. New York, 1982.

Brett, Michael. *The Rise of the Fatimids: The World of the Mediterranean and the Middle East in the Tenth Century CE*. Leiden, 2001.

Briffault, Robert, *The Making of Humanity*. Lahore, 1980.

al-Bukhārī, Muḥammad b. Ismāʿīl. *Ṣaḥīḥ al-Bukhārī: Arabic-English*, tr. Muhammad Muhsin Khan. Chicago, 1976.

Burckhardt, Titus. *Moorish Culture in Spain*, tr. Alisa Jaffa. London, 1970.

Cassirer, Ernst, Paul Oskar Kristeller, John Herman Randall, ed. *The Renaissance Philosophy of Man*. Chicago, 1948.

Chandra, S. *Mughal Religious Policies, the Rajputs, and the Deccan*. New Delhi, 1993.

Chittick, William C. *The Sufi Path of Knowledge: Ibn al-ʿArabī and the Metaphysics of the Imagination*. Albany, NY, 1989.

——*Imaginal Worlds: Ibn al-ʿArabī and the Problem of Religious Diversity*. Albany, NY, 1994.

——*Supplications: Amīr al-Muʾminīn*. London, 1995.

Chodkiewicz, Michel. *Un Océan sans rivage : Ibn Arabî, le livre et le loi*. Paris, 1992.

——*The Spiritual Writings of Amir ʿAbd al-Kader*, tr. James Chrestensen and Tom Manning. Albany, NY, 1995.

Churchill, Charles Henry. *The Life of Abdel Kader*. London, 1867.

Cohen, Mark R. 'Islam and the Jews: Myth, Counter-Myth, History', in *Jerusalem Quarterly*, 38 (1986), pp. 125–137.

Collins, Roger. *Early Medieval Spain: Unity in Diversity, 400–1000*. London, 1995.

Coope, Jessica A. *The Martyrs of Cordoba: Community and Family Conflict in an Age of Mass Conversion*. Lincoln and London, 1995.

Corbin, Henry. *En Islam iranien*. Paris, 1971.

——*Cyclical Time and Ismaili Gnosis*, trans. R. Manheim and J. W. Morris. London, 1983.

Daftary, Farhad. *A Short History of the Ismailis*. Edinburgh, 1998.

——*The Ismāʿīlīs: Their History and Doctrines*. 2nd ed., Cambridge, 2007.

Dakake, David, 'The Myth of a Militant Islam', in Joseph E. B. Lumbard, ed., *Islam, Fundamentalism and the Betrayal of Tradition*. Bloomington, IN, 2009, pp. 3–38.

Dallmayr, Fred. *Beyond Orientalism: Essays on Cross-Cultural Encounter*. Albany, NY, 1996.

——*Dialogue Among Civilizations: Some Exemplary Voices*. New York and Basingstoke, 2002.

Dalrymple, William. *From the Holy Mountain: A Journey among the Christians of the Middle East*. New York, 1999.

——'Of Saints and Sufis in the Near East: Past and Present', in Roger Boase, ed., *Islam and Global Dialogue: Religious Pluralism and the Pursuit of Peace*. Aldershot, 2005, pp. 91–101.

Daniel, Norman. *Islam, Europe and Empire*. Edinburgh, 1966.

D'Costa, Gavin. *The Meeting of Religions and the Trinity*. Edinburgh, 2000.

Al-Djazairi, S. E. *The Hidden Debt to Islamic Civilisation*. Oxford, 2005.

Dunlop, D. M. *Arabic Science and the West*. Karachi, 1958.
Eaton, Gai. *Islam and the Destiny of Man*. Cambridge, 1994.
El-Fadl, Khaled Abou. *Conference of the Books: The Search for Beauty in Islam*. Lanham, 2001.
——*Speaking in God's Name: Islamic Law, Authority and Women*. Oxford, 2001.
——*The Place of Tolerance in Islam*. Boston, 2002.
——*The Great Theft: Wrestling Islam From the Extremists*. New York, 2007.
Ernst, Carl W. *Following Muḥammad: Rethinking Islam in the Contemporary World*. Chapel Hill, NC, 2003.
Fletcher, Richard. *The Cross and the Crescent: Christianity and Islam from Muhammad to the Reformation*. New York and London, 2004.
Forty Hadith Qudsi, tr. E. Ibrahim and D. Johnson-Davies. Beirut and Damascus, 1980.
Friedmann, Yohanan. *Tolerance and Coercion in Islam: Interfaith Relations in the Muslim Tradition*. Cambridge, 2003.
Gammer, Moshe. *Muslim Resistance to the Tsar: Shamil and the Conquest of Chechnia and Daghestan*. London, 1994.
al-Ghazālī, Abū Ḥāmid Muḥammad. *Fayṣal al-tafriqa bayna al-Islam wa al-zandaqa*, tr. Sherman Jackson as *On the Boundaries of Theological Tolerance in Islam*. Oxford, 2002.
——*The Book of Knowledge*: Kitāb al-ʿilm *of al-Ghazzālī's* Iḥyāʾ ʿUlūm al-dīn, tr. Nabih Amin Faris. Lahore, 1970.
——'Kitāb ādāb al-maʿīsha wa akhlāq al-nubuwwa', tr. L. Zolondek, *Book XX of al-Ghazālī's* Iḥyāʾ ʿUlūm al-dīn. Leiden, 1963.
Ghurar al-ḥikam, ed. Sayyid Ḥusayn Shaykh al-Islāmī. Qom, 2000.
Gibb, H. A. R. ed. *Whither Islam? A Survey of Modern Movements in the Moslem World*. New York and London, 2000.
Glick, Thomas F. *Islamic and Christian Spain in the Early Middle Ages*. Leiden, 2005.
Glubb, John. *The Life and Times of Muhammad*. New York, 1971.
Goddard, Hugh. *A History of Christian–Muslim Relations*. Edinburgh, 2000.
Goichon, A. M. *The Philosophy of Avicenna and its Influence on Medieval Europe*. Delhi, 1969.
Goitein, S. D. *Jews and Arabs: Their Contacts Through the Ages*. New York, 1964.
——*A Mediterranean Society: The Jewish Communities of the World as Portrayed in the Documents of the Cairo Geniza*. Berkeley, 1967.
Goldziher, Ignaz. *Introduction to Islamic Theology and Law*. New Jersey, 1981.
Griffith, Sidney. *The Church in the Shadow of the Mosque: Christians and Muslims in the World of Islam*. Princeton and Oxford, 2008.
Guénon, René, *Fundamental Symbols: The Universal Language of Sacred Science*, tr. Alvin Moore, Jnr. Cambridge, 1995.

——*Introduction to the Study of the Hindu Doctrines*, tr. Marco Pallis. New York, 2001.
——*Man and his Becoming according to the Vedanta*, tr. Richard C. Nicholson. New York, 2001.
Halm, Heinz. *The Empire of the Mahdi*, tr. Michael Bonner. Leiden, 1996.
——*The Fatimids and their Traditions of Learning*. London, 1997.
Hodgson, Marshall G. H., *The Venture of Islam: Conscience and History in a World Civilization*, vol. 2: *The Expansion of Islam in the Middle Periods*. Chicago and London, 1974.
al-Ḥusaynī, 'Abdallāh Sirājuddīn. *Our Master Muhammad, the Messenger of Allah: His Sublime Character and Exalted Attributes*, tr. Khalid Williams. Amsterdam, 2009.
Ibish, Yusuf. 'Traditional Guilds in the Ottoman Empire' in R. Shah-Kazemi, ed., *Turkey: The Pendulum Swings Back*. London, 1996, pp. 22–30.
Ibn al-ʿArabī, Muḥyī al-Dīn. *Fuṣūṣ al-ḥikam*. Cairo, 1903.
——*al-Futūḥāt al-Makkiyya*. Cairo, 1329/1911.
——*The Ringstones of Wisdom* (Fuṣūṣ al-ḥikam), tr. Caner K. Dagli. Chicago, 2004.
——*The Tarjumān al-Ashwāq: A Collection of Mystical Odes*, tr. R. A. Nicholson. London, 1978.
Ibn al-Bābawayh, Abū Jaʿfar Muḥammad (al-Shaykh al-Ṣadūq). *Kitāb al-tawḥīd*. Beirut, 1967.
Ibn al-Haytham, Abū ʿAbd Allāh Jaʿfar. *Kitāb al-Munāẓarāt*, ed. and tr. Wilferd Madelung and Paul E. Walker as *The Advent of the Fatimids: A Contemporary Shiʿi Witness*. London, 2000.
Ibn Isḥāq, Muḥammad. *The Life of Muḥammad: A Translation of Ibn Isḥāq's Sīrat Rasūl Allāh*, tr. Alfred Guillaume. Oxford, 1968.
Ibn Kathīr, Ismāʿīl. *Tafsīr al-Qur'ān al-ʿaẓīm*. Riyadh, 1998.
Ikram, S. M. *Muslim Civilization in India*. New York, 1964.
Inalcık, Halil. *The Ottoman Empire: The Classical Age, 1300–1600*, tr. Norman Itzkowitz and Colin Imber. London, 1973.
ʿIyāḍ Abu'l-Faḍl (al-Qāḍī). *Kitāb al-shifā bi-taʿrīf ḥuqūq sayyidinā'l-Muṣṭafā*. Mecca, 1993; tr. Aisha Abdarrahman Bewley as *Muḥammad, Messenger of Allāh: Ash-Shifa of Qadi ʿIyad*. Inverness, 1991.
Izutsu, Toshihiko. *Sufism and Taoism: A Comparative Study of Key Philosophical Concepts*. Berkeley, CA and London, 1983.
——*Ethico-Religious Concepts in the Qur'an*. Lahore, 2002.
——*God and Man in the Qur'ān: Semantics of the Qur'ānic Weltanschauung*. Kuala Lumpur, 2002.
Jiwa, Shainool. 'Inclusive Governance: A Fatimid Illustration', in Amyn Sajoo, ed., *A Companion to the Muslim World*. London, 2010, pp. 157–175.

Kahteran, Nevad. 'Ḥanīf', in *The Qur'an: An Encyclopaedia*, ed. Oliver Leaman. Oxford, 2006, pp. 242–244.
Kamali, Mohammad Hashim. *Freedom of Expression in Islam*. Cambridge, 1997.
——*Moderation and Balance in Islam: The Qur'ānic Principle of Wasaṭiyyah*. Kuala Lumpur, 2010.
——*The Dignity of Man: An Islamic Perspective*. Cambridge, 2002.
Kassis, Hanna. 'The Arabicization and Islamicization of the Christians of al-Andalus: Evidence of their Scriptures' in Ross Brann, ed., *Languages of Power in Islamic Spain*. Bethesda, MD, 1997, pp. 136–155.
Khan, Iqtidar Alam. 'The Nobility under Akbar and the Development of his Religious Policy', in *Journal of the Royal Asiatic Society*, 1 (1968), pp. 29–36.
Khushalani, Gobind. *Chachnamah Retold: An Account of the Arab Conquest of Sindh*. New Delhi, 2006.
Kiser, John W. *Commander of the Faithful: The Life and Times of Emir Abd el-Kader*. Cambridge, 2008.
Klein, Eliahu. *Kabbalah of Creation: The Mysticism of Isaac Luria, Founder of Modern Kabbalah*. Berkeley, CA, 2005.
al-Kulaynī, Muḥammad Ya'qūb. *al-Uṣūl min al-kāfī*. Tehran, 1376 Sh./1997.
Lane-Poole, Stanley. *The Speeches and Table Talk of the Prophet Muhammad*. Delhi, 1987.
Lazarus-Yafeh, H. *Studies in Ghazzali*. Jerusalem, 1975.
Lev, Yaacov. *State and Society in Fatimid Egypt*. Leiden, 1991.
Lévi-Provençal, E. *Histoire de l'Espagne musulmane: La Conquête et l'émirat hispano-umaiyade (710–912)*. Paris and Leiden, 1950.
Lewis, Bernard. *Origins of Ismā'īlism: A Study of the Historical Background of the Fāṭimid Caliphate*. Cambridge, 1940.
——*The Jews of Islam*. Princeton, NJ, 1984.
——*Semites and Anti-Semites: An Inquiry into Conflict and Prejudice*. London, 1986.
——*The Multiple Identities of the Middle East*. New York, 1998.
Lings, Martin. *Muḥammad: His Life Based on the Earliest Sources*. Cambridge, 1984.
——*What is Sufism?* Cambridge, 1993.
——*Ancient Beliefs and Modern Superstitions*. Cambridge, 1996.
Locke, John. 'A Letter Concerning Toleration' in John Horton and Susan Mendus, ed., *A Letter Concerning Toleration: In Focus*. London and New York, 1991.
Makdisi, George. *The Rise of Colleges: Institutions of Learning in Islam and the West*. Edinburgh, 1981.
——*The Rise of Humanism in Classical Islam and the Christian West: With Special Reference to Scholasticism*. Edinburgh, 1990.

——'Scholasticism and Humanism in Classical Islam and the Christian West', in *Journal of the Americal Oriental Society*, 109 (1989), pp. 175–182.

Mardin, Şerif. 'Islam in the Ottoman Empire and Turkey' in R. Shah-Kazemi, ed., *Turkey: The Pendulum Swings Back*. London, 1996, pp. 7–21.

Matar, Nabil. 'John Locke and the Turbanned Nations' in *Journal of Islamic Studies*, 2 (1991), pp. 67–77.

Matt, Daniel Chanan. *Zohar: The Book of Enlightenment*. New Jersey, 1983.

Maycock, A. L. *The Papacy*. London, 1927.

McAuliffe, Jane D. *Qur'anic Christians: An Analysis of Classical and Modern Exegesis*. Cambridge, 1991.

Menocal, Maria Rosa. 'Culture in the Time of Tolerance: Al-Andalus as a Model for our Own Time', in *Palestine-Israel Journal of Politics, Economics and Culture*, 8 (2001), pp. 173–180.

——*Ornament of the World: How Muslims, Jews and Christians Created a Culture of Tolerance in Medieval Spain*. New York, 2002.

Mirandola, Giovanni Pico della. *On the Dignity of Man*, tr. Charles Glenn Wallis. Indianapolis, 1998.

Mitchell, D. W. and J. Wiseman, ed. *The Gethsemani Encounter*. New York, 1999.

Morris, James W. 'Ibn al-'Arabī's Spiritual Ascension', in Michel Chodkiewicz et al, ed., *Les Illuminations de La Mecque*. Paris, 1988, pp. 351–381.

Myers, Eugene A. *Arabic Thought and the Western World in the Golden Age of Islam*. New York, 1964.

Nasr, Seyyed Hossein. *An Introduction to Islamic Cosmological Doctrines*. London, 1978.

——*Islamic Art and Spirituality*. Cambridge, 1987.

——'The Cosmos and the Natural Order,' in S. H. Nasr, ed., *Islamic Spirituality*, vol. 1: *Foundations*. London, 1987, pp. 345–357.

——*Science and Civilization in Islam*. Cambridge, 1987.

——*Islam and the Plight of Modern Man*. Lahore, 1988.

——*Religion and the Order of Nature*. New York and Oxford, 1996.

——*The Heart of Islam: Enduring Values for Humanity*. New York, 2002.

Nahj al-balāgha, ed. Shaykh 'Azīzullāh al-'Uṭārdī. Tehran, 1993.

al-Nīsābūrī, al-Ḥākim. *al-Mustadrak 'ala'l-ṣaḥīḥayn*. Beirut, 2002.

Nizami, K. A. *On History and Historians of Medieval India*. New Delhi, 1982.

——*Akbar and Religion*. Delhi, 1989.

O'Leary, De Lacy. *Islamic Thought and its Place in History*. New Delhi 2001.

Philip, Neil, ed. *In a Sacred Manner I Live: Native American Wisdom*. New York, 1997.

Pickthall, M. M. *The Meanings of the Glorious Qur'an*. London, 1976.

Plato. *The Republic of Plato*, tr. Francis MacDonald Cornford. Oxford, 1969.

Qureshi, I. M. *Ulema in Politics*. Karachi, 1972.

Ramadan, Tariq. *In the Footsteps of the Prophet: Lessons from the Life of Muhammad*, tr. Claude Dabbak. Oxford, 2007.

Rayshahrī, Muḥammad, ed. *Mīzān al-ḥikma*, ed. and tr. N. Virjee et al as *The Scale of Wisdom: A Compendium of Shi'a Hadith*. London, 2009.

al-Rāzī, Abū Ḥātim. *A'lām al-nubuwwa*, ed. Salah al-Sawy and Gholam-Reza Aavani. Tehran, 1381 Sh./2002.

Ritchie, Susan, 'The Islamic Ottoman Influence on the Development of Religious Toleration in Reformation Transylvania', in *Seasons: Semiannual Journal of Zaytuna Institute*, 2 (2004), pp. 59–70.

Rizvi, S. A. A. *Muslim Revivalist Movements in Northern India in the Sixteenth and Seventeenth Centuries*. Agra, 1965.

——*Religious and Intellectual History of the Muslims in Akbar's Reign*. New Delhi, 1975.

Rogerson, Barnaby. *The Prophet Muhammad: A Biography*. London, 2003.

——*The Heirs of the Prophet Muhammad*. London, 2006.

Rosenthal, Franz. *Knowledge Triumphant: The Concept of Knowledge in Medieval Islam*. Leiden and Boston, 2007.

Rūmī, Jalāl al-Dīn. *Kitāb fīhi mā fīhi*, tr. A. J. Arberry as *Discourses of Rūmī*. London, 1961.

——*The Mathnawī of Jalāl ud-Dīn Rūmī*, trans. R. A. Nicholson. London, 1930.

——*Selected Poems from the Dīvāni Shamsi Tabrīz*, trans. R. A. Nicholson. Cambridge, 1976.

Sahas, Daniel J., 'The Face to Face Encounter between Patriarch Sophronius of Jerusalem and the Caliph 'Umar ibn al-Khaṭṭāb: Friends or Foes?', in Emmanouela Grypeou, Mark Swanson, and David Thomas, ed., *The Encounter of Eastern Christianity with Early Islam*. Leiden, 2006, pp. 33–44.

Santillana, Giorgio de. *The Age of Adventure: The Renaissance Philosophers*. New York, 1970.

Schimmel, A. *Islam in the Indian Subcontinent*. Leiden, 1980.

——*Islam in India and Pakistan*. Leiden, 1982.

——*And Muḥammad is His Messenger*. Chapel Hill and London, 1985.

——*The Empire of the Great Mughals*, tr. Corinne Atwood. London, 2004.

Schuon, Frithjof. *The Transcendent Unity of Religions*, tr. Peter Townsend. London, 1953.

——*Understanding Islam*, ed. Patrick Laude. Bloomington, IN, 2011.

Shah-Kazemi, Reza. *Justice and Remembrance: Introducing the Spirituality of Imam 'Alī*. London, 2006.

——*The Other in the Light of the One: The Universality of the Qur'an and Interfaith Dialogue*. Cambridge, 2006.

——*My Mercy Encompasses All: The Koran's Teachings on Compassion, Peace and Love*. Amory, 2007.

——*Common Ground between Islam and Buddhism*. Louisville, 2010.

——'God "The Loving"' in Miroslav Volf, Ghazi bin Muhammad and Melissa Yarrington, ed., *A Common Word: Muslims and Christians on Loving God and Neighbour*. Grand Rapids, MI and Cambridge, 2010, pp. 88–109.

——'Tolerance' in Amyn Sajoo, ed., *A Companion to Muslim Ethics*. London. 2010, pp. 167–186.

Shalṭūṭ, Maḥmūd. *Al-Qurān wa'l-qitāl*, tr. F. E. Peters as 'A Modernist Interpretation of Jihad: Mahmud Shaltut's Treatise, *Koran and Fighting*' in Peters, *Jihad in Classical and Modern Islam*. Leiden, 1977, pp. 59–101.

Sharafuddin, Mohammed. *Islam and Romantic Orientalism*. London and New York, 1996.

Sharma, Sri Ram. *Religious Policy of the Mughal Empire*. London, 1962.

——*Mughal Government and Administration*. Bombay, 1965.

Shaw, Stanford, *History of the Ottoman Empire and Modern Turkey*, vol. 1: *Empire of the Gazis: The Rise and Decline of the Ottoman Empire 1280–1808*. Cambridge, 1976.

Sirāj ad-Dīn, Abū Bakr. *The Book of Certainty*. Cambridge, 1992.

Smith, Wilfred Cantwell. *The Meaning and End of Religion: A Revolutionary Approach to the Great Religious Traditions*. London, 1978.

Stern, Samuel M. *Studies in Early Ismāʿīlism*. Leiden, 1983.

Stillman, Norman. *The Jews of Arab Lands: A History and Source Book*. Philadelphia, PA, 1979

al-Suyūṭī, Jalāl al-Dīn. *al-Jāmiʿ al-Ṣaghīr*. Beirut, 1972.

al-Ṭabarī, Abū Jaʿfar Muḥammad b. Jarīr. *The History of al-Ṭabarī*, vol. 12, tr. Y. Friedmann. Albany, NY, 1985.

——*Jāmiʿ al-bayān*. Beirut, 2001.

Ṭayy, Muḥammad. 'Ru'yat al-Imām 'Alī wa muwaqqifuh min waḥdat al-umma wa ḥuqūq al-aqalliyyāt al-siyāsiyya wa al-dīniyya' ['The vision of Imam 'Alī and his establishment of the unity of the Umma and the rights of political and religious minorities'], in Mehdi Golshani, ed., *Proceedings of the Congress on Imam Ali and Justice, Unity and Security*. Tehran, 1423/2002, vol. 2, pp. 55–77.

Watt, M. Montgomery. *Muḥammad at Medina*. Oxford, 1956.

——*Muḥammad's Mecca: History in the Qur'an*. Edinburgh, 1988.

Winter, Tim (under the name Abdal Hakim Murad). 'The Last Trump Card: Islam and the Supersession of Other Faiths', in *Studies in Interreligious Dialogue*, 9 (1999), pp. 133–155.

——'Islam and the Threat of Europe' in *World Faiths Encounter*, 29 (2001), pp. 4–12.

——'Faith in the Future: Islam after the Enlightenment'. First Annual Altaf Gauhar Memorial Lecture. Islamabad, December, 2002. http://www.masud.co.uk/ISLAM/ahm/postEnlight.htm.

——'Ishmael and the Enlightenment *Crise de Coeur*' in Basit Koshul and Steven Kepnes, ed., *Scripture, Reason and the Contemporary Islam-West Encounter: Studying the 'Other', Understanding the 'Self'*. New York, 2007, pp. 149–175.

——'Spiritual Life in Ottoman Turkey', in R. Shah-Kazemi, ed., *Turkey: The Pendulum Swings Back*, pp. 32–41.

Ye'or, Bat. *The Decline of Eastern Christianity Under Islam: From Jihad to Dhimmitude, Seventh-Twentieth Century*, tr. Miriam Kochan and David Littman. New Jersey and London, 1996.

Yusuf, Hamza. 'Buddha in the Qur'ān?', in R. Shah-Kazemi, ed., *Common Ground between Islam and Buddhism*. Louisville, 2010, pp. 113–136.

——'Generous Tolerance in Islam,' in *Seasons: Semiannual Journal of Zaytuna Institute*, 2 (2005), pp. 26–42.

al-Zamakhsharī, Maḥmūd b. 'Umar. *Tafsīr al-Kashshāf*. Beirut, 1995.